FULFILLING GOD'S MISSION FOR
AMERICA IN THESE LAST DAYS

Salt & LIGHT

Bob Fraley

Copyright 2007
Robert R Fraley
All rights reserved
ISBN 978-0-9612999-5-8

Published by
Christian Life Outreach
6438 East Jenan Drive
Scottsdale, Arizona 85254
www.christianlifeoutreach.org
www.campaignsaveamerica.com

Printed in the United States of America

Cover design and book layout by Paul Annan

What you are going to read in this book is probably going to challenge everything you've ever heard or read about Bible prophecy, and specifically what the Bible says about America's future. Pray that God will give you wisdom and discernment to evaluate what I am saying. Understanding these truths is the key to understanding the enemy's plan to attack and defeat us—and to defeating him.

For you to get the benefit of the message in this book it is essential that you read this book by starting at the beginning and reading it in it's entirely in the order in which the information is presented. There are many important and vital spiritual concepts. These spiritual concepts are an important foundation to an understanding of the prophetic Scriptures about America and are why the information is presented in a very specific order. If you jump ahead or jump around trying to find an immediate answer you could miss the central theme of Campaign Save Christian America. But if you will read this book from start to finish be assured, by the time you finish, you will understand the root cause of Satan's spiritual warfare in America and why he has experienced the success in tearing down our Christian values over this last generation.

Bob Fraley

CONTENTS

AMERICA, which had such a strong Christian foundation and where so much Christian teaching has taken place, has experienced an overwhelming increase in the spirit of lawlessness, permissiveness, rebellion and selfishness in this last generation. **WHY?**

Many Christian leaders, as well as church members are falling into sexual sin. **WHY?**

Addiction to pornography has reached epidemic levels for both Christian and non-Christian men and women. **WHY?**

The divorce rate has climbed to epidemic levels among both Christians and non-Christians in our country. **WHY?**

We are seeing moral actions in America that were "unthinkable" 30-40 years ago now become "commonplace." **WHY?**

Crime, violence, and drugs are at epidemic levels in America. We have the largest prison population in the world. Our rate of incarceration is over seven times higher than most other countries. **WHY?**

The percentage of young American adults who have biblical based values has dropped since W.W.II from 65% to 4%. **WHY?**

In the history of mankind, there has never been a society whose moral values have deteriorated so drastically in such a short period of time as those of Americans have during the past 50-60 years...and that trend shows no sign of stopping.

Dr. Billy Graham, Dr. Henry Blackaby, David Wilkerson, James Robison, Pat Robertson, Tommy Barnett, Bill McCartney, and other Christian leaders have expressed concern that America is racing toward God's judgment. America's rapid deterioration in moral values continues, and nothing—whether new programs, education, counseling or anything else—seems to have any effect on the problem. Why have all of our efforts failed to solve this problem?

Why has Satan had so much success in his attacks against the body of Christ in America? God's Word tells us WHY! "…**My people are destroyed** (overcome, defeated) **for lack of knowledge**" (Hosea 4:6).

We see and hear many reports that warn us about the negative fruit our society has produced in this last generation. It is important for us to be knowledgeable of this fruit. However, that is only a portion of the knowledge we need if we are going to be victorious in the spiritual warfare now taking place in America. Christians are being overcome today because of **lack of knowledge about how Satan is attacking the body of Christ <u>in these last days</u>**. Therefore, we are <u>not addressing the root cause</u> of this warfare that is causing so much spiritual defeat. That is what is important, and why I have written this book!

Satan is well aware of America's great spiritual history. America has been God's geographical base in the world for Christianity in the last 300 plus years. Therefore, our living in the last days and his seeing that time is short; he has launched an all out vicious spiritual attack against Christians in our country. His plan is to destroy every Christian standard that we hold. Christians must be aware of this, and must also be knowledgeable about how he is attacking. Only then will we understand why he is having so much success in causing so much spiritual defeat in the body of Christ. This is the only way we can prepare ourselves to stand against what the Bible warns will be the enemy's attack methods for believers living in these end-times.

A few years ago, there was a surge in interest in the end times, but now it seems the subject has taken a back burner for many Christians and Christian teachers. Maybe this is because the materials that were popular and which were being taught about the last days were <u>not</u> preparing Christians by telling them how to be overcomers in these troubled times.

The destructive fruit of spiritual warfare reveals that most Christians have <u>not</u> been taught and are not spiritually prepared to stand against the deceptive battles currently taking place in our society. Many Christians readily admit they do not understand the root cause of the rapid breakdown in our society's moral fiber or how the enemy has conducted such a successful campaign of spiritual warfare against our country.

It is a sad thing to see the hundreds of thousands of Christians who have been hurt in this warfare. The divorce rate among Christians has exploded in this generation. Sexual immorality, dishonesty, and greed are running rampant in the body of Christ. Bill McCartney, founder of Promise Keepers, told me addiction to pornography has become a national epidemic among Christian men. Christian leaders are falling into sin, right along with laypeople. Christian families have been devastated and many individual Christian lives afflicted with hurt and pain. The most alarming thing is the fact that the pace of this process is accelerating all over the country.

You need to realize this: we are living in one of the toughest times in history to be a committed Christian. Never before has our spiritual enemy had the ability to tempt and teach so many people the standards of the world as American society can through TV, radio, movies, the Internet, dozens of publications, and the secular educational system.

No longer do you and I have to go out into the world in order to make contact with it. The world's influencing power comes right into our homes. It searches us out! The Christian family has never felt the power and pull of a worldly society like the one we must contend with today in America. We are being hit daily in every way imaginable to bend and compromise biblical standards. We are living in the middle of a spiritual war zone, and many Christians have become casualties and suffered major spiritual defeats in their lives. Dr. Billy Graham said a few years ago that, according to his research, at least 90 percent of all Christians in America are living defeated spiritual lives.

My entire working career has been in the corporate business world, most of that at the executive level. In 1997, I founded ALEXCO, a major manufacturer of high tech aluminum extruded alloys for the aerospace industry. Every Tuesday we hold a meeting of all of the managers and other personnel to review the company's performance from the previous week. A corrective action plan is quickly implemented if an area of weakness has developed in any of the departments. That plan specifically targets the area of weakness. Just as Jesus taught, your fruit or performance is the sign of success or failure in whatever you do. This is equally true for an individual, a company, or a country.

As we evaluate what has been produced in our country during the last generation, we see the fruit of an evil work. You cannot afford to hide your head in the sand. Fruit reveals truth! By looking at the negative fruit we can see that America is headed in the wrong direction. We are in danger of spiritual bankruptcy!

It is time for Christians to take a stand! I know that spiritual warfare is never going to be one of our favorite subjects to discuss, especially if the circumstances of our own personal life appear to be just fine. Warfare can be exhausting! It is usually stressful. It is expensive and dangerous at times. Warfare requires skill and discipline to emerge victorious, much less unscathed. That is why few of us seek out conflict. It puts us at risk, and this goes against our natural impulse toward self-preservation. Therefore, our human tendency, even as Christians, is to sit out conflict unless we are pushed beyond a reasonable limit. As you look around, I think you will agree with me—that time has come!

As a Christian living in America today, you really do not have a choice. We are involved in this warfare whether we like it or not. There is a spiritual battle taking place to destroy the biblical standards that the majority of Americans once honored and lived by. No matter how hard you try, you cannot avoid the effects of this battle. The worldly standards that are being taught through our mass communication system are just too wide-reaching and strong.

The many defeats taking place in the body of Christ tell us that Christians today have very little knowledge about the tactics and methods of our spiritual enemy in these last days. Most Christians go out into the world everyday unprepared to face the enemy and the snares of his worldly system. We <u>have not</u> developed a successful battle plan to <u>counter-attack</u> and destroy the roots of Satan's strategic plan of deception that is being used against Christians. Being a <u>businessman</u> I know the necessity of understanding your opposition's tactics so that you can carefully prepare to counter them.

<u>What we need is not a generic program, but a specific corrective action plan.</u> If we do not quickly develop one, we are going to continue to fall away from fulfilling God's special calling for America in these last days. That is what Satan wants—to defeat God's purpose. That is why he has launched such a heavy and deceptive spiritual attack against our country. Satan has been successful in his warfare against America because we have not addressed the root cause underlying his attack.

Every day we hear about the war against terrorism. However, very few Americans, including Christians, are knowledgeable about the spiritual warfare taking place. That is true even though that spiritual warfare has been far more detrimental to our country. My purpose in writing this book is to help give you the knowledge you need to understand this spiritual warfare and the deceptive tactics and methods that Satan is using.

Every "born again" Christian is called to act in a way that goes against conventional wisdom, against social expediency and often against the popular will. We have a mission to fulfill and a responsibility to make our country, and the world, a better place by preserving all that is good as given to us through God's Word. We are to be people <u>not</u> to make others proud of us—but who think of and put the "Kingdom of God" first. That is what being "salt" and "light" is all about! However, we can only do this if we are prepared.

I have founded Campaign Save Christian America to implement a specific corrective action plan against this warfare that Satan is conducting. It will help us realize God's special calling for America. **This corrective action plan is new and different from anything that has been implemented before. It will work!** This plan is based completely on the teachings of Scripture, including prophetic Scriptures about the last days.

This book will give you the knowledge that you need to know how to prepare yourself to stand firm against the enemy. The knowledge and understanding will help you develop the spiritual character and courage you need to fulfill God's mission statement to be "salt" and "light" in the face of today's tremendous pressures. The objective of this book is to equip you to stand firm.

A PERSONAL WORD

My wife, Barbara, and I are devoted to family values. In 2007 we celebrated 50 years of marriage. We have three children of our own and in 1969 the Lord called us to take six children into our home to rear whose parents had been tragically killed in an automobile accident. Being fairly young at the time, we became very dependent on the Lord to lead us for such a task of raising our expanded family.

As we trained and raised these children many things began to happen that made it very obvious that the Lord and the truth of His Word were directing us in a miraculous way (that is another story). Not only can we testify of this, but so can others who were close to our situation. Jesus said, **"You did not choose me, but I chose you to go**

and bear fruit—fruit that will last. Then the Father will give you whatever you ask in my name" (John 15:16).

The Lord has been faithful in fulfilling His Word. One of the major things He did to help equip us to raise our children was to open our eyes to the tremendous spiritual warfare that Satan had launched for the hearts and minds of the American people. It was this insight that became the foundation the Lord used to guide us in raising godly children in an increasingly godless society. As I write this book (early 2007) we have 54 in our family including spouses, grandchildren and great grandchildren, and every one except for the few that are too young, have made a commitment to serve our Lord Jesus Christ.

Although we were very busy with nine children, I was convicted by the Lord to share the things He was teaching my wife and me about this spiritual warfare in America. Since the early 1970s this directive has motivated me to research America's secular and spiritual history. Along with that research, I began to study the Scriptures about the characteristics of the Christian life and its prophecies about the last days.

My research and study revealed that Christians are not being taught some of the most important prophetic Scriptures about how the enemy will spiritually attack Christians in these end-times. Yet, if we want to avoid suffering a major spiritual defeat, an understanding of these prophetic Scriptures is vital. These prophetic Scriptures give us the insights we need to stand against the enemy in these last days and fulfill our **God given mission to be salt and light**. Again I want to tell you that what you will read as we open the prophecies of Revelation will challenge your thinking. I trust that it will also open your eyes to the battle we are facing and the way forward to victory.

Over the years I have written 6 books (including this one), along with several booklets and newsletters, about this spiritual warfare the enemy is conducting to destroy America's Christian heritage, and why Christians in our country are experiencing so many spiritual defeats. Nearly two million copies of my writings have been distributed.

Never before in the history of mankind has a society changed its moral values so drastically in such a short period of time as we Americans have in this past generation. The American people have changed the way we think, raise our families, run our public schools, run our government, set moral standards, and establish our social order. The guidelines that the majority of American people have lived by for generations have been thrown off and replaced with a new code of conduct that goes against the Word of God.

If Bible prophecy is true, and we know that it is, then it must be our priority to learn how the enemy will be attacking the Christian community in these last days. That is the only way we can know how to prepare ourselves to stand firm against the enemy's attacks.

I was recently called by the Lord to start Campaign Save Christian America (www.campaignsaveamerica.com), to inform people about the spiritual warfare and the principles of Scripture. The mission of this campaign is to preserve God's special calling for Christians in America in these last days. I recently wrote a booklet that introduces Campaign Save Christian America, which is available through our website. America is in danger! The Lord is calling you to help by sharing this message.

The Bible says that as it was in the days of Noah so will it be in our day (see Luke 17:26-30). **"By faith Noah, when warned about things not yet seen, in holy fear built an ark to save his family"** (Hebrews 11:7).

According to the Bible we are now living in the final days of the current Church Age. In chapter three I briefly explain how we know that we are living in the last days. The material in this book will help to provide you the building materials you need to build a spiritual ark for you and your family. Giving you knowledge of these building materials is the core of my corrective-action plan for Campaign Save

Christian America that will help save God's special call for Christians in America. I know that this plan will work.

Fear not the days to come, but fear this only: That you shall walk in a manner pleasing to the Lord. This is not a verse of Scripture but a word the Lord spoke to my heart about living in these last days.

Bob Fraley

I have been asked, "Why would you want to save America with all of the filthy fruit that our country is now producing?" First and foremost it is because Scripture reveals that that is the heart of God. God has always tried to save, not destroy. Regardless of what the spiritual conditions were in Israel when Jesus began His ministry the Bible says, **"For God did not send his Son into the world to condemn the world, but to save the world through him"** (John 3:17). Examine the heart of God as revealed through the prophets. The fruit being produced by God's chosen people was terrible, but before sending judgment God tried over and over to save them through the messages proclaimed by the prophets. God even sent Jonah on a mission to save the city of Nineveh, though it was completely evil. The heart of God is love, which means His first desire is to seek and save. Of course the greatest example of this is His heart to save all of mankind.

The spiritual history of America is unique. Please note that I said our spiritual history. It is important to make a distinction between our spiritual and secular history and not mix them together. Doing so can cause confusion and mistakes.

God has had a special place in His heart for America and the American people. Even a casual look at the history of our nation confirms this. America has been the world's center of Christianity for over 300 years. God has used our people and our resources to take the Gospel of Jesus Christ throughout the world.

To understand the way God has worked through American history, we need to look at the history of Israel. That history is familiar to most of us because of the historical record found in the Old Testament and the many books written, and movies and documentaries made, about Israel's history. God's Word centers on these people and their history!

As you travel through the history of Israel, it is clear that God often intervened and corrected the spiritual commitment of the Jewish people so that His mission for them would be accomplished. They would often get caught up in the ways and standards of the world and as a result would fall away from serving the God of Abraham.

There are many spiritual lessons for us to learn from the history of the Jewish people and their relationship with the Lord. The history of our country's spiritual development confirms that we, too, have a special calling from God. I am not saying that it is to the same degree as the nation of Israel, but the spiritual history of America is very unique compared to the history of other countries. Other than the nation of Israel there has never been another country where God has directly intervened like He has in the spiritual development of America. Let me share some of those interventions with you.

INTERVENTION NUMBER ONE

It is common knowledge that Christopher Columbus discovered America in 1492. What is not common knowledge is his own personal call from God to venture out and discover the New World. The following quotation is from the explorer's own writings, Columbus' Book of Prophecies. For many years, this work was only available in Spanish. These words were translated by August J. Kling, and quoted in an article in the October 1971 issue of Presbyterian Layman.

Columbus wrote, *"It was the Lord who put into my mind (I could feel his hand upon me) the fact that it would be possible to sail from here to the Indies. All who heard of my project rejected it with laughter, ridiculing me. There is no question that the inspiration was from the Holy Spirit, because He comforted me with the rays of marvelous inspiration from the Holy Scriptures... I am a most unworthy sinner, but I have cried out to the Lord for grace and mercy, and they have covered me completely... For the execution to the Indies, I did not make use of intelligence, mathematics or maps. It is simply the fulfillment of what Isaiah had prophesied... No one should fear to undertake any task in the name of our Savior, if it is just and if the intention is purely for his Holy service."*

INTERVENTION NUMBER TWO

The Church of England was established by Henry VIII in 1534 when the Pope refused to grant him a divorce from Catherine of Aragon. When it became the official state religion, all of the people were placed under the authority of the bishops of the Church. These bishops began to create power positions and lord it over their congregations, becoming harsh and cruel. By the late 1500s, it was difficult for committed Christians in England to worship and serve God with freedom and follow the writings of the Scriptures.

One group of Christians moved to Holland for about 12 years, but found a hard and difficult life there. The Lord used the difficult lives of these Christians to encourage them to explore the possibilities of going to the New World. In the land called America, they could worship in freedom and serve the Lord according to His Word.

They began to lay plans for a move to this new land. Their search for a way to the New World, and a means to ship their supplies led them to a group of businessmen who owned merchant ships. One hundred and two passengers set sail for America on a cargo ship that had been arranged for by these businessmen. The name of the ship was the *Mayflower*. They were nicknamed "Pilgrims" since a pilgrim is someone who goes on a long, long journey. The *Mayflower* was not designed to carry passengers; therefore, living conditions on the ship were miserable. The food consisted of salted beef, pork or fish and hard dry biscuits. Sleeping quarters were on the wet floor below the main deck; many of the people on board became deathly ill. Sanitary facilities were non-existent. The passengers had to wear the same clothes day after day for the entire voyage. The Pilgrims knew it was only by God's mercy that any of them survived such a voyage.

On the morning of November 9, 1620, 66 days after setting sail, the *Mayflower* reached the sandy beaches of Cape Cod in what today is the State of Massachusetts. The Pilgrims were in a strange land where there were no homes, no towns, and no friends to greet them. But they were obedient to the call of God and would be able to worship Him, and pray and sing songs with complete freedom.

There were many trials in building this first Christian settlement in America. Besides the miserable trip on the *Mayflower*, the Pilgrims had to contend with the cold and snow, lack of food, sickness, death, loneliness, and conflicts with the Indians. By spring, half of the Pilgrims had died. The rest were alone, except for their commitment to God and their faith in Jesus Christ to give them the courage and strength to carry on.

During that first summer the Pilgrims were able to build several homes. A friendly Indian named Squanto who had learned the English language, taught them how to plant crops. The Pilgrims said he had been sent to them by God. Because of his advice their garden crops flourished. Along with the wild game that was available they now had plenty to eat. In the autumn of 1621, nearly a year after their arrival, the Pilgrims decided to set aside a special time to give thanks to the Lord for His faithfulness—a commemoration we now call Thanksgiving.

INTERVENTION NUMBER THREE

The next major event in the development of our country's spiritual heritage was the arrival of the Puritans. While the

Pilgrims were establishing the first Christian settlement at Plymouth, Massachusetts, the Puritans living in England continued to come under mounting pressures through persecution and advanced moral decay. Like the Pilgrims before them, they found conditions made living a Christ-like life extremely difficult.

The Puritans had much more than the Pilgrims—that is, more money, more friends in high places, more education and more business experience. They attracted people from all social classes and walks of life. They too began to search for the leading of the Lord in how to deal with their spiritual problem of living out their life in England and serving the Lord. Like the Pilgrims before them, they saw an alternative in America. God began to move among the Puritans and in the year of 1628 a massive exodus to America began. This migration lasted for about 16 years and more than 20,000 Puritans packed up and moved to America.

The Pilgrims had brought the first light of Jesus Christ to America. However, the Puritans above all others laid America's foundation as a Christian nation. The Puritans had submissive spirits, and were willing to face the reality of their own sinful natures. They recognized the harm that sin caused in their relationship with Jesus Christ and their relationships with one another. This willingness to submit to the Lord produced not only a compassion for one another, but a remarkable maturity in the handling of spiritual matters.

The Puritans placed a great deal of emphasis on the matter of parental responsibility, accountability and authority in the home. They believed it was their God-given responsibility to protect their children, raise and teach them in the way the Lord would have them go. The Bible was the guide for the Puritan people. The older men and women taught the younger ones how to establish and develop this proper spiritual atmosphere and teaching in their homes. Christian love and caring for the souls of others characterized the family lives of our forefathers; it also contains the answer for our family problems today. As one of the outstanding Puritan leaders, Cotton Mather, put it, *"Well-ordered families naturally produce a good order in society."*

The commitment of the Puritans shows us why God anointed and directed them to be His light bearers in establishing America's spiritual direction. The main reason many of us today do not know their story is the revisionist history that began in the last century. Relatively few negative comments about the Puritans can be found in earlier histories. In fact, early historians gave the Puritans credit for setting the course of this nation. Why we find such a prejudice in the hearts of so many American people today against the Puritans and their reported self-righteousness perhaps stems from the fact that in 20th century America the spirit of rebellion has gained such a tight hold on our minds and on our wills.

We have a tendency to rebel against the kind of commitment to God that the Puritan people had, which resulted in their submission to biblical authority and teaching. I am sure that our spiritual enemy, Satan, hates the Puritan example of submissiveness more than any other of their spiritual qualities. He has tried to eradicate the true picture of their role in the history of our country and their contribution. Rebellion was foreign to the Puritans, and since rebellion is Satan's specialty, it is no wonder the Puritans have received bad press here in our country over the last 50 years.

INTERVENTION NUMBER FOUR

The Puritan's obedience of the Word grew from their deep commitment to Christ. However, this strong initial light of submitting to the teachings of Jesus Christ by the Puritans had become a faint glow by 1700. That light dimmed because our faith is not automatically passed on to our children. This pattern is seen over and over in the Old Testament lives of the Israelites. Succeeding generations quickly fell away from the faith of their fathers. The Puritans of the second and third generations had not personally experienced the original call and commitment, and became spiritually indifferent. They had not forsaken their homes in faith and followed the Lord's leading to a new land. Instead they enjoyed the fruit of the blessing the Lord poured out on their ancestors. Though they still attended church, their hearts and minds were on worldly affairs rather than the things of God. This spiritual darkness brought an intervention by God in the 1700s that is called the Great Awakening.

By the end of the 1700s, there had not been any significant spiritual developments in America for some fifty years. However God was beginning to move in a miraculous way to bring an end to this period of spiritual inactivity. Possibly the first glimmer of light that began to dawn on this nation's state of spiritual apathy began in 1734 in North Hampton, Massachusetts where Jonathan Edwards was pastor. Soon it became obvious that the Spirit of God was sweeping over other preachers who began to preach the Word with tremendous anointing and great spiritual power. Among them were John and Charles Wesley, George Whitefield, Theodore Freilinghuysen, Samuel Davis and David Brainerd. As these men proclaimed the message of Jesus Christ, thousands came to the knowledge of Jesus as their Savior. The people were in awe at the power of God that fell on one village after another as these men preached. Wherever they went, revival would accompany them in a dramatic way.

These evangelists of the Great Awakening performed a magnificent service in the spiritual development of our country. Riding the main roads and through the backwoods on horseback, these men traveled hundreds of miles. George Whitefield preached more than 18,000 sermons between 1736 and 1770. John Wesley traveled up to 8,000 miles per year on horseback and preaching over 40,000 sermons in his lifetime. God was preparing America to become a new nation. The principles of her foundation were being established through the preaching of the Word of God. The spiritual health of her people was being formulated to meet the special calling that God had planned. <u>Our special calling is to fulfill God's mission of being the "salt of the earth" and the "light to the world" in these last days of the Church Age.</u> America was being prepared to become the geographical nerve center from which God would take the Gospel of Jesus throughout the world.

America was definitely a "new event" in the spiritual history of mankind. Historians agree it was the powerful preaching during the "Great Awakening" that set the tone for the Revolution and later for our Constitution. The body of Christ in America did not let secular society form our government, although our government was designed to be secular—to be the government of all. Christians were involved in forming our Constitution, Bill of Rights, and every other aspect of our republic form of government. They were given wisdom and inspiration from God.

The reason why the original laws of our government were founded upon the teachings of the Bible is that Christian men led the way in forming our government. Because the foundation of Jesus Christ had been set so firmly in the believers in America, they knew the importance of their freedom in Christ, and recognized that they could never again submit to the yoke of slavery. That is what the new Americans would have been guilty of if they had allowed themselves to go back under the rule of England.

Our Founding Fathers protested for eleven years before they wrote the Declaration of Independence, which listed 27 violations of biblical principles among their complaints against King George of England. This document concludes with the statement, *"We...pledge our lives, our fortunes, and our sacred honor."* Fifty-three out of the fifty-six signers of The Declaration of Independence confessed a personal relationship with Jesus Christ as their Lord and Savior. Twenty-four of these men were lawyers and jurists, eleven were merchants, nine were farmers and large plantation owners, men of means and educated, yet by putting their signature on this Declaration they knew full well that the penalty would be death if the British government captured them.

Five of the signers were captured as traitors in the Revolutionary War with the British and tortured before they died. Twelve had their homes ransacked and burned, seven lost their sons, nine fought and died from wounds or hardships of the War, ten had all of their property seized and burned. Some lost their wife through death and several ended up bankrupt living in poverty. These men and their families were singled out by the government of England and suffered heavy persecution and hardships for signing this act of freedom. Yet they were willing to risk everything for the freedom they rightly believed came only from God. Many of them suffered great hardships during the Revolutionary War, but to them it was worth the price. Some of us take our liberties for granted, but we shouldn't. We should never forget that <u>freedom has never been free</u>!

A majority of the militia units in the Revolutionary War were composed of a pastor and the men from his congregation. In George Washington's first address to his troops he stated: *"The time is now at hand which must probably determine whether Americans are to be free men or slaves...consigned to a state of wretchedness from which no human efforts will deliver them. The fate of unborn millions will now depend, under God, on the courage of this Army. Our cruel and unrelenting enemy leaves us on the choice of brave resistance or the most abject submission. We have therefore to resolve to conquer or die."*

One of our Founding Fathers and 2nd president, John Adams, said, *"Our Constitution was made only for a moral and a religious people. It is wholly inadequate to the government of any other."* His son, John Quincy Adams, the 6th president, stated, *"The highest glory of the American Revolution was this: It connected in one indissoluble bond, the principles of civil government with those of Christianity."* Christianity has been the dominant religious faith in America from the beginning.

In the year 1892, in the case of *The Church of the Holy Trinity vs. The United States*, the Supreme Court stated: *"Our laws and institutions must necessarily be based upon and embody the teachings of the Redeemer of mankind. It is impossible that it should be otherwise and in this sense and to this extent our civilization and our institutions are emphatically Christian. This is historically true from the discovery of this continent to the present hour; we find everywhere a clear recognition of the same truth. These and many other matters add a volume of unofficial declarations to the mass of organic utterances that this is a Christian nation."*

INTERVENTION NUMBER FIVE

After the victory of our Forefathers in the American Revolutionary War and the framing and adoption of our Constitution, which was put into effect March 4, 1789, the next major move of God was the establishment of thousands of churches during the 1800s and 1900s. The revivals that started during the Great Awakening period in the 1700s continued in the 1800s. Men like Dwight L. Moody, Charles Finney, A. B. Earle and others continued the work of revival. The effect of Moody's work in Christian education continues to this day. Charles Finney saw 100,000 give their lives to the Lord in one two-year period, 1857-58. Even during the Civil War, great revivals broke out among the soldiers on both sides. The history of our nation is a history that cannot be told without referring to our spiritual heritage. During the 1900s this movement continued and today there are over 300,000 Christian churches across our land. God has continued to raise up men and women with a special calling like Dr. Billy Graham, David Wilkerson, the late Bill Bright, the late Larry Burkett, Bill Gothard, James Dobson, Bill McCartney, my friend Tommy Barnett, musicians Bill and Gloria Gaither and many others. American history is filled with Christian men and women who have taken the Gospel of Jesus Christ throughout the world and raised up ministries to meet the various spiritual needs of the people. Today you can hear the Gospel preached every day through every communication media available.

I know that <u>not</u> all of the teaching and preaching heard on radio and TV is the true Christian message found in the Bible. As the Apostle Paul warns us, we are to examine the Scriptures ourselves so we can determine if what we are being taught is the true Word of God.

The way God has spiritually developed our country makes it clear that He has a special calling for Christians in America in these last days. <u>Campaign Save Christian America's mission statement is to save this special calling</u>. I appreciate and support the many excellent ministries that are helping provide for the people and families that have been devastated by the rapid deterioration of our country's moral standards. But we must do more! We are <u>not only</u> to be the doctor who treats the pain; we must also be the doctor who treats the disease that is causing the pain.

Campaign Save Christian America is a campaign that has developed a corrective plan to treat the disease. It uses the same method that Jesus used to successfully overcome Satan's attack against Him—that is to prepare to respond to Satan's attacks by studying and knowing the Word of God. <u>Through this book, my objective is to review with you God's special calling for Christians in America during these last days, which I did in this chapter: review the fundamentals of the Christian faith, which I do in the next few chapters: follow that with an examination of the tactics and methods the enemy is using in these last days to overcome Christians in our country: and then to show you through prophetic Scriptures how the enemy is implementing his plan of spiritual warfare.</u> This will equip you with the knowledge to resist his temptations and counterattack against him. Then you can help fulfill our mission to be salt and light as the enemy's spiritual attacks escalate in these end times.

CHAPTER TWO

It is a common thing in our day for organizations and corporations to have a mission statement. In Matthew 5:13-14 Jesus makes two of the most penetrating statements about Christians that you can find anywhere in Scripture. He said, **"You are the salt of the earth"** and **"You are the light of the world."** Jesus gave us our <u>perfect mission statement</u> in these two phrases. They carry a tremendous amount of responsibility, require a lot of courage and are very demanding. This mission statement should cause us to realize what a remarkable and glorious thing it is to be a Christian.

Jesus was saying that Christians are the only people in this world who can preserve the good (our function as salt) and have the understanding to give help and advice in those areas that really matter the most in life (our function as light). What a glorious adventure Christians are to have in this life on Earth, being God's servants of salt and light. This has been the mission statement for every Christian since the beginning of the church.

SALT

For Jesus to use the word **salt** to describe one of the key functions in the life of a Christian is amazing. At the time He made this statement only the wisdom of God could have known what we know today about salt. Salt is one of the most stable compounds on Earth. It will <u>not</u> lose its saltiness on its own. Salt becomes non-effective only when it becomes contaminated. Contamination occurs if salt becomes mixed or diluted with some other material or chemical.

Salt must be kept pure for it to be effective in its purposes. To keep it from losing its effectiveness, or its saltiness, salt has to remain essentially different from the medium in which it is placed. When it is kept in a pure condition it only takes a small amount of salt to be effective and accomplish its purpose of adding flavor or acting as a preservative.

Jesus was telling His people that if we will not become contaminated—that contamination is usually caused by walking to close and mixing with the standards and things of the world—this same principle will hold true. We will succeed in functioning as the **salt of the earth** and preserve that which is good in this evil world. And if we remain in a pure state it will only take a few of us to make a major difference. History records this happening in the first century during the beginning of the church.

"You are the salt of the earth. But if the salt loses its saltiness, how can it be made salty again? It is no longer good for anything..." (Matthew 5:13). There is a principle of life that Jesus is teaching us through this parable about salt. If we Christians assimilate something other than the purity of God's Word in our life, we face great danger of becoming contaminated. Our influence of God's goodness and keeping His standards in this world will only happen if we are distinctively different. We cannot be identical! We must separate ourselves from the world. **"Do not be yoked together with unbelievers. For what do righteousness and wickedness have in common? Or what fellowship can light have with darkness? What harmony is there between Christ and Belial? What does a believer have in common with an unbeliever? What agreement is there between the temple of God and idols? For we are the temple of the living God. As God has said: 'I will live with them and walk among them, and I will be their God, and they will be my people.' 'Therefore come out from them and separate, says the Lord. Touch no unclean thing, and I will receive you.' 'I will be a Father to you, and you will be my sons**

and daughters, says the Lord Almighty'" (II Corinthians 6:14-18).

Mixing the standards of the world with God's standards is one of the strongest temptations that the enemy is using today to cause Christians to become contaminated and lose their "saltiness." It is vitally important to our mission that we understand what being **"the salt of the earth"** entails. We must be a preserver of the good, for He said that for us to lose our effectiveness and influence, or our saltiness, would be to render ourselves kingdom-rejects.

LIGHT

Jesus then made the statement that Christians **"are the light of the world."** This tells us that the world is living in a state of darkness, even though the people of the world are always talking about their enlightenment. There are many Scriptures that confirm this truth. **"For he has rescued us from the dominion of darkness and brought us into the kingdom of the Son he loves..."** (Colossians 1:13). **"For you were once darkness, but now you are light in the Lord"** (Ephesians 5:8). **"But you are a chosen people...a people belonging to God...who called you out of darkness into his wonderful light"** (I Peter 2:9). Only Christians have been brought into the light; the people of the world live in darkness.

The world does not recognize its darkness however. They are convinced of their own enlightenment. One of the catchphrases of the Renaissance in the 15th and 16th centuries was that "knowledge brings light." But many replaced God's knowledge with man's reasoning, placing human insight above God's revealed wisdom. They turned away from truth and replaced the worship of God with the worship of man's intellect.

The majority of people living in the world today believe that all we need to solve our difficulties is more knowledge. Mankind does not realize that our knowledge has only increased our understanding of *things*; scientific, biological, business, commerce, pleasure, etc., not the *real factors* that are critical to the makeup of a successful and peaceful life. That is why the world's vast accumulation of knowledge has brought us to the many predicaments that we see around us today. We humans have failed in the most important area of all. <u>We do not know what to do with our knowledge</u>. People with great worldly knowledge have little enlightenment on how to live. Look around you at the failed relationships between people and between nations. What people don't seem able to take hold of is the truth that **knowledge only gives us the ability to analyze. It does <u>not</u> give us the wisdom, therefore, the answers as to what to do.** Knowledge does <u>not</u> give us the light that is needed for a successful, peaceful, happy life. History has proven this over and over. Jesus said nobody but the Christian can give off the light that this world needs to truly understand those areas that really matter in life.

The world does not have light because Jesus, and He alone, is the light of the world. **"...he said, "I am the light of the world. Whoever follows me will never walk in darkness, but will have the light of life"** (John 8:12). Only Christians can be a reflection of the light and life of Jesus Christ. Jesus is God in the flesh. When a person is born again into His spiritual Kingdom, the Spirit of Jesus Christ, is born into that person and the Holy Spirit begins to live in and through that individual. **"Don't you know that you yourselves are God's temple and that God's Spirit lives in you?"** (I Corinthians 3:16).

Christians are <u>not</u> the light of the world because of who we are, but because we become transmitters of the light of Jesus Christ as we reflect the nature and character of Him who now lives in us by His Spirit. Jesus said, **"And I will ask the Father, and he will give you another Counselor to be with you forever—the Spirit of truth. The world cannot accept him, because it neither sees him nor knows him. But you know him, for he lives with you and will be in you. I will not leave you as orphans; I will come to you. Before** long, the world will not see me anymore, but you will see me. Because I live, you also will live. On that day you will realize that I am in my Father, and you are in me, and I am in you" (John 14:16-20).

The wisdom of the world is foolishness to God. Scripture tells us, "For the wisdom of this world is foolishness in God's sight …The Lord knows that the thoughts of the wise are futile (I Corinthians 3:19-20). I will destroy the wisdom of the wise; the intelligence of the intelligent I will frustrate. Where is the wise man? Where is the scholar? Where is the philosopher of this age? Has not God made foolish the wisdom of the world?" (I Corinthians 1:19-20). Speaking about those with worldly wisdom the Lord states, "You turn things upside down, as if the potter were thought to be like the clay! Shall what is formed say to him who formed it, "He did not make me"? Can the pot say of the potter, "He knows nothing?" (Isaiah 29:16).

Jesus said, "This is the verdict: Light (speaking of Himself) has come into the world, but men loved darkness instead of light because their deeds were evil. Everyone who does evil hates the light, and will not come into the light for fear that his deeds will be exposed. But whoever lives by the truth comes into the light, so that it may be seen plainly that what he has done has been done through God" (John 3:19-21).

Light exposes the hidden things of darkness. That is what the Christian life is meant to do in this world. As the light of Jesus Christ shines through us, it brings the error and failure of man's way of thinking and of living in darkness. That is why the Pharisees and scribes who supposedly had all the answers hated Jesus so much. It is why the people of the world today who think they have the answers hate the teachings and standards of living found in the Scripture. Such a light exposes and condemns the sins of mankind that they do not want revealed.

OUR PERFECT EXAMPLE

Salt describes our state of <u>being</u> and **light** describes our state of <u>doing</u>. Our perfect example of these two words that Jesus chose to describe our mission was Jesus Himself. He did not have the attributes that most people would think are necessary to accomplish greatness. He lived in poverty and was reared in obscurity, never received any formal education, never possessed wealth or widespread influence or traveled extensively, yet the effects of His life on mankind in just three and one-half years of ministry is greater than anyone else in history.

In childhood He puzzled the religious leaders with His wisdom; in manhood He ruled the course of nature, walked upon the waves, and hushed the sea to sleep. He never wrote a book. Yet His life has inspired more books than any other man. He never wrote a song. Yet He has furnished the theme for more songs than all the songwriters combined. He never marshaled an army, nor drafted a soldier, nor fired a gun. Yet no leader ever had more rebels surrender to Him without a shot fired.

All of the armies that ever marched, all the navies that have ever set sail, all the rulers that have ever ruled and all of the kings that have ever reigned on this Earth, all put together have not effected the lives of mankind like this one solitary man. The names of great statesmen have come and gone. Scientists, philosophers, and theologians are soon forgotten. But the name of this man Jesus abounds more and more. Once each week the wheels of commerce cease their turning, and multitudes gather to pay homage and respect to Him. His enemies could not destroy Him, and the grave could not hold Him. He was God on Earth in the form of a human being. He truly proved the statement that it only takes a small amount of light to make a major difference in a completely dark world. The same Spirit of God that lived in Him lives in all Christians who have truly been born again. **"Don't you know that you yourselves are God's temple and that God's Spirit lives in you?"** (I Corinthians 3:16).

It is the duty of all Christians to be an ambassador for Christ in this life by fulfilling God's mission to be **the salt of the earth** and **the light of the world.** However, according to Bible prophecy there will be a tremendous spiritual warfare carried on by the enemy in these last days of the Church Age. The enemy wants to defeat Christians, to keep us from fulfilling our mission and duty to be salt and light. God has given us these prophetic Scriptures to warn us so that we will have knowledge of how the enemy will conduct his attacks. That way we can prepare ourselves to overcome his schemes.

MANKIND LOVES DARKNESS

Since the fall of man, man by nature loves darkness rather than light. Why? Because he likes it that way! It is his nature. The trouble with mankind is not our intellect; it is with our nature. The Bible says since the fall of Adam and Eve everyone born is born with a sinful nature. **"Therefore, just as sin entered the world through one man,** (speaking of Adam) **and death through sin, and in this way death came to all men, because all sinned"** (Romans 5:12).

The world in its makeup is offensive to God. It is a rotten, foul, polluted place in its fallen, sinful state with a tendency to immorality, evil and wars. Left to itself, the world would fester and destroy itself. It needs a preservative or an antiseptic to return to the standards of God and a light that shines brightly and shows forth the love of God. Jesus stated that Christians and Christians alone are that preservative and that light. No one else can fulfill these two functions of being salt and light regardless of how educated they may be, or how hard they may try. That is because, as the Scriptures teach, the people of the world live in spiritual darkness. As you look back throughout history and see the evil way that mankind has lived and treated his fellowman, it is clear that knowledge does not equal goodness. Every difficulty in the world can be traced to the selfishness and self-seeking sin nature of mankind.

God, and God alone, has the wisdom that provides the answers to the problems of this world. Those with all of the knowledge hate to hear they do not have the answers, even though history proves they have not solved mankind's problems. In fact those problems have gotten worse over the years even though everything man knows to do has continually been tried: education, political enactments, international conferences and more. The only way this dark world will find the answers is from the light coming from the life and teachings of Jesus Christ! Only Christians are **"the light of the world."** The truth of this statement is why Jesus tells us that our light <u>must</u> shine before men, that they may see our good deeds. **"...let your light shine before men, that they may see your good deeds and praise your Father in heaven"** (Matthew 5:16).

By bringing up the biblical truth that knowledge and education is <u>not</u> the answer to mankind's problems I don't want to leave the impression that I don't support education. Quite the contrary! I have a college degree, our own three children and the six children we took to raise all went to college. Eight out of the nine received their college degrees, and three received a masters' degree. My wife and I founded what is now one of the major Christian schools in Phoenix, Arizona. I served as president of this school for seventeen years and served on the board of Phoenix Christian High School for ten years.

Education is important. However, Scripture makes it clear that it is the Spirit of God and the Word of God that enlightens mankind with the <u>wisdom</u> we need to understand and apply what knowledge we have. Of course the philosophy of the world disagrees with this statement and promotes the idea that all we need to find the answer is more education in worldly things and worldly knowledge.

FULFILLMENT OF OUR MISSION

To be the **salt of the earth** and the **light of the world** is a wonderful and exciting challenge for every Christian; however, it does not happen just because the words are spoken. There must be a continued audit of the fruit of any mission statement; otherwise how can you know if it is being fulfilled? This principle applies to any organization including the people in the Kingdom of God, His church, and the fulfillment of our mission statement.

Properly fulfilling the mission statement of any organization requires proper training, discipline and commitment on the part of each individual. The same holds true in Christianity. Paul relates the Christian life to the training and discipline required to run a marathon, and then at the end receive the prize.

The Bible summarizes the directive for the fulfillment of the Christian's mission statement in Romans 12:1-2. It states, **"Therefore, I urge you, brothers, in view of God's mercy, to offer your bodies as living sacrifices, holy and pleasing to God—which is your spiritual worship. Do not conform any longer to the pattern of this world, but be transformed by the renewing of your mind. Then you will be able to test and approve what God's will is—his good, pleasing and perfect will."**

It was God's mercy that implemented His perfect plan of salvation by grace; a free gift to everyone who believes in and accepts Jesus Christ as personal savior. In response to this gift, every born again Christian is to offer up his being as a sacrifice unto God. If we are going to fulfill His perfect will in our life in this dark world, which is to be salt, a preserver of good by living according to biblical standards, and light, by the good deeds which we accomplish, this must be our commitment.

As you proceed through this book, you will see that I often make the statement that in these last days we are living in one of the toughest times ever for Christians to fulfill their mission statement to be salt and light. This is especially true in America! In the history of mankind there has never been a world society with so much power to teach so many people its standards as the American society has now to teach and influence people in the ways of the world. Remember, accepting the world's philosophy is what causes contamination that prevents us from being salt.

That is one of the reasons why God warns us several times in different places in the Bible about the ways and things of the world. The world is the enemy's main attack vehicle to spiritually contaminate the strength of Christians, thereby weakening our ability to function as salt and light in this dark world. I will cite a couple of these warnings here, and we will be discussing the "kingdom of the world" in more detail in chapter five. **"You adulterous people, don't you know that friendship with the world is hatred toward God? Anyone who chooses to be a friend of the world becomes an enemy of God"** (James 4:4). **"Do not love the world or anything in the world. If anyone loves the world, the love of the Father is not in him. For everything in the world—the cravings of sinful man, the lust of his eyes and the boasting of what he has and does —comes not from the Father but from the world"** (I John 2:15, 16).

God warns us in Scripture that the systems and things developed by mankind that make up a society, called the world, are controlled by our spiritual enemy. He uses them as his attack vehicle to wage warfare against Christians. His world systems may attack us directly through persecution, either physically or verbally, or indirectly through deception. Both of these methods work toward the enemy's purpose to weaken us spiritually by "shooting out" our being light and contaminating our being salt.

We are told in Scripture that we are to live in the world, but if we spiritually have been born again, we are not to be of the world. That is because spiritually we are no longer citizens of the kingdom of this world, but have become citizens of the Kingdom of God. The apostle Paul considered this world dead to him and himself dead to this world, as did Jesus. Paul said, **"May I never boast except in the cross of our Lord Jesus Christ, through which the world has been crucified to me, and I to the world"** (Galatians 6:14). And Jesus said, **"You** (speaking to the Pharisees) **are from below; I am from above. You are of this world; I am not of this world"** (John 8:23).

When we accept Jesus Christ into our hearts as our personal savior, we experience a spiritual rebirth—what we refer to as being born again—by the power of the Holy Spirit. From that point on, we are no longer a part of the world's spiritual family. Colossians 1:13 states, **"For He has rescued us out of the darkness and gloom of Satan's kingdom and brought us into the kingdom of His dear Son"** (Living Bible). Satan's objective is to prevent us from carrying out God's mission to function as salt and light. Satan uses his kingdom—the world, or society, as one of his key attack vehicles to contaminate our being salt and to dim our light. However, all Christians are equipped with a power greater than the influence of Satan's world system and its standards so that we might fulfill our mission. **"You, dear children, are from God and have overcome them, because the one who is in you** (speaking about the Holy Spirit—God Himself) **is greater than the one who is in the world** (speaking about Satan)" (I John 4:4).

As we look at prophetic Scriptures that reveal the roots of Satan's methods and tactics that he is using in his spiritual warfare against America, we will see how he is trying to destroy God's special call for Christians in America in these last days. As we have already seen, his methods have been very successful in this last generation in overcoming the body of Christ. We have not preserved many of the godly standards that the majority of people in our society lived by since the founding of our country.

Before discussing these prophetic Scriptures, however, it is important that we review some of the fundamental principles and characteristics that make up the Kingdom of God and the kingdom of the world. Our understanding of the major differences between these two spiritual kingdoms is important to build a proper foundation so that you might understand the prophetic Scriptures about these last days.

CHAPTER THREE

The majority of Christians believe we are in the last days of the Church Age. There are several biblical reasons why this truth is widely believed. I will not review all of them but I do want to share a few. This is because it is important that we be well grounded in this truth and do not waiver in realizing that <u>according to Scripture we are living in the most critical and deceptive time of spiritual warfare that the church has encountered</u>.

THE AGES OF TIME

According to the Bible the time that God created Adam and Eve was around 4000 B.C. It can also be determined from the Bible that the time span from Adam and Eve to when God called Abraham was around 2000 years. From the time of Abraham, which was the beginning of the Jewish Nation, to the beginning of the Church Age and the time of the Gentiles, we know from Scriptures that the time span was also about 2000 years. And, of course, from the beginning of the Church Age to our present time is now nearing 2000 years.

God has dealt with mankind in <u>three distinct</u> periods of time, each of which has been approximately 2000 years. This is significant. The number <u>three</u> throughout Scripture <u>denotes</u> something that is of <u>divine perfection</u>. For example, the Trinity of the Godhead: God the Father, Jesus Christ and the Holy Spirit. Another example is the fact that the universe is made up of three distinct things: Space, time and matter. Even these three things can be broken down into three different parts. Space is length, depth and height. Time is past, present and future. Matter is solid, liquid or gas.

We know very little about the first 2000-year period that God dealt with mankind. All that God chose to tell us about this first period of time is found in the first eleven chapters of the Bible. In this time, God dealt with mankind through select individuals, called patriarchs. That is why this period is called the Patriarchal Dispensation.

The second period of 2000 years began in Genesis chapter 12 when God called Abraham. God shifts His emphasis from the history of mankind in general and begins to focus on the development of a single individual and his descendants, who became the Jewish race. From this race, Jesus Christ, God's Son, would be born. This second period of 2000 years is called the Jewish Dispensation.

During this second period of 2000 years, God's dealings with mankind were focused on one nationality, the Jewish nation, whose founder was Abraham. **"The Lord had said to Abram, "Leave your country, your people and your father's household and go to the land I will show you. I will make you into a great nation and I will bless you; I will make your name great, and you will be a blessing. I will bless those who bless you, and whoever curses you I will curse; and all peoples on earth will be blessed through you"** (Genesis 12:1-3). This second period consumes all of the Old Testament except for the first 11 chapters of Genesis.

The third way that God has dealt with mankind completely changed with the death and resurrection of Christ. That was the beginning of the Church Age. During this period of time God changed from dealing with mankind through a nation and began to deal personally with each individual. He does this by taking up His residence in each person through the Holy Spirit when they accept Jesus Christ as their personal Savior. Every person who becomes a Christian is spiritually born again into the Kingdom of God, and becomes a temple of the Holy Spirit, **"Don't you know that you yourselves are God's temple and that God's Spirit lives in you?"** (I Corinthians 3:16). This is uniquely different than how God dealt with mankind in the previous 4000 years. In those periods only a select few received the gift of the Holy Spirit. This last period of 2000 years is called the Church Age or the Spiritual Dispensation, because all who become Christians receive the Holy Spirit. In this period of time, God deals primarily with the Gentiles.

The history of these three distinct periods of time is one of the reasons we know that we are living in the last days of the Church Age. This last age is now approaching 2000 years, the same amount of time that the other two distinct periods of time lasted. As the period we are now living in comes to a close, we do not want to be foolish like the Jewish people who did not recognize the prophetic events that God had warned them about. We need to recognize the biblical prophesies about the end of our dispensation, the Church Age. This is critical to understanding Satan's spiritual warfare going on against the body of Christ in America. We will discuss these prophetic warnings later in this book.

THE SIGNIFICANCE OF 6000 YEARS

Another significant indication that we are living in the last days of the Church Age is that mankind has been living on Earth for about 6000 years. Like the three 2000-year periods of time, this too can be calculated from Scripture. Though scientists attempt to pre-date man to long before Adam, only God knows the exact time of mankind's origin and He has shared that information with us in His Word. The effects of the flood make it impossible for man's wisdom and instruments to accurately test and determine the chronology of what took place before the flood.

The number six is a significant number to mankind because in the Bible it is associated with all that relates to human beings and their labor. Man was created on the sixth day; he was commanded to work for six days and rest on the seventh; he was to work the ground for six years and then let it rest in the seventh. In Revelation 13:18 we are told that the number of man is 666, which people commonly refer to as the mark of the beast. Six signifies "secular completeness."

According to the Bible record, the time of human beings on Earth has now spanned nearly 6000 years. There is still one more period of time that God deals with mankind in the future. It will be quite different from the other three. The last period of time that God will deal with mankind is called the millennium, and the book of Revelation seems to indicate it will last for 1000 years. It will begin at the end of this current Church Age. No longer will mankind run the affairs on this Earth, but Christ will rule the Earth in peace. Before that happens we must realize there is still a lot to take place in the few remaining years of the Church Age—however many years that may be. Christians need to be well informed about the prophetic warnings given to us in Scripture and how they apply to these last days as mankind runs the affairs on this Earth. One of the major reasons why the body of Christ has suffered so many spiritual defeats in recent years is because we lack an understanding of those prophetic Scriptures about the last days. I repeat the words of the prophet Hosea, **"My people are destroyed** (defeated or overcome) **from lack of knowledge"** (Hosea 4:6).

THE SIGNIFICANCE OF 7000 YEARS

When we add the 1000-year period of the millennium that Christ will reign to the 6000 years that mankind has run the Earth it equals 7000 years. Throughout Scripture the number seven denotes divine perfection or completeness. For example, it took seven days for God to complete His creation. On the seventh day He rested, which is one indication why the last 1000 year period of mankind on Earth will be one of peace and rest. I know there are many questions one would like answered about this millennium period of 1000 years, but just like those who lived in previous time periods, mankind has never been given much insight into how God is going to work with mankind in the next period of time.

Joshua had the children of Israel march around the wall of Jericho for seven days with seven priests carrying trumpets. On the seventh day they marched around the city seven times with the seven priests blowing their trumpets before God collapsed the wall around Jericho. The prophet Elisha in the Old Testament told Naaman, the commander of Syria's army, that the Lord would heal him of leprosy if he would go wash himself seven times in the Jordan River. Naaman did not receive his healing until he came up out of the water the seventh time. Seven denotes completeness.

RETURN OF THE JEWS TO PALESTINE: A MAJOR PROPHETIC SIGN

The return of the Jewish people to Palestine and the development of their nation after 1900 years of dispersion throughout the World are considered by many to be the greatest fulfillment of Bible prophecy other than those fulfilled in the birth, life, death and resurrection of Jesus Christ. Both the Old and New Testaments speak of this prophetic sign. Nearly 2000 years ago Jesus stated that Jerusalem would be trampled down by the Gentiles until the end of this the Church Age. From 70 AD until 1967, Jerusalem was under the control of other nations. The restoration of Israel as a nation in 1948 serves as a major prophetic sign that helps us understand from God's prophetic timetable that we are now living in the last days of the Church Age.

Because the Jews rejected their Messiah, God allowed the Roman army to swoop down on Jerusalem in 70 A.D. and destroy the city and the temple. The Jews were then dispersed throughout the world, scattered to more than 100 countries for nearly 1900 years. Yet even though the Jewish people were dispersed among many nations, God remained faithful to His Word. He kept His promise to Abraham and protected his descendants, their nationality and their heritage. We have full evidence of this today. The Jews are the only people in the history of mankind to be without a country of their own for so long who have kept their identity.

From 70 A.D. to 614 A.D. the Romans ruled the land of Palestine. The Persians conquered Palestine in 614 A.D. and ruled it until about 700 A.D. when Islam spread from Spain to India. The Arabs took control around 700 A.D. and maintained control of the Holy Land, except for brief periods of time during the Crusades directed by the Roman Church during the period of the Dark Ages.

During the years from 1500 A.D. to 1800 A.D. Palestine fell into disuse. There were only 1500 Jewish people in the entire land. During the 1800s the population began to slowly increase. By 1865, Jerusalem had a population of 18,000. About one half of the inhabitants were Jewish. In the late 1800s, the Jewish people began to suffer persecution in many of the lands where they had been living. God used this persecution to cause the Jews to think about returning to their own national homeland. This concept was intensified through the distribution of a pamphlet called "The Jewish State," written by Theodore Herzl in 1897.

By 1914 there were 90,000 Jews in Palestine. God was moving to bring about the second restoration of Abraham's descendants just as the Old Testament prophets had written. The next major event occurred in November of 1917 when an English statesman, Arthur Balfour, wrote the Jewish Federation, stating that England would make a declaration to help the Jewish people return to Palestine. England was able to fulfill that commitment after World War I when they gained control of Palestine from the Turkish government.

England's commitment to help the Jewish people owed much to a Jewish scientist, Chaim Weizmann. The August 1982 issue of *Gospel Truth* magazine reported: *"Weizmann was a brilliant research chemist, and became the first president of the modern state of Israel. However, he was born in Russian Poland. He lectured in the University of Geneva in biochemistry, and in 1904 at Manchester,*

England. The thrilling thing in this romantic story is that when World War I broke out in 1914, God had raised up Weizmann in Poland, brought him over to England, and when it looked as though Britain might not be able to terminate the war victoriously, Weizmann worked in the British laboratories from 1916 to 1918 on acetone—a colorless, flammable, volatile liquid. In that capacity, he performed a notable service for the British government during the latter years of World War I by discovering and developing a method for synthesizing acetone (a substance essential to the manufacture of a smokeless powder called cordite). The discovery of this secret gave him national recognition. In 1917 Prime Minister David Lloyd George offered him a reward for this spectacular achievement. Weizmann chose that the British government provide a national, geographical home for the Jewish people. In November, 1917, Britain issued the celebrated Balfour Declaration in which it formally announced its favorable attitude towards the establishment in Palestine of a national home for Jews."

The next 30 years saw the Jewish population in Israel mushroom to 710,000. It appears God used the same method to detach the Jewish people from their homes among the Gentile nations that He used to wean them from Egypt in the days of Moses. In Egypt, it was persecution from the hands of Pharaoh. In the 1920s, 30s and early 40s it was persecution from Nazi Germany and the Communist government in Russia.

It was 30 years to the month from the Balfour Declaration that a United Nations mandate returned part of the land of Palestine to the Jewish people, in November 1947. I do not believe this period of 30 years was just happenstance. Thirty years has always denoted maturity in God's dealings with the Jewish people. There are many examples of this in Scripture—the most significant being that Jesus was 30 years old when He began His ministry. Another is King David, the king of Israel whose life and history is discussed more than anyone else in the Old Testament. David became king when he was 30 years old.

On May 14, 1948 the mandate that had been issued by the United Nations became effective and Abraham's descendants once again possessed Israel. This restoration is one of the greatest miracles and fulfillment of prophecy of all time. Several Old Testament writers prophesied about this second restoration of the Jews to the land of Palestine. **"In that day the Lord will reach out his hand a second time to reclaim the remnant that is left of his people from Assyria, from Lower Egypt, from Upper Egypt, from Cush, from Elam, from Babylonia, from Hamath and from the islands of the sea** (islands of the sea is a prophetic phase that means many nations). **He will raise a banner for the nations and gather the exiles of Israel; he will assemble the scattered people of Judah from the four quarters of the earth"** (Isaiah 11:11-12). By the words of Isaiah we can know that God is <u>not</u> referring to the first restoration of the Jews to Palestine, which was from their 70 years of captivity by the Babylonian Empire. Not only does Isaiah specifically say the <u>second</u> restoration, but he also mentions the Israelites returning from many nations, which was <u>not</u> the case in the first restoration when they returned from Babylon.

In a similar way both Jeremiah and Ezekiel prophesied of the second restoration by referring to the Jews returning from many countries and nations. **"'However, the days are coming,' declares the Lord, 'when man will no longer say, 'as surely as the Lord lives, who brought the Israelites up out of Egypt,' but they will say, 'as surely as the Lord lives who brought the Israelites up out of the land of the north and out of the countries where he had banished them.' For I will restore them to the land I gave their forefathers"** (Jeremiah 16:14-15). **Therefore say: 'This is what the Sovereign Lord says: Although I sent them far away among the nations and scattered them among the countries, yet for a little** while I have been a sanctuary for them in the countries where they have gone.' Therefore say: 'This is what the Sovereign Lord says: I will gather you from the nations and bring you back from the countries where you have been scattered, and I will give you back the land of Israel again'" (Ezekiel 11:16-17).

Ezekiel also made one of the best-known prophecies about the second return of the Jewish people to the land promised to Abraham in Ezekiel 37:1-12. **"The hand of the Lord was upon me, and he brought me out by the Spirit of the Lord and set me in the middle of a valley; it was full of bones. He led me back and forth among them, and I saw a great many bones on the floor of the valley, bones that were very dry. He asked me, "Son of man, can these bones live?" I said, "O Sovereign Lord, you alone know."** The dry bones Ezekiel saw were representative of the Jewish people. They were as dead people, because they were not fulfilling their purpose as Abraham's descendants because they had been scattered throughout the Earth.

Ezekiel continues: **"Then he said to me, "Prophesy to these bones and say to them, 'Dry bones, hear the word of the Lord!' This is what the Sovereign Lord says to these bones: 'I will make breath enter you, and you will come to life. I will attach tendons to you and make flesh come upon you and cover you with skin; I will put breath in you, and you will come to life. Then you will know that I am the Lord.'**

So I prophesied as I was commanded. And, as I was prophesying there was a noise, a rattling sound, and the bones came together, bone to bone. I looked, and tendons and flesh appeared on them and skin covered them, but there was no breath in them.

Through the message of Herzl's pamphlet and the Balfour Declaration in England (1917) the Jewish people began to return to Israel en masse ... to take the form of a nation once again.

"Then he said to me, "Prophesy to the breath; prophesy,

51

son of man, and say to it, 'This is what the Sovereign Lord says: Come from the four winds, O breath and breathe into these slain, that they may live.'" So I prophesied as he commanded me, and breath entered them; they came to life and stood up on their feet—a vast army." On May 14, 1948 the Jewish people came to life as a nation once again in Israel as the mandate which had been issued by the United Nations became effective.

Then he said to me: "Son of man, these bones are the whole house of Israel. They say, 'Our bones are dried up and our hope is gone; we are cut off.' Therefore, prophesy and say to them: 'This is what the Sovereign Lord says: O my people, I am going to open your graves and bring you up from them; I will bring you back to the land of Israel'" (Exekiel 37:1-12). "...This is what the Sovereign Lord says: 'I will take the Israelites out of the nations where they have gone. I will gather them from all around and bring them back into their own land. I will make them one nation in the land, on the mountain of Israel...'" (Ezekiel 37:21-22).

For centuries, the Lord hid His face from Abraham's descendants. But God's faithfulness prevailed. Because of the promise God made to Abraham He has kept His covenant with Abraham over these past 4000 years. The land of Israel is again the home of the Israelites, Abraham's descendants. The nation once again is alive! The fulfillment of the prophecies found in the Old Testament is now written in our history book.

BATTLING FOR THEIR HOMELAND

There have been several wars that have taken place in Israel since May 14, 1948 when the Jewish people regained control of the land. The Arab nations that surround them have tried to destroy them repeatedly, and that effort continues today. Studying the way the Jewish people won those wars, even though the odds were greatly against them, is like reading about the miraculous victories that took place in the days of Joshua in the Old Testament when they went in to possess the land. Within hours of the declaration of the Jewish state, Arab forces began dropping bombs to rid the land of its 710,000 Jews. However, God had different plans, and the Israelites gained the upper hand in this first conflict with the Arabs. An armistice followed, even though the Arabs still had control of the old city of Jerusalem and the remains of the temple wall.

The next conflict occurred in 1956, when President Gamal Abdel Nasser of Egypt called for a holy war against Israel. The Egyptian army, equipped with Soviet weapons, moved into the Sinai and began the second round of fighting against this new nation of Israel. However, this second conflict was again brief, with the Israelites teaching the Arabs a dramatic lesson.

By 1958, only ten years after the establishment of the new Jewish state, major progress had been made in several areas: The Jewish population had risen to 1.8 million. Most of the people were employed and self-sufficient. Agricultural productivity was up 600%. To house the growing population, 150,000 new dwellings had been completed. Other areas of progress included: national insurance, several welfare and health services, roads, water, electricity, sanitary facilities, irrigation and participation in free elections.

In 1967, a third conflict broke out as Arab resentment again exploded, beginning what came to be known as the Six-Day War. The Arabs launched an all-out attack this time, but the Israelites retaliated with lightning speed, again soundly defeating them. The war started on June 4. On June 5, Israel bombed the airfields of Egypt, Syria, Jordan and Iraq, destroying 452 planes in three hours. The same day their ground forces moved against Egyptian forces at four different points in the Sinai.

On June 6, Israel counterattacked against Jordanian troops in Jerusalem and took everything except the old city. On June 7, Israel gained possession of the old city of Jerusalem for the first time since

70 AD, and a quarter of a million Jews streamed into the old city, headed for the Wailing Wall. The site where Solomon built the temple for the Lord was back in Jewish hands. On June 9, Israel drove the Syrians from the Golan Heights, penetrated the Sinai to the Suez Canal and took the Gaza strip. On June 10 all parties agreed to a cease-fire.

The fourth conflict started on October 6, 1973, which was Yom Kippur, the most holy day of the year for the Jews—their Day of Atonement. It looked extremely bad at first. In the south, Egyptian aircraft and artillery bombarded the Sinai and 70,000 of their troops and 1,000 tanks crossed the Suez Canal. In the north, 40,000 Syrian troops with 800 tanks attacked the Golan Heights. Within a few days Israel stopped all advances on both fronts and began to penetrate enemy lines with amazing speed, moving to within 62 miles of Cairo, Egypt. The Arab nations again faced defeat and within 20 days from the war's beginning, October 25, 1973, a cease-fire was proclaimed.

The next conflict began on June 6, 1982, when the State of Israel launched a massive thrust into Lebanon aimed at removing PLO (Palestine Liberation Organization) terrorist gunners from the northern border of Israel. During this brief war, 86 Soviet-built MIG fighters were shot down by the Israeli air force without a single loss of their own. Business Week, September 20, 1982 reported: *"The latest air war was lopsided, too, but this time in Israel's favor. When Syria sent up 60 Soviet built MIG fighters to defend its SAM batteries, 90 U.S. made Israelite jets pounced on and shot down 36 MIGS without a single loss. On the following day, Syria dispatched 50 more MIGS to challenge the Israeli air force—and not one of those jets returned to base, the Israelis claim."*

The purpose of this brief review is to further help us understand that we are living in the prophetic times the Bible calls the last days of the Christian dispensation. Sometimes we fail to remember the important part the Jewish people have played in God's plan for man.

Because of God's faithfulness in keeping His promise to Abraham, the Jewish people have been a tremendous blessing. They gave us all of the Scriptures. They are the race God chose to use for Jesus, God himself in the flesh, to come to Earth in the form of man. The majority of God's Word centers on the history of the Jewish people. They began the early church.

The prophet Ezekiel also foretells their ending. Speaking of things to come after their second restoration, he says: **"My servant David** (making reference to Jesus) **will be king over them, and they will all have one shepherd. They will follow my laws and be careful to keep my decrees** (we know this has not yet happened). **They will live in the land I gave to my servant Jacob,** (remember, Jacob was the father of the 12 sons who formed the twelve tribes of Israel) **the land where your fathers lived ... I will make a covenant of peace with them; it will be an everlasting covenant. I will establish them and increase their numbers, and I will put my sanctuary among them forever. My dwelling place will be with them; I will be their God, and they will be my people. Then the nations will know that I, the Lord, make Israel holy, when my sanctuary is among them forever"** (Ezekiel 37:24-28).

The Jewish people will someday acknowledge and accept Jesus, as foretold by Zechariah, another Old Testament prophet. Speaking of the end-times he says: **"On that day, when all the nations of the earth are gathered against her, I will make Jerusalem an immovable rock for all the nations ... on that day I will set out to destroy all the nations that attack Jerusalem. And I will pour out on the house of David and the inhabitants of Jerusalem a spirit of grace and supplication. They will look on me, the one they have pierced,** (what they did to Jesus at the crucifixion) **and mourn for him as one grieves for a first born son"** (Zechariah 12:3,9-10).

There can be no doubt as to the prophetic times in which we

live. However, the main message of this book is not just to establish God's prophetic timetable. We cannot just observe the Jewish people fulfill end-time Scriptures. God also recorded some crucial scriptural prophecies for Christians during this same period. These were given to help guide us spiritually so that we might properly prepare ourselves to fulfill our mission to be the "salt of the earth" and the "light of the world" in these troubled times.

Prior to World War II, one could scarcely have imagined or visualized that there would ever be a nuclear age, a space age or a computer age such as we are now experiencing. Obviously, all the things taking place on Earth at this time are no accident; everything is happening for a purpose. God has not been caught off guard. He has known all along just what was to take place, and when and how. That is why He has warned His people through the prophetic Scriptures about these last days. It is especially important for us in America to understand these key prophetic Scriptures because we have been the geographical center of the Church these last 300 years. Because of that truth, it is easy to understand why Satan's attacks against the church that are foretold in the Bible for our day will be the most severe against Christians in our country.

CHAPTER FOUR

The next fundamental truth that is important in order to have a proper understanding of is the relationship between the prophetic warnings that are found in Scripture about these end times and what it means to be born again. Salvation is the most significant truth of the Christian faith. Being born again is a requirement to enter the Kingdom of Heaven. Understanding what it means to be born again shows us why Christians are the only people who can truly function as the **salt of the earth** and the **light of the world.**

"**After dark one night a Jewish religious leader named Nicodemus, a member of the sect of the Pharisees, came for an interview with Jesus. 'Sir,' he said, 'we all know that God has sent You to teach us. Your miracles are proof of this.' Jesus replied, 'With all the earnestness I possess I tell you this: Unless you are born again, you can never get into the Kingdom of God.' 'Born again!' exclaimed Nicodemus. 'What do You mean? How can an old man go back into his mother's womb and be born again?' Jesus replied, 'What I am telling you so earnestly is this: Unless one is born of water** (meaning the normal process of physical birth) **and the Spirit,** (meaning spiritual rebirth) **he cannot enter the Kingdom of God. Men can only reproduce human life, but the Holy Spirit gives new life from heaven; so don't be surprised at My statement that you must be born again!**" (John 3:1-7 LB).

Today many people, like Nicodemus, do not understand what is meant by the phrase "born again." We live in the physical world; therefore, our natural tendency is to think of things more in the physical realm. It is difficult for us to think of things in the spiritual realm, which is necessary to comprehend spiritual truths. However, keep in mind the fact that every human being is **primarily a spiritual being**. It is the only part of our being that will live forever; the physical does not. The physical is secondary and returns to the elements of the Earth. This physical life is like a vapor compared to our spiritual life, which will last for an eternity.

When God created mankind the Bible says that He made us in His own image. **"Then God said, 'Let us make man in our image, in our likeness,'…So God created man in his own image, in the image of God he created him; male and female he created them"** (Genesis 1: 26-27). God is a spiritual being. Therefore, to be created in His image would have to mean that mankind was created in God's spiritual image. Our body, or the physical flesh that God gave man when He created him, is made up from the physical elements of this Earth and that is what it will return to after we die. Its main purpose is to house our spiritual being for the duration of time that we live here on Earth as we prepare for our life hereafter.

Both Paul and Peter referred to our physical body as a tent, something that is temporary. Paul said, **"Now we know that if the earthly tent we live in is destroyed, we have a building from God, an eternal house in heaven, not built by human hands"** (II Corinthians 5:1). **"I think it is right to refresh your memory as long as I live in the tent of this body, because I know that I will soon put it aside, as our Lord Jesus Christ has made clear to me"** (II Peter 1:13). In Heaven the mortal body that we now have to house our spiritual being will be replaced with an immortal body.

To understand the fundamental truth that we must be born again, we must understand that there are **two completely different spiritual Kingdoms.** Every person is a member of one of these two different spiritual Kingdoms. You cannot be a member of both at the same time. **I cannot over emphasize this important spiritual truth.** One of the spiritual Kingdoms to which we can belong is the

Kingdom of God, or Kingdom of Heaven, whose ruler is Jesus Christ. The other spiritual kingdom that we can belong too is the kingdom of the world, whose ruler is Satan. To help you comprehend the spiritual warfare that the Bible prophesies for these last days, it is important for you to be fully aware of the fundamental differences between these two spiritual Kingdoms.

THE TWO SPIRITUAL KINGDOMS

KINGDOM OF THE WORLD: RULER IS SATAN

KINGDOM OF GOD OR OF HEAVEN: RULER IS JESUS

YOU MUST SPIRITUALLY BE BORN AGAIN TO ENTER THE KINGDOM OF GOD.

JOHN 3:5-7

COL 1:13

JOHN 3:16-19

JOHN 1:12-13

The phrase **"unless you are born again"** used by Jesus in His conversation with Nicodemus is referring to a spiritual birth, not a physical birth. Every baby is born not only with a physical body but also as a spiritual being into a spiritual family. The Bible teaches that the disobedience of Adam and Eve didn't just bring about physical death, but also spiritual death to all of their descendants. Death means separation! Therefore, every newborn baby is born spiritually separated from the Kingdom of God. We are all born spiritually as a member of the kingdom of the world. No one at birth is part of the Kingdom of Heaven. This is the spiritual condition everyone inherited from Adam and Eve. **"Therefore, just as sin entered the world through one man,** (referring to our forefather Adam) **and death through sin, and this way death** (separation from God) **came to all men, because all sinned—"** (Romans 5:12).

One of the strongest statements of this truth came from Jesus in His reply to Nicodemus. For emphasis I will repeat these verses, **"What I am telling you so earnestly is this: Unless one is born of water** (referring to our physical birth) **and the Spirit,** (conceived by the Holy Spirit and reborn spiritually into the Kingdom of God) **he cannot enter the Kingdom of God. Men can only reproduce human life, but the Holy Spirit gives new life from heaven; so don't be surprised at My statement that you must be born again!"** (John 3:5-7 LB).

We are born spiritually on the wrong side of the tracks, so to speak. We are born as members of the kingdom of the world with a sinful nature. This is why we must be born again spiritually to enter the Kingdom of God. We are sinners by nature. The Bible says in Romans chapter 7 that it is a spiritual law—we sin because of our heritage. Our natural instinct is to be self-centered. A young child, for example, will naturally lie or cheat, bite, scratch, and hit as they look after and seek after their own self interest. Parents do not teach them to be this way. I am not saying that God holds children responsible for being born into the kingdom of the world and their actions while they are young. If a child should die while he is young, he is saved into the Kingdom of Heaven not because he is innocent of sin, but because of his innocence in not knowing. Even though they have not spiritually been born again God does not hold someone accountable until they reach an age of accountability, which varies with each child or individual.

The natural instinct of every person, being a member of the kingdom of the world, is to pursue self-exaltation, self-glorification and self-satisfaction. We are born with a self-centered nature! It was this same self-centered attitude that brought about the fall of Satan and explains why God cast him out of His Kingdom, even though Satan had held a high position in God's Spiritual Kingdom. Speaking of Satan the Bible states, **"You said in your heart, "I will ascend to heaven; I will raise my throne above the stars of God; I will sit enthroned on the mount of assembly, on the utmost heights of the sacred mountain. I will ascend above the tops of the clouds; I will make myself like the Most High"** (Isaiah 14:13-14). Notice the use of the word "I," "I," "I," "I." I will do this and I will do that.

Because we are born as members of the kingdom of the world we have this same natural instinct that caused Satan to fall. We live to serve ourselves. When we set ourselves up to decide what is right and wrong rather than following the teachings of God, it really means that we want to take the place of God. Examine the nature of our Lord and Savior Jesus Christ who walked here on Earth in the fullness of the Holy Spirit. He is the only person to ever be conceived by the power of the Spirit of God in a woman's womb; the only one born as a member of the Kingdom of God. He said, **"I tell you the truth, the Son can do nothing by himself; he can do only what he sees his Father doing, because whatever the Father does the Son also does"** (John 5:19). **"By myself I can do nothing; I judge only as I hear, and my judgment is just, for I seek not to please myself but him who sent me"** (John 5:30). If Jesus did not do anything by Himself, surely it is obvious that we too are dependent upon the Father and His Word. Satan's plan of attack is to use his kingdom, the world or society, to take away this dependence and thus remove our ability to be the **salt of the earth** and the **light of the world**.

FREEDOM FROM THE KINGDOM OF THE WORLD

We all need to be freed from the spiritual kingdom of the world into which we have been born. The Bible teaches there is only one way out. After reaching the age of accountability, we all must experience being born again spiritually, just as Jesus told Nicodemus. We must be convicted of sin by the Holy Spirit and spiritually born again to get into the Kingdom of God. This is the only way to Heaven. How are we born again? The Word of God states that this spiritual rebirth takes place when we accept Jesus Christ as our personal Savior. **"Before anything else existed, there was Christ, with God. He has always been alive and is Himself God. He created everything there is—nothing exists that He didn't make. Eternal life is in Him, and this life gives light to all mankind....But although He made the world, the world didn't recognize Him when He came. Even in His own land and among His own people, the Jews, He was not accepted. Only a few would welcome and receive Him. But to all who received him, He gave the right to become children of God. All they needed to do was to trust Him to save them. All those who believe this are reborn!—not a physical rebirth resulting from human passion or plan—but from the will of God"** (John 1:1-4, 10-13 LB). **"Jesus answered, "I am the way and the truth and the life. No one comes to the Father except through me. If you really knew me, you would know my Father as well. From now on, you do know him and have seen him...Anyone who has seen me has seen the Father..."** (John 14:6, 7-9).

When we have been spiritually born again of the Holy Spirit of God, that same Holy Spirit literally takes up residence in our being, just as He is in the being of Jesus. This is what the apostle Peter was referring to when he preached on the day of Pentecost. He told the crowd of people that all who received Jesus Christ as their personal Savior would **"...receive the gift of the Holy Spirit. The promise is for you and your children and for all who are far off—..."**

(Acts 2:38-39). Speaking to Christians Paul said later, **"Don't you know that you yourselves are God's temple and that God's Spirit lives in you?"** (I Corinthians 3:16).

Praise be to God that He has made a way for us to escape from the spiritual kingdom called the world by being born again spiritually into His Kingdom, the Kingdom of Heaven. This is what the Gospel of Jesus Christ is all about. **"For he has rescued us from the dominion of darkness and brought us into the kingdom of the Son he loves, in whom we have redemption, the forgiveness of sins"** (Colossians 1:13). **"If you believe that Jesus is the Christ— that He is God's Son and your Savior—then you are a child of God....All who believe this know in their hearts that it is true. If anyone doesn't believe this, he is actually calling God a liar, because he doesn't believe what God has said about His Son. And what is it that God has said? That he has given us eternal life, and that this life is in His Son. So whoever has God's Son has life; whoever does not have his Son, does not have life. I have written this to you who believe in the Son of God so that you may know you have eternal life"** (I John 5:1, 10-13 LB). **"For God so loved the world that he gave his one and only Son, that whoever believes in him shall not perish but have eternal life. For God did not send his Son into the world to condemn the world, but to save the world through him. Whoever believes in him is not condemned, but whoever does not believe stands condemned already because he has not believed in the name of God's one and only Son"** (John 3:16-19).

WHY JESUS IS THE ONLY TRUTH
THAT LEADS TO HEAVEN

We serve a loving and just God, who the Bible says **"...wants all men to be saved and to come to a knowledge of the truth"** (I Timothy 2:4). In today's world, there are many types of religions, including different groups calling themselves Christians. We need to know the difference between these different types of religions because only one leads to Heaven. **True biblical Christianity is not necessarily what society presents it to be or for that matter what some churches present it to be.** The **"knowledge of the truth"** the Bible speaks of in I Timothy 2:4 is given in the next verse. It states, **"For there is one God and one mediator between God and men, the man Christ Jesus"** (I Timothy 2:5).

True Christianity is based on all of the teachings of the Bible—the Gospel of Jesus Christ. It is to experience a personal encounter—a personal relationship—with Jesus Christ as Savior and Lord. That is true biblical Christianity! That is the only truth that will take you to Heaven.

Though we may not understand all that happens in the spiritual world, it is when we accept God's Son, Jesus Christ, as our personal Savior that the power of God is released in our lives. We experience a spiritual rebirth that is brought about by the power of the Holy Spirit. We are born again, and become members of the spiritual Kingdom of God and Heaven. God's Word tells us that it will only be those in the Kingdom of God who will spend eternity with Him in that special place that He has prepared for them—the place called Heaven.

We also need to be aware of the fact that there is in the world today what I call the religion of Christianity. Many people practice the religion of Christianity, but it is not based upon biblical principles and the Gospel of Jesus Christ. It directs our faith towards manmade concepts and practices, just like the religion of Israel did when Jesus was here on Earth. A Christian commitment to things, doctrines, ordinances, traditions, structures, and personalities will not stand the test of true biblical teachings. Our commitment cannot be to anything other than Jesus Christ and His teachings as found in the Scriptures. This non-biblical type of Christianity has caused much confusion. Even more importantly, it has caused many people to miss being born again into the Kingdom of God; therefore, miss Heaven.

I would never point you in the direction of some weak-kneed, shallow Christianity that is not the true way to Heaven. Heaven is too valuable for that. Unfortunately in today's religious environment it is easy for people to get involved in what may be called Christianity, but which does not necessarily mean a commitment to Jesus Christ and His teachings. There is a vast difference. It is very easy to be involved; involvement only requires activity. Many people are committed to a lot of different ideas and philosophies. They can even be doing many works in the name of Jesus, but that may not mean they have experienced a personal relationship with Jesus Christ and spiritually been born again into the Kingdom of God.

The Apostle Paul was involved full time in the religion of his day, but he said, **"...whatever was to my profit I now consider loss for the sake of Christ. What is more, I consider everything a loss compared to the surpassing greatness of knowing Christ Jesus my Lord, for whose sake I have lost all things. I consider them rubbish, that I may gain Christ and be found in Him, not having a righteousness of my own that comes from the law** (being able to keep all of the commandments) **but that which is through faith in Christ..."** (Philippians 3:7-9).

Jesus Christ was the true and living God in the flesh, the God who created all things, including you and me. When the Virgin Mary gave birth to Jesus, an angel said to the shepherds living out in the fields near His birthplace of Bethlehem, **"'Do not be afraid. I bring you good news of great joy that will be for all the people. Today in the town of David** (that was Bethlehem) **a Savior has been born to you; he is Christ the Lord. This will be a sign to you: You will find a baby wrapped in cloths and lying in a manger.' Suddenly a great company of the heavenly host appeared with the angel, praising God and saying, 'glory to God in the highest, and on earth peace to men on whom his favor rests'"** (Luke 2:10-14). Jesus is the Savior for all of mankind who come to Him. He will save their souls from

Hell. The angels knew how important this was for mankind; it was good news of great joy!

The earthly ministry of Jesus only lasted for about three and one-half years; yet, the effect of His life on the history of mankind has been far greater than that of anyone else who ever lived. Why did Jesus have so much influence on the history of mankind? He was God on Earth in the form of a human being. If you want to know God, look at the life of Jesus Christ.

In the Bible Jesus is called: **"The Alpha and the Omega"** (Revelation 1:8); **"Anointed"** (Psalms 2:2); **"Bread of Life"** (John 6:48); **"The Bright and Morning Star"** (Revelation 22:16); **"Chosen and Precious Corner-stone"** (I Peter 2:6); **"Wonderful Counselor"** (Isaiah 9:6); **"Mighty God"** (Isaiah 9:36); **"Deliverer"** (Romans 11:26); **"Emmanuel"** (Isaiah 7:14—it means God is with us); **"Eternal Life"** (I John 5:20); **"Firstborn"** (Psalms 89:27); **"Foundation"** (Isaiah 28:16); **"Friend of Sinners"** (Matthew 11:19); **"Good Shepherd"** (John 10:11); **"High Priest"** (Hebrews 4:14); **"I Am"** (John 8:58); **"Our God"** (Isaiah 40:3); **"King of Kings"** (I Timothy 6:15); **"Lamb"** (Revelation 5:12); **"Light of the World"** (John 8:12); **"Living Bread"** (John 6:51); **"Messiah"** (John 1:41); **"Most Holy"** (Daniel 9:24); **"Physician"** (Matthew 9:12); **"Prince of Peace"** (Isaiah 9:6); **"Rabbi"** (John 1:49); **"Rock"** (I Corinthians 10:4); **"Rose of Sharon"** (Song of Songs 2: 1); **"Descended from David"** (II Timothy 2:8); **"Sun of Righteousness"** (Malachi 4:2); **"Teacher"** (John 3:2); **"The Way, The Truth, The Life"** (John 14:6); **"Word"** (John 1:1). No one can come to the Father, except through Him (see John 14:6).

One of the greatest problems many people have as human beings in becoming a genuine Christian is that they don't think they can possibly be good enough. Others see sin in the lives of Christians, which causes them to reject Christian teachings, thinking that can't be the way to God. If you think that you can't be good enough, you're right! No one is ever good enough for God. We are all sinners, born into the kingdom of the world. You can't pile up brownie points and somehow hope they make you acceptable in God's sight. That is not the way to gain favor with God. Our salvation and becoming a member of God's Kingdom is not based on our being good enough, it is based upon the righteousness of Jesus Christ. This is why, **"Salvation is found in no one else, for there is no other name under heaven given to men by which we must be saved"** (Acts 4:12).

Jesus is the only one who was ever good enough to qualify for Heaven. He lived a sinless life! That is how people like you and me are made right with God—that is where we get the righteousness we need to be saved. That is why **"Salvation is found in no one else..."** as the above verse states. The righteousness of Jesus Christ is **credited to our account** in the eyes of God when we truly believe in and accept Jesus as our personal Savior. This is the gospel of Jesus Christ. That is the Great News!

"But now a righteousness from God, apart from law (our keeping all of God's commandments and never sinning) **has been made known, to which the Law and the Prophets testify. This righteousness from God comes through faith in Jesus Christ to all who believe** (to all who accept Him as their Savior—emphasis added). **There is no difference, for all have sinned and fall short of the glory of God, and are justified freely by his grace** (our salvation is a free gift) **through the redemption that came by Christ Jesus. God presented him as a sacrifice of atonement, through faith in his blood..."** (Romans 3:21-25).

God can't pretend that sin doesn't exist. Yet because of the love that He has for mankind He did something to break the power of sin and its condemnation over us. He sent His Son Jesus to rescue us—redeem us from the spiritual kingdom of the world. This was accomplished when Jesus shed His blood on the cross as a sacrifice to pay the penalty for all of mankind's sins. This is how He became the Savior of mankind and set us free from the spiritual kingdom of the world. To those who will believe this and receive God's free payment for the penalty of their sins by what Jesus Christ did, God does a wonderful thing. He justifies us by applying the righteousness of Jesus Christ to our record. That is how our relationship with God is changed. That is how we fit His standards and qualify for spiritual rebirth into the Kingdom of Heaven. It is not because of my goodness, but because of Jesus Christ's sinless life, death and resurrection and that God counted Jesus' righteousness as my righteousness when I accepted Jesus as my Savior. **"Know that a man is not justified by observing the law, but by faith in Jesus Christ...because by observing the law** (never sinning by always keeping all of God's commandments) **no one will be justified"** (Galatians 2:16).

Do we deserve this? No, it is by God's grace and His love for mankind that He has made this marvelous gift of salvation from the kingdom of the world and Hell available to us through Jesus Christ. It is a free gift from God. And best of all, it assures us of an eternity in Heaven. How are you going to respond to such a gift? I trust you receive it thankfully and with a repentant heart.

For all of those who know the Lord Jesus as their Savior, the grave has been transformed from a foe to a friend. With the backing of the Bible we can say, *"we need to have no fear of death."* It will be a wonderful experience. Our last breath here will result in instantaneous complete healing and exquisite joy there on the other side in a better world. Jesus and Heaven are ours! In a word, sunset here is sunrise there! As Paul said, **"For to me, to live is Christ and to die is gain"** (Philippians 1:21).

To the natural person, death is the final pauperizing blow; to die is loss. Nothing bankrupts humans so completely as death. Death is the greatest loss, for in that instant, every thrill and ambition is extinguished. What a contrast is Paul's statement, **"...to die is gain."** Only a Christian like Paul could say this with confidence based on certified guarantees. He knew, as we can know, how soundly factual the basis of the Christian faith and hope really is. Paul actually encountered the risen Jesus on the road to Damascus, and he became a vehicle through which Jesus worked many miracles, even raising the dead.

Paul had searched the sacred Scriptures with scholarly carefulness and had found in them the birth, life, miracles, death, resurrection, and ascension of Christ all clearly foretold centuries in advance through the Hebrew prophets. He knew how true the ful-fillment of those prophecies was. His knowledge of this and more was behind Paul's commitment and victory cry, **"...to die is gain."**

What Heaven represents is unmistakable. To be there will be the highest fulfillment of all pure hopes, ageless vitality and every sorrow healed. Gone forever will be the burdens of mortal flesh and earthly troubles, weakness, pain, temptation, grief, limitation, and frustration. Heaven is a place where there is no unholy thought, desire, fear, doubt, or anxiety. No more hungering and thirsting, every tear wiped away, drinking "living waters" of immortality. Peter describes it as **"...an inheritance that can never perish, spoil or fade—kept in heaven for you ..."** (I Peter 1:4).

All around us will be those shining "clouds of witnesses"—the redeemed of all the centuries. The saints of the Old and New Testament will gather there. Added to that will be the reward of reunion with our own departed loved ones. Every blemish, every disfigurement, every mark of age or weakness will be gone forever. There will be neither any fading of identity nor any blurring of personality. You will always be you. I shall always be me.

A common question is what happens to young children who die. The Bible nowhere says or implies that young children who die are lost. Although all that are born are sin-infected and born into the kingdom of the world, they are not guilty. There is no such thing as inherited guilt. Those who die as children are not saved by their innocence, but they are saved because of it. I believe the Bible teaches that we do not become responsible; therefore, accountable for our transgressions until we reach a responsible age where we knowingly commit wrong. That, and only that, makes us transgressors and consequently guilty.

No words, however vivid would allow me to properly communicate to any mind limited by sense and time the vastness of all the riches that God has in store for those who love Him enough to put their faith in His Son Jesus Christ. We all have a choice to make, and we will choose either Heaven or Hell. Whichever one you choose will be for eternity; it will never end. There are many people who do not want to hear such a statement, but we will all choose one or the other, even if it is by our silence. There are many people who will ignore the reality that they ultimately have to make a choice. They do not want to think about it. There are people who avoid making a choice by convincing themselves that they don't believe in either Heaven or Hell.

If there is even a possibility of a Heaven and a Hell, it is far too critical a decision for anyone to pass it off lightly by not thinking about it, by ignoring it, or by not trying to find out all that it involves. That is poor judgment. We are talking about something that is for eternity.

You do not want to miss Heaven.
God does not want you to miss Heaven.
I do not want you to miss Heaven.
You do not have to miss Heaven.

You must come to grips with the reality that you are a sinner because every person is born into the kingdom of the world with a sinful nature (see Romans 7: 14 - 8:4). By our own life experiences, we know that this is true. Certainly, we would not have wanted to have been born with a sinful nature. But the Bible says we had no choice in the matter; it has been handed down to us from our forefather Adam. Sin is a part of our nature because he fell into sin (read Romans 5:12-19). Therefore none of us can ever be good enough to qualify for

Heaven. That is why we need a Savior. Otherwise our lot is to remain in the kingdom of the world and spend our eternity in Hell. Jesus changed all of that by becoming mankind's Savior. He provided the means for our salvation by coming to Earth and living a sinless life.

God's plan for salvation is simple. If we believe in and accept His Son Jesus, who lived a sinless life, as our Savior He will credit the sinless life of Jesus to our life. That is what qualifies us for Heaven. That is not only good news, it is great news! Mankind has no authority to alter God's plan by using or believing in some other method that is humanly-developed or created.

Is God's plan fair? It is more than fair! It required a great sacrifice on the part of both God the Father and His Son, Jesus. Remember that it has always been mankind who has turned his back on God; God never turned against mankind. We are the party that is guilty. God didn't have to save us! We should be thankful that He loved us enough to provide such a simple plan so that we might be saved from spending our eternity in Hell, despite the fact that we make mistakes and often live contrary to His standards. The reason God's plan is a just plan is that He took the entire burden upon Himself through His Son Jesus Christ. Who can argue with that?

A portion of Scripture that I think is very meaningful is found in Romans 5:12-20. In essence what God's Word is saying is that because of one man, Adam's sin, all mankind inherited a sinful nature and therefore spiritual death or condemnation and separation from God. The Bible says that it is therefore a right and just plan that all mankind can be justified or saved, reunited with God, by one man, Jesus Christ's, righteousness. **"Consequently, just as the result of one trespass was condemnation for all men, so also the result of one act of righteousness was justification that brings life for all men. For just as through the disobedience of the one man the many were made sinners, so also through the obedience of the one man the many will be made righteous"** (Romans 5:18-19).

Would you look at and consider a simple point of logic with me. If you are the typical individual who believes that you will go to Heaven and you are right in your belief, following God's plan by accepting Jesus Christ as your Savior in order to go to Heaven won't hurt you. However, if what you believe is wrong and the Bible is right, that only those who accept Jesus Christ as their personal Savior will go to Heaven, then your choice not to accept Jesus Christ as your Savior will dramatically crush and affect you for all eternity.

One belief has the potential of terrible consequences, the other way, accepting the Gospel of Jesus Christ as presented in the Bible, has none. One choice won't hurt you regardless of what the truth is; the other choice will cost you your soul in Hell for an eternity if it is not correct. Since we must choose one or the other, logically, which is the wise choice? The choice is yours. Like it or not, each of us makes a choice that will decide our state of being for eternity. That may sound harsh, but it is the truth. Soon enough all of us must pass over to that other side of the grave. To talk about death is not being morbid; it is rational because death is inescapable. The Bible says there is coming a final Judgment Day and that every person will be judged according to the way they lived of their own free will. It says those who are not believers in the gospel of Jesus Christ are condemned. **"Whoever believes in him is not condemned, but whoever does not believe stands condemned already because he has not believed in the name of God's one and only Son"** (John 3:18).

That is a fearful thought! Every human being should stop, listen, and consider while the opportunity lingers. Be done with perilous procrastination. I am not playing on your emotions. I am addressing your intelligence, conscience, and free will. Death has a way of striking unexpectedly and then the last chance is gone. There is no second chance. Receive the risen and living Savior Jesus Christ into your heart now. To possess Him is the only way to be eternally saved. God loves every person and His plan of salvation is available to everyone regardless of what they may have done up to this point in their life. He wants everyone to know the truth. No one was ever worse than the Apostle Paul before he learned the truth of Jesus Christ. He hated the Gospel and was even a leader in trying to kill Christians, but God saved and transformed him.

Repent (decide in your heart to change your way of thinking) and accept Jesus Christ into your heart as your Savior and Lord. That is what Paul did on the Road to Damascus, and what millions have done since. It is the only way to know for sure that you are going to Heaven. If you are sincere and mean it from the heart, you will experience a spiritual rebirth—being spiritually born again into the Kingdom of Heaven. You do not have to understand all that this means. But you will know that it happened and you will be in the Kingdom of God and on your way to Heaven.

God knows your heart and He is not as concerned with your words as He is with the attitude of your heart. The following is a suggested prayer:

"Lord Jesus, I want to know You personally. Thank You for sacrificing Your life on the cross for my sins, paying for the penalty that I owe, making it possible for me to spend my eternal life in Heaven. I open the door of my heart and receive You as my Savior and Lord. Take control of the throne of my life and make me the kind of person You want me to be." If these words express the desire of your heart, pray this prayer right now, and Christ will come into your life as He promised. It is then important that you locate a church that believes in and follows true biblical Christianity so that you can become grounded in the Word of God and be active in Christian service and fellowship.

The Bible promises eternal life in Heaven to all that receive and remain faithful to Christ. **"And this is the testimony: God has given us eternal life, and this life is in his Son. He who has the Son has**

life; he who does not have the Son of God does not have life. I write these things to you who believe in the name of the Son of God so that you may know that you have eternal life" (I John 5:11-13).

I have reviewed the basic plan of salvation and what we must do to be rescued from the kingdom of the world and become a member of the Kingdom of God. Next I want to discuss some of the fundamental differences between the two spiritual Kingdoms, the kingdom of the world and the Kingdom of Heaven. This knowledge will help us understand the prophetic Scriptures that warn us about the tactics and attack methods Satan is using to tempt and cause Christians to experience so much defeat during these last days of the Church Age.

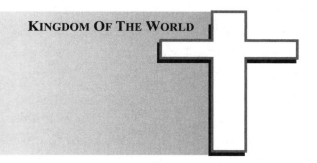

KINGDOM OF THE WORLD

Remember that the kingdom of the world is the spiritual kingdom that we are born into. It was somewhat amazing to find that the word *world* is used more than 200 times in the New Testament. It is mentioned more than either the words Holy Spirit or love. Therefore, I have to conclude that if God used that much space in the New Testament on the subject of *"the world"* it must be important for us to have some understanding of its meaning. The Greek word in Scripture for *world* is "kosmos." It has three primary meanings.

One: The word *world* in Scripture is used to reference the material universe or Earth. **"I will open my mouth in parables, I will utter things hidden since the creation of the world"** (Matthew 13:35). The word *world* is used in a similar way in Acts 17:14, John 1:10 and Mark 16:15.

Two: The word *world* in Scripture is used to reference the inhabitants or people of the world. **"For God so loved the world that He gave His one and only Son, that whoever believes in Him shall not perish, but have eternal life"** (John 3:16). Similar Scriptures that use the word *world* to focus on the whole race of mankind are found in John 12:19 and 17:21.

Three: The word *world* in Scripture is used to reference the moral and spiritual systems we call <u>human society</u>. Society is that realm of the world, which has been developed through the efforts of mankind rather than created by God. It consists of man-made religious systems, political and governmental systems, economic systems, educational systems, business and financial systems, pleasures, entertainment, medicine and the arts, legal systems, science and technology, endowments, riches, advantages, and so forth. Eliminate these things and you eliminate a society. The Bible has much to say about this third meaning of *world*. The Bible has reference to this third use *world* when it says that Satan is its ruler. **"We know that we are children of God** (referring to Christians)**, and that the whole <u>world</u>** (societies) **is under the control of the evil one"** (I John 5:19). This verse is referring to **those things developed by mankind, not created by God.**

Until a person has been conceived by the Holy Spirit and spiritually born again, the Bible says he is a member of the kingdom of the world, which is under Satan's spiritual influence and control. This means that those things developed by mankind who are members of this spiritual kingdom falls into the realm of the kingdom of the world, or society. They are not of God's Kingdom under the control and influence of the Holy Spirit. **"As for you, you were dead in your transgressions and sins, in which you used to live when you followed the ways of this <u>world</u>, and the ruler of the kingdom of the air, the spirit** (Satan) **who is now at work in those who are disobedient. <u>All of us</u> also lived among them at one time, gratifying the cravings of our <u>sinful nature</u>, and following its desires and thoughts. Like the rest, we were <u>by nature</u>** (born this way) **objects of wrath. But because of his great love for us, God, who is rich in mercy, made us alive with Christ even when we were dead in transgressions—it is by grace** (a free gift from God) **you have been saved"** (Ephesians 2:1-5).

There is a mind behind society—a controlling spiritual influence—referred to in the Bible as the "prince of this world," and "he that is in the world." **"For we are not fighting against people made of flesh and blood, but against persons without bodies—the evil rulers of the unseen <u>world</u>, those mighty satanic beings and great evil princes of darkness who rule this <u>world</u>; and against huge numbers of wicked spirits in the spirit world"** (Ephesians 6:12 LB). When Satan tempted Jesus the Bible says, **"Then Satan took Him up and revealed to Him all the kingdoms of the <u>world</u> in a moment of time; And the Devil told Him, 'I will give you all these splendid kingdoms and their glory—for they are mine to give to anyone I wish..."** (Luke 4:5-6 LB). Jesus did not contest Satan's statement that all of the kingdoms of this world, what we call society, were under Satan's authority.

This is not to say that the things of the world that mankind develops as members of the kingdom of the world cannot be converted out of the world system and used for the glory of God, just as man can be. But on the whole, God warns us through Scripture that our spiritual enemy controls the systems and things that make up a society. This is important to remember because the world system is one of Satan's key attack vehicles to tempt and wage spiritual warfare against Christians. It is through the things of the world or society that he tempts us in his efforts to keep Christians from fulfilling God's mission to be the **salt of the earth** and the **light of the world**.

This is why we find several Scriptures in God's Word that warn us to no longer conform to the pattern of this *world (society);* to keep ourselves unspotted from the *world (society)*; to avoid friendship with the *world (society)* and its standards; to only be **in** but not **of** the *world (society)*; and not to love—become attached to—this *world (society)*.

Here are just a few of the warnings from Scripture. **"Do not conform any longer to the pattern of this <u>world</u>, but be transformed** by the renewing of your mind. Then you will be able to test and approve what God's will is" (Romans 12:2). **Religion that God, our Father, accepts as pure and faultless is this: to look after orphans and widows in their distress and to keep oneself from being polluted** (spotted) **by the world"** (James 1:27). **"You adulterous people, don't you know that friendship with the world is hatred toward God? Anyone who chooses to be a friend of the world becomes an enemy of God"** (James 4:4). Jesus said, **"My prayer is not that you take them out of the world, but that you protect them from the evil one. They are not of the world** (speaking about our no longer being a member of the spiritual kingdom of the world), **even as I am not of it"** (John 17:15-16). **"Do not love the world** (become attached to the things of society) **or anything in the world. If anyone loves the world, the love of the Father is not in him. For everything in the world** (referring to the things of society) **... comes not from the Father** (they are under Satan's influence) **but from the world"** (I John 2:15-16). **"The god** (referring to Satan) **of this age** (world) **has blinded the minds of unbelievers"** (II Corinthians 4:4). **"Finally, be strong in the Lord and in his mighty power. Put on the full armor of God so that you can take your stand against the devil's schemes. For our struggle is not against flesh and blood, but against rulers, against the authorities, against the powers of this dark world"** (Ephesians 6:10-12).

Since the day Adam opened the door for evil to enter God's creation, the whole world order (which includes all societies) has shown itself to be hostile to God. Jesus said, **"If the world hates you, keep in mind that it hated me first. If you belonged to the world, it would love you as its own. As it is, you do not belong to the world, but I have chosen you out of the world** (Jesus is talking about the spiritual kingdom of the world.) **That is why the world hates you"** (John 15:18-19). He also said, **"In this world you will have trouble. But take heart! I have overcome the world** (the pressures and influence of society)" (John 16:33).

There is a mind behind every society—a controlling spiritual influence governing from behind the scenes—which of course is Satan. This is why Jesus, Stephen and others down through the ages have said, *"Forgive them* (talking about people who did them harm) *for they know not what they do."* Those who felt this way knew their conflict was not with people or the establishment—it was against Satan and his angels who were working through various individuals and society systems.

The Apostle Paul sums up the Christian's position toward society when he said—talking about himself—that spiritually he was dead to the world and that it was dead to him. He said, **"May I never boast except in the cross of our Lord Jesus Christ, through which the <u>world</u> has been crucified to me, and I to the <u>world</u>"** (Galatians 6:14). After we have been conceived by the Holy Spirit and born again, we too are dead to the kingdom of the world and alive in the spiritual Kingdom of God. Our function here on this Earth is to represent God's Kingdom; to be a shining **light** and a preservative **salt**. There is a reason why there are such strong warnings in Scripture about society or the kingdom of the world. Although we have been born again spiritually, **"...rescued...from the dominion of darkness and brought...into the kingdom of the Son he loves..."** (Colossians 1:13), Christians retain that <u>sinful nature</u> that we are born with, which we inherited from our forefather Adam. God knows that after we become Christians, Satan will constantly tempt our <u>sinful nature</u> using the kingdom of the world as his vehicle to get us to disobey God's standards and accept society's standards. That is the spiritual warfare that we face every day!

We need to constantly remind ourselves that society is one of **Satan's main attack vehicles** to tempt Christians. We only have to look at our own society and see what has happened to the living standards of the majority of people in recent years to know this is true.

One of the greatest causes of the change in the people's standards in America in recent years has come about through the influence of our society's entertainment industry. This has been primarily through the electronic media such as TV, movies, and the Internet, which come right into our home every minute of the day. It has filtered down through our churches, our schools, our businesses and just about every other influencing element in society.

SINFUL NATURE

It was not until after the Apostle Paul became a Christian that he discovered the truth about this sinful nature that everyone has at birth. He discussed this nature in Romans chapter seven stating that it is a natural law of our being. He said, **"I know that nothing good lives in me, that is, in my sinful nature. For I have the desire to do what is good, but I cannot carry it out. For what I do is not the good I want to do; no, the evil I do not want to do—this I keep on doing. Now if I do what I do not want to do, it is no longer I who do it, but it is sin living in me that does it. So I find this law at work...another law at work in the members of my body, waging war against the law of my mind and making me a prisoner of the law of sin at work within my members. What a wretched man I am! Who will rescue me from this body of death? Thanks be to God—through Jesus Christ our Lord! So then, I myself in my mind am a slave to God's law, but in the sinful nature a slave to the law of sin. Therefore, there is now no condemnation for those who are in Christ Jesus, because through Christ Jesus the law of the Spirit of life set me free from the law of sin and death"** (Romans 7:18-21, 23-25 & 8:1-2).

After becoming a Christian Paul discovered the truth that mankind has a sinful nature in his being, which he referred to as the law of sin. This is why everyone sins and falls short of the glory of God. **"There is no difference, for all have sinned and fall short of the** glory of God" (Romans 3:23). The characteristics of the spiritual kingdom of the world include: **Lover of ourselves, lovers of money, boastful, proud, abusive, disobedient, rebellious, permissive, ungrateful, immoral, unforgiving, slanderous, without self control, brutal, not lovers of good, treacherous, rash, conceited, anger, jealousy, and lovers of pleasure rather than God** (see 2 Timothy 3:2-4). I am sure you can add to this list. This is not to say that all of these characteristics are a part of every human being all the time. Some of these characteristics will only be displayed in our personalities under certain circumstances and conditions. Some of these worldly characteristics are determined by the society in which we are raised and what is considered acceptable by the standards of its environment. They are easily discovered when we examine both the history of mankind throughout the centuries and the differences in his character in different parts of the world under different social environments. It is actually difficult to imagine how evil the history of mankind has been down through the ages.

These natural tendencies that make-up our sinful nature that we are born with as members of the kingdom of the world cause us to emphasize personalities, natural abilities, appearance, family heritage, nationality, natural temperaments, intelligence, wealth, worldly position and authority. It is our sinful nature that promotes self-reliance, self-confidence, self-expression, self-exaltation, self-glorification, and self-satisfaction rather than our complete dependence on God, which is what Jesus lived and taught. Paul knew that in his sinful nature he was a wretched man. However, because he had accepted Jesus Christ as his Savior, he was no longer condemned because of his sinful nature, but had been set free from condemnation. This truth applies to all of mankind. I will point out again, as emphasized here in these particular verses in Romans chapters seven and eight, that the only ones who have been set free from the condemnation brought about by this law of sin in our nature are those who have accepted Jesus Christ. It is not religion or anything else that sets us free!

Having an understanding of our <u>sinful nature</u> is of vital importance in being fully equipped to understand the prophetic Scriptures about the last days and how Satan is attacking Christians. Our sinful nature, which is a critical part of our make-up as a member of the kingdom of the world, is carried over into the Kingdom of God when we are born again. Although we are born again, this law of our sinful nature remains with us. We do not lose it! That is what Paul is telling us in Romans chapter seven. I am sure all of us can identify with Paul's discovery through our own personal experiences.

Christians may wonder why this sinful nature that we inherited from Adam is not removed when we are reborn into the Kingdom of God. I certainly do not know all the reasons, but I do know that God in His wisdom is correct. One thought is that there is a principle found throughout all of Scripture in mankind's relationship with God that in anything relating to Him, God always keeps mankind dependent upon Him. He knows that man within himself is no match spiritually with our spiritual enemy, the Devil. Even Jesus, who was God in the flesh, said He was totally dependent on the Father. He could do nothing on His own.

Instead of removing our sinful nature, God had a better plan, which is to take up residence within our being through the Holy Spirit, a power greater than the power of Satan and our sinful nature. **"You dear children, are from God and have overcome them, because the one who is in you is greater than the one who is in the <u>world</u>** (referring to Satan)" (I John 4:4). Yes, every Christian becomes a battleground for spiritual warfare when he enters the Kingdom of God. And we must become dependent on God alone through the power of the Holy Spirit to resist as our sinful nature is tempted by the elements of the world, or society.

UNDERSTANDING THE ELEMENTS OF
OUR SINFUL NATURE

Since the fall of Adam and Eve everyone is born with a nature that is self-centered. There are <u>three main elements that make up our self-serving sinful nature</u> that are subject to Satan's temptations. John breaks them down when he says, **"Do not love the world** (referring to society) **or the things in the world. If any one loves the world, love for the Father is not in him. For all that is in the world, <u>the lust of the flesh</u>** (1ˢᵗ element) **and <u>the lust of the eyes</u>** (2ⁿᵈ element) **and <u>the pride of life</u>** (3ʳᵈ element), **is not of the Father but is of the world"** (I John 2:15-16 RSV).

It was these three elements, **the lust of the flesh, the lust of the eyes and the pride of life,** that were used by Satan to deceive Eve, then Adam, which caused them to sin. **"When the woman saw that the fruit of the tree was good for food** (lust of the flesh) **and pleasing to the eye** (lust of the eyes), **and also desirable for gaining wisdom** (pride of life), **she took some and ate it. She also gave some to her husband, who was with her, and he ate it"** (Genesis 3:6). God had told Adam and Eve that they were not to eat the fruit from this particular tree or they would die. After they had disobeyed and eaten the fruit, **"Then the Lord God said to the woman, "What is this you have done?" The woman said, "The serpent** (referring to Satan) **deceived me, and I ate"** (Genesis 3:13).

Satan used the lust of the flesh, lust of the eyes and the pride of life to get Adam and Eve to disobey God's Word. The sinful nature of mankind has always been subject to these three key methods of temptation. All three appeal to the self-serving life, which has always been the center of Satan's attacks against mankind to get us to be disobedient and go against the standards of God.

It was with these same three self-serving attractions that Satan tried to trap and deceive Jesus into sinning. The first temptation was with the lust of the flesh. **"Jesus, full of the Holy Spirit, returned** from the Jordan and was led by the Spirit in the desert, where for forty days he was tempted by the devil. He ate nothing during those days, and at the end of them he was hungry. The devil said to him, "If you are the Son of God, tell this stone to become bread." Jesus answered, "It is written 'Man does not live on bread alone'" (Luke 4:1-4). In the second temptation, Satan used both the lust of the eyes and the pride of life. **"The devil led him** (referring to Jesus) **up to a high place and showed him in an instant all the kingdoms of the world. And he said to him, "I will give you all their authority and splendor, for it has been given to me, and I can give it to anyone I want to. So if you worship me, it will all be yours." Jesus answered, "It is written: 'Worship the Lord your God and serve him only'"** (Luke 4:5-8). Through the third temptation Satan tempted Jesus with the pride of life in that he tried to get Him to do a self-serving miracle to prove that He was a child of God and that God would save Him. **"The devil led him to Jerusalem and had him stand on the highest point of the temple. "If you are the Son of God," he said, "throw yourself down from here. For it is written: "'he will command his angels concerning you to guard you carefully; they will lift you up in their hands, so that you will not strike your foot against a stone.'" Jesus answered, "It says: 'Do not put the Lord your God to the test'"** (Luke 4: 9-12). Jesus stood firm and responded to all three of these temptations by quoting the Word of God. This tells us how important it is to know the Word of God if we are going to win the battles in spiritual warfare.

As you explore the Bible and examine the reasons why men of God like Samson, King Saul, King David, King Solomon and others fell into sin, you will always find that they were tempted and fell into deception through one or more of these three tempting elements: **the lust of the flesh, the lust of the eyes and the pride of life**. If you examine why spiritual leaders and lay people are being defeated and falling into sin today, the basic cause is still these same three tempting elements that John warns us about when he said, **"For all that is in the world** (society)**, the lust of the flesh and the lust of the eyes and the pride of life, is not of the Father but is of the world"** (I John 2:16).

It is critical that you keep these three methods of temptation in mind when we begin to examine how Satan is carrying out his spiritual warfare in these last days, especially against America. We learn from prophetic Scripture that Satan will attempt to destroy every possible spiritual influence in our nation through his kingdom of the world, to keep Christians in America from fulfilling our end time mission to be **salt** and **light**. Why is Satan having so much success? Too many Christians are not prepared for the battles. As in the example given to us by Jesus, we must learn how to answer the enemy's temptations that come out of the world system by knowing and stating the Word of God as Jesus did.

There is a part of our natural makeup that enjoys things that are sinful—things that are a part of the world and contrary to God's standards. Satan is fully aware of the sinful nature that mankind is born with, the lust of the flesh, the lust of the eyes and the pride of life. Notice how often the lust of the flesh, the lust of the eyes and the pride of life are at the core of entertainment, advertising, and many other things that we are involved with throughout the day as we live in the world.

I think all of us can identify with Paul when he said, **"What a wretched man I am! Who will rescue me from this body of death? Thanks be to God—through Jesus Christ our Lord! So then, I myself in my mind am a slave to God's law, but in the sinful nature a slave to the law of sin"** (Romans 7:24-25).

"Since we have now been justified by his blood, how much more shall we be saved from God's wrath through him! For if, when we were God's enemies, we were reconciled to him through the death of his Son, how much more, having been reconciled, shall we be saved through his life! Not only is this so, but we also

85

rejoice in God through our Lord Jesus Christ, through whom we have now received reconciliation. Therefore, just as sin entered the world through one man, (speaking of Adam) and death through sin, and in this way death came to all men, because all sinned...how much more will those who receive God's abundant provision of grace and of the gift of righteousness reign in life through the one man, Jesus Christ. Consequently, just as the result of one trespass was condemnation for all men, so also the result of one act of righteousness was justification that brings life for all men. For just as through the disobedience of the one man (Adam) the many were made sinners, so also through the obedience of the one man (Jesus Christ) the many will be made righteous" (Romans 5:9-12 & 17-19).

CHAPTER SIX

KINGDOM OF GOD
AND HEAVEN

When we are spiritually born again by the Holy Spirit of God, we are redeemed from the kingdom of the world and become members of the spiritual Kingdom of God and Heaven whose ruler is Jesus Christ. **"I pray also that the eyes of your heart may be enlightened in order that you may know the hope to which he has called you, the riches of his glorious inheritance in the saints, and his incomparably great power for us who believe. That power is like the working of his mighty strength, which he exerted in Christ when he raised him from the dead and seated him at his right hand in the heavenly realms, far above all rule and authority, power and dominion, and every title that can be given, not only in the present age but also in the one to come. And God placed all things under his feet and appointed him to be head over everything for the church, which is his body, the fullness of him who fills everything in every way"** (Ephesians 1:18-23). **"For in Christ all the fullness of the Deity lives in bodily form, and you have been given fullness in Christ, who is the head over every power and authority"** (Colossians 2:9-10). **"...the mystery that has been kept hidden for ages and generations, but is now disclosed to the saints. To**

them God has chosen to make known among the Gentiles the glorious riches of this mystery, which is Christ in you, the hope of glory" (Colossians 1:26-27).

We are a new spiritual creation. **"Therefore, if anyone is in Christ, he is a new creation the old has gone** (being a member of the kingdom of the world)**, the new has come** (being a member of the Kingdom of God)**!"** (II Corinthians 5:17). We have entered into a new life as spiritual babies in a completely different Kingdom with completely different characteristics, principles, and standards than those which rule the kingdom of the world. Most of the New Testament is written to help us learn how to grow and thrive in this new Kingdom. God has blessed us with the Scriptures and the gift of the Holy Spirit to make this possible. The Scriptures are like a road map to guide us in the ways and standards of the Kingdom of God and the Holy Spirit is living in us to teach, convict and transform the character of our old nature into the character of God's nature. This change in the character of our being and the standards by which we are to live as members of God's Kingdom is an ongoing process for the rest of our lives regardless of what physical age we may have been when we were born again. As we grow older in the Lord, there are always going to be areas where we are not as spiritually mature as we would like to be. Every Christian knows this from personal experience.

It is a glorious adventure to serve the Lord. I was raised in a strong and committed Christian family. I was the youngest of 13 children. I accepted the Lord Jesus as my personal Savior at the age of 9. I had a close walk with the Lord during most of my teens, but somewhat fell away from my strong commitment during most of my 20s. When I was nearly 30, both my wife and I recommitted our lives to serve the Lord on a daily basis.

The Apostle Paul stated, **"Do you not know that your body is a temple of the Holy Spirit, who is in you, whom you have received from God? You are not your own, you were bought at a** price. Therefore honor God with you body" (I Corinthians 6:19-20). And, **"Therefore, I urge you, brothers, in view of God's mercy, to offer your bodies as living sacrifices, holy and pleasing to God—which is <u>your spiritual worship</u>"** (Romans 12:1). As a new member of the Kingdom of God we are a temple of the Holy Spirit of God. We are not our own anymore; we were bought at a price by the blood of Jesus Christ. We are Christ's ambassadors in this world to fulfill the mission that every Christian is called to fulfill, which is to be the **salt of the earth** and the **light of the world.** This world is no longer our home as we are just passing through with a mission to fulfill for God. This doesn't mean that we should not work, play and raise our families in this world, but as Jesus said, **"...you do not belong to the world, but I have chosen you out of the world..."** (John 15:19). And **"...they are not of the world any more than I am of the world. My prayer is not that you take them out of the world but that you protect them from the evil one. They are not of the world, even as I am not of it"** (John 17:14-16). The characteristics that are to govern our new spiritual life are completely different than those characteristics that governed our old spiritual life in the kingdom of the world.

Jesus gave us the ruling characteristics of the spiritual Kingdom of God and then illustrated how they are to be carried out by those who are members of His Kingdom. These are found in Scripture in the greatest sermon ever preached, The Sermon on the Mount. This sermon that was given by Jesus is recorded in Matthew chapters 5 thru 7. It is the one place that gives us an overview of the general characteristics of the Kingdom of God. It was in this sermon that Jesus stated that we are to be the **salt of the earth** and the **light of the world.**

SERMON ON THE MOUNT

There is no place in Scripture that more clearly outlines the general characteristics of a Christian than the teaching that is found in the Sermon on the Mount. All of the Lord's teaching in this Sermon is meant for Christians today. The Sermon on the Mount is a great, grand, and perfect elaboration of the Lord's 'new commandment,' which was that we are to love one another even as He has loved us. It is here in this Sermon that Jesus illustrates how we are to do it. This Sermon is not telling us that if we live like this we will become a Christian; rather it tells us that, because we are Christians, we are to live like this. The teachings in this sermon lay out the characteristics that governed the life of Jesus. It tells us what it means to be Christ-like. This is why it is important that we study this Sermon and why we should try to live it! Jesus died to enable us to live the Sermon on the Mount. As the Apostle Paul said, **"Who** (referring to Jesus) **gave himself for us to redeem us from all wickedness and to purify for himself a people that are his very own, eager to do what is good"** (Titus 2:14).

In this chapter, we are only going to look at the first part of this Sermon, called the Beatitudes, as they outline the general characteristics of a Christian, or the spiritual characteristics that rule God's Kingdom. You will see that it would crush us to the ground if we had to live this way through our own strength. You will see how utterly helpless we are to live out these characteristics without the gracious operation of the Holy Spirit.

Jesus lists these general spiritual characteristics that are to govern the life of a Christian at the beginning of this Sermon. The word **"blessed"** before each of these characteristics means happy. Jesus said, **"Blessed** (happy) **are the poor in spirit, for theirs is the kingdom of heaven. Blessed** (happy) **are those who mourn, for they will be comforted. Blessed** (happy) **are the meek, for they will inherit the earth. Blessed** (happy) **are those who hunger and thirst for righteousness, for they will be filled. Blessed** (happy) **are the merciful, for they will be shown mercy. Blessed** (happy) **are the pure in heart, for they will see God. Blessed** (happy) **are the**

peacemakers, for they will be called sons of God" (Matthew 5:3-9). Poor in spirit, mourning, meekness, hunger and thirst for righteousness, merciful, pure in heart and a peacemaker—these are the characteristics of members of the Kingdom of God. It is the work of the Holy Spirit to develop each one of these characteristics in every born again Christian. In the next chapter I will discuss the meaning of each one of these characteristics. It is important to note that Jesus lists these characteristics just a few verses before He makes His proclamation that we are to be the **salt of the earth** and the **light of the world.** He is telling us that developing these spiritual characteristics is a prerequisite for fulfilling the call to be salt and light.

As we progress through this book it is also important for you to remember Satan's spiritual warfare against Christians is designed to keep these spiritual characteristics from being developed in our nature or to destroy them if they have been. This is because he knows that the degree to which these characteristics are controlling our nature will determine how successful we will be in fulfilling God's mission to be the **salt of the earth** and the **light of the world.** Therefore, he is going to do every thing he can, using the things of his kingdom, the world or society, to keep these characteristics at a minimum in their development in any Christian. Our knowing this is a key to help us understand the spiritual warfare now taking place in America.

Another reason it is good to review these spiritual characteristics is that the more we live and practice them, along with the teachings from the rest of this Sermon, the more we shall experience God's blessing and be happy. If we want to have power in our life and be blessed we need to go straight to this message. Every one of these spiritual characteristics begins with the promise of a blessing. If we want to receive God's blessings and be happy we don't have to seek some other method. Those don't work anyway!

Finally I want to mention that we should study this Sermon and these spiritual characteristics because as we learn its message and live it, our lives will become a powerful witness for the message of Christianity—tools for the Lord to use for evangelism. If Christians would live the Christian life as taught by Jesus in this Sermon, there would become a great drawing attraction, and we would see men and women crowding into our church buildings.

The Sermon on the Mount is divided into two different subdivisions. First we have the general part which occupies Matthew chapter 5:3-16 where Jesus makes statements with regard to the character of a Christian. In the remainder of the Sermon He gives us examples of how these characteristics are lived out in the Christian life. From Matthew 5:17 through the end of Matthew chapter seven, Jesus gives us specific examples and illustrations of how a person with these spiritual characteristics will carry out the function of being the **salt of the earth** and the **light of the world**.

One important thing to remember about the teachings of Jesus in this Sermon is these spiritual characteristics are not a code of ethics or of morals. It is not a set of rules and regulations which are to be carried out by us—but rather a description of what Christians are meant to be. It is as if Jesus is saying, "Because of who and what you are, a child of God and a member of His Kingdom, this is how you will face the law of God and how you will live it." As a Christian living in dependence on our Father and truly drawing from Him through the power of the Holy Spirit, this is how we would react and fulfill God's standards in every situation. His message is not a rule book to force us to react in the stated manner through the power of the flesh.

AN OVERVIEW OF THE SPIRITUAL CHARACTERISTICS THAT RULE GOD'S KINGDOM

In the next chapter I explain the meaning of each one of these seven spiritual characteristics that rule God's Kingdom: poor in spirit, mourning, meekness, hungering and thirsting for righteousness, merciful, pure in heart, and a peacemaker. However, before doing that there are a few general comments I want to make that applies to each of these characteristics.

First: These spiritual characteristics apply to all Christians. These characteristics are a description of the characteristics that are to rule the nature of every single person who is born again and becomes a member of the Kingdom of God. We often have a tendency to divide people into two separate groups when it comes to character: The leaders, or pastors, and the ordinary believers who are involved in secular affairs. That is completely unscriptural. There is no such distinction in the Bible.

There is distinction in offices—apostles, prophets, teachers, pastors and so on. But the Beatitudes are a description of spiritual character. They do not apply just to the Hudson Taylors, George Müllers, Whitefields, Wesleys, Finneys, Moodys, Billy Grahams, or David Wilkersons. These are the spiritual characteristics that are to be developed in every Christian.

Second: Each one of these characteristics is meant to be manifested in every Christian. Some Christians are not meant to manifest some of these spiritual characteristics, while others manifest different traits. These Beatitudes describe a completeness of the character of a Christian, and you really cannot divide them. God's desire and design for the body of Christ is not to expect one person to have some of these spiritual characteristics and someone else to have others.

Third: Very important. Not one of these spiritual characteristics refers to what we might call a natural biological tendency. Each one of them is completely dependent upon grace alone and the operation of the Holy Spirit within us. No one can conform to the description of any one of these spiritual characteristics in the Kingdom of God, let alone all of them, by the natural power of the flesh.

There are people who may appear to be **poor in spirit** or **meek** or one of these other characteristics who are not even Christians. If they do, it is purely natural and physical, not spiritual. Just as people differ in their physical appearance, so they differ in their temperament. This has nothing to do with their relationship with God and it is not what Jesus is describing. These characteristics in the Beatitudes are spiritual qualities. They are not natural qualities; nobody by birth and biological natural temperament is like this.

Four: These descriptive spiritual characteristics recorded in Matthew 5:3-10 indicate perhaps more clearly than anything else in Scripture the essential, absolute difference between the Christian and the non-Christian—the difference between those in the kingdom of the world and those in the Kingdom of God. Today this difference has become blurred; the world has come into the Church and as a result the Church has become worldly. The line is not as distinct as it was. There are those today who believe that you have to make the church worldly in order to attract people from the outside. History proves it has never happened that way. What ends up happening when we do this is that we end up with worldly Christians. And too often we are afraid to admit this fact and talk about it.

I have prepared a simple graph that illustrates how the biblical standards Christians live by in our society have systematically been lowered or removed in the last few years.

BIBLICAL STANDARDS

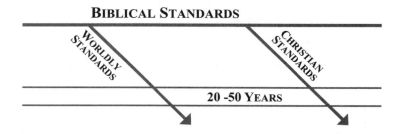

As illustrated by the top line on this graph, biblical standards always remain the same. The line on the left illustrates how over the last fifty years or so the worldly standards in our society have been ⸱⸱riorating. The line on the right illustrates how over the same period of time many Christian standards have also deteriorated. The deterioration of Christian standards has come about because during this last generation, many of us began to set our Christian standards by comparing them to the world's standards rather than by using only biblical truths to make our comparison. We have maintained the same distance between world's standards and Christian standards. We are not as bad as the world, so to speak. But this false comparison is a deceptive trick of the enemy. This has caused us to lower many of the Christian standards in our society. The net result is that what was considered a worldly standard in American society 20 to 30 years ago has now become an acceptable Christian standard.

This deceptive trick of Satan has caused us to become more tolerant and indifferent toward many of the sins described in the Bible. It has brought devastation to the lives of many Christians because sooner or later, sin always leads to broken lives. The Bible puts it very bluntly; **"the wages of sin is death..."** (Romans 6:23). This truth does not only apply to salvation. Sin is the cause for broken relationships and the inner hurt and pain we suffer.

Satan is using the same deceptive strategy on Christians today that he used on Adam and Eve. Satan tricked Eve to reason in her own mind what was right rather than trusting and being obedient to the truth of God's Word. Working through the power of our society to influence us via the communication media and various other means that are available to him today, Satan is doing the same thing to Christians. He is breaking down our resistance to those standards of the world that are contrary to the biblical truths that are found in God's Word both in the Sermon on the Mount and other teachings.

His ability to do this seems overwhelming at times. If we begin to reason in our mind and become tolerant of some of the world's standards, we have opened the door for Satan to move in. He will bring about defeat to the unsuspecting in this day of tremendous temptation. The fruit that our society has produced in this last generation point to the fact that many of us have fallen into his trap of **spiritual deception.**

One of the symptoms of having the **disease of spiritual deception** is that we become indifferent, and therefore, complacent about our own moral standards as well as the rapid deterioration of our country's moral standards. **The world's influence on Christians has been much greater in this generation than the influence of Christians on the world.** The proof of this is illustrated by the graph above and in the fruit being produced both by the world and by the body of Christ. Remember that deception is determined by examining the fruit being produced.

For the moral character of the people in the world to change is understandable. History reveals the majority of non-Christians usually follow the trends of a society, but for Christians it is supposed to be different. We are a new creation, born again into the Kingdom of God to be the righteousness of God and live by His code of morals. As with Eve, then Adam, Satan's scheme of **spiritual deception** has been very successful in America in this past generation.

I am no different than most people. I would rather dwell on the positives than the negatives. However, when you see that you are continually losing the battle, you cannot continue to hide your head in the sand. We need to stand up and take appropriate corrective action steps now. The only way you can make the positives more common than the negatives is to address and confront the negative issues and correct them. To dwell on the positives and ignore the truth of the negatives may sound good, but it only changes lives temporarily rather than permanently. This is one of the reasons I founded Campaign Save Christian America.

The glory of the Gospel is that when the Church is absolutely different from the world, it invariably attracts the world. The world may hate the message at first, but it has been proven time and again that the world will listen when they see a true difference. That is how revival comes. This same principle applies to each individual Christian. Our ambition should not be as much like everybody else, but be as much different from everybody who is not a Christian. Remember that we belong to a different Kingdom. Our ambition is to be like Christ, the Ruler of the Kingdom to which we now belong. The more we are like Him the better. And the more like Him we become, the more we shall be <u>unlike</u> those who are <u>not</u> Christian and are still members of the kingdom of the world.

There are those in the world who say that a Christian is a weakling, someone who needs a crutch. The world believes in self-confidence, self-expression and the mastery of life. You will never find anything that is further removed from these spiritual characteristics of the Kingdom of God, listed in the Beatitudes, than that which appeals to the natural person. The natural person likes an element of boastfulness. We are born self-centered, but that is the very thing that is condemned in these spiritual characteristics of the Christian.

Look at the difference in what they seek. The Beatitudes proclaim, **"Blessed** (happy) **are those who hunger and thirst for righteousness"...** (Matthew 5:6). After what? Is it wealth, money, status, position, or publicity? No! It is righteousness! Righteousness is being right with God. We admire and seek after different things than the people of the world. Therefore, the life of a Christian must be a totally different life than that of a non-Christian. We are not living for the world, but regard the world (society) as that which we are just passing through into something vast and eternal and glorious.

We are not here to try and make sure we get everything we can get out of this world. Peter states, **"Dear friends, I urge you, as aliens and strangers in the world, to abstain from sinful desires, which war against your soul. Live such good lives among the pagans that though they accuse you of doing wrong, they may see your good deeds and glorify God on the day he visits us"** (I Peter 2:11-12). The sinful desires that Peter mentions would include all kinds of earthly desires that fall into the realm of our sinful nature: **the lust of the eyes, the lust of the flesh and the pride of life.** These continually battle against the soul to bring it into worldly captivity.

The Bible teaches us that the objective and operation of Satan is to use every earthly and sensual desire that we have to tempt and defeat us from living a victorious Christian life. We can see how he uses the things of the world to the ruin of those of the world. But as a Christian we are seeking a heavenly home, and must not get entangled in the world by setting our affections on earthly things. We are not like the people of the world who live in the kingdom of darkness and spend all of their time and employ all their skills on earthly things, while totally neglecting the salvation of their souls.

POINTS TO REMEMBER ABOUT THE SPIRITUAL CHARACTERISTICS OF A CHRISTIAN

1. Each of these spiritual characteristics applies to all Christians.

2. All Christians are meant to manifest every one of these characteristics.

3. None of these descriptions of the Christian character refers to what we may call a natural tendency. They all are spiritual qualities and are only developed through the power of the Holy Spirit.

4. These descriptive Christian characteristics indicate as clear as anything the difference between the character of a Christian and the non-Christian.

5. These characteristics teach us very clearly the truth that the Christian and non-Christian belong to two entirely different realms; two different Kingdoms.

The first and the last promise given in these characteristics offer the same reward—"**for theirs is the kingdom of heaven.**" Jesus starts and ends with this statement because the first thing we have to realize about ourselves is that we belong to a different Kingdom. We are in this world, but we are not of it. We live among the people of the world, but we are citizens of another Kingdom.

We are here on Earth; we obey the laws of the land in which we live as the Scriptures tell us we are to do. We work, play and raise our families in the ways the Lord directs. We live our lives here, but our true citizenship is in Heaven. Paul states; **"For he has rescued us from the dominion of darkness and brought us into the kingdom of the Son he loves"** (Colossians 1:13). **May I never boast except in the cross of our Lord Jesus Christ, through which the world has been crucified to me, and I to the world"** (Galatians 6:14). And **"But our citizenship is in heaven. And we eagerly await a Savior from there, the Lord Jesus Christ, who, by the power that enables him to bring everything under his control, will transform our lowly bodies so that they will be like his glorious body"** (Philippians 3:20).

We should not get into a materialistic way of looking at the Kingdom of God as the Jews were looking for an earthly king. They were thinking that the Messiah would return them to political and military power as in the days of King David. Our Lord's whole objective in His teachings was to show that His Kingdom is primarily a spiritual one. The teachings of Jesus focused on the heart. His Kingdom is not a part of anything here on this Earth. His Kingdom is certainly going to affect the world in many different ways as His Kingdom is here among us through the presence of the Holy Spirit, but it is a spiritual Kingdom. The Kingdom is Christ in us!

He told the disciples He sent out to preach, to tell the cities that did not receive them, **"...be sure of this, that the kingdom of God is come nigh unto you."** (Luke 10:11KJV). Wherever the reign of Christ is being manifested, the Kingdom of God is there. The Kingdom of God is present at this very moment in all of us who are true believers. We represent the Kingdom of God here in this world and we are meant to live like citizens of that Kingdom, not like the people who are a part of the kingdom of this world.

One other thing we need to remember is that as we look at the meaning of these characteristics, they are a mirror for us to look at ourselves, not something that we use to evaluate or judge other people. I will be the first to admit that I personally have not nearly arrived in the development of these characteristics. Another thing I want to remind you about as we examine these spiritual characteristics of the Kingdom of God is they are <u>not</u> a new moral code or law by which we are saved or become a member of the Kingdom of God. **"It is by grace you have been saved, through faith—and this not from yourselves, it is the gift of God—not by works, so that no one can boast"** (Ephesians 2:8). **"Therefore, there is now no condemnation for those who are in Christ Jesus"** (Romans 8:1). Jesus gave these to us so that we may know what the spiritual characteristics are that make up His Kingdom.

Now we are ready to venture into an examination of the characteristics of a Christian to see how we are meant to live here on Earth as citizens of God's Kingdom. As we do I think you will better understand why I make the statement that I believe we are living in one of the toughest times ever to live the committed Christian life in America and carry out our mission of being the **salt of the earth** and the **light of the world.** However, with God all things are possible regardless of the fact that the world and its mass communication system is waging one of the hardest, fiercest spiritual warfare's ever known against the body of Christ in our country to keep us from developing and living out these characteristics.

CHAPTER SEVEN

"**B**lessed are the poor in spirit, for theirs is the kingdom of heaven. Blessed are those who mourn, for they will be comforted. Blessed are the meek, for they will inherit the earth. Blessed are those who hunger and thirst for righteousness, for they will be filled. Blessed are the merciful, for they will be shown mercy. Blessed are the pure in heart, for they will see God. Blessed are the peacemakers, for they will be called sons of God. Blessed are those who are persecuted because of righteousness, for theirs is the kingdom of heaven"** (Matthew 5:3-10).

The word "blessed" in these verses means happy. Happiness is one of the great challenges confronting mankind. The whole world longs for happiness and it is tragic to observe the many ways in which people seek it. Many people get involved in activities that only bring happiness for a short time. And as we know many of these are sinful and actually end up bringing misery. The Lord tells us through the teachings of these spiritual characteristics He lists in Matthew 5:3-9 that if we really want to be happy, this is the way. The person who has these traits is truly going to be happy, the one who is really blessed.

Think of the development of these spiritual characteristics in God's Kingdom as if you were climbing a rugged mountain. As the old spiritual characteristics that we are born with as members of the kingdom of the world are burned out of our nature, we will grow in these spiritual characteristics of our new nature. One of the greatest examples of this in the Old Testament was Moses. For forty years in the wilderness, God burned the old nature out of Moses to prepare him for the tremendous task for which He was going to be used. God knew that Moses would have to be completely dependent upon Him if Moses was going to be successful. It is the same for us—we cannot develop these characteristics and live them out apart from the power of the Holy Spirit.

As we climb our spiritual mountain and God burns out our old nature, these first three characteristics that Jesus lists make us conscious of a <u>deep need</u> we humans have. The character traits of being **poor in spirit**, **mourning** because of our sinfulness, and **meekness** as the result of a true understanding of the nature of self and its great ego emphasize the vital importance of a deep awareness of our need.

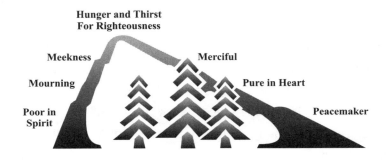

As we grow spiritually we will realize this need by seeing the true character of our old <u>sinful nature</u> and these first three characteristics of the Kingdom of God which will cause us to **hunger and thirst after righteousness**. God's provision to satisfy this hunger and thirst is **they shall be filled.** The result of this filling is the development of the characteristics on the downside of the mountain. We become **merciful, pure in heart, and peacemakers**. After that, as Jesus warns us beforehand in the next verse, we may be **persecuted because of righteousness.** This is because Satan hates and wars against these godly characteristics in the lives of those who belong to the Kingdom of God.

DEVELOPMENT OF CHRISTIAN CHARACTER

God develops our Christian character by: One—making us

aware of our need; Two—filling that need as we hunger and thirst for righteousness and; Three—the outpouring or the results of this need being satisfied, which will be the development of the characteristics of mercy, pure in heart, and a peacemaker.

1. Need. **2**. Satisfaction. **3**. Results.

Our old nature in the kingdom of the world is just the opposite of our new nature in God's Kingdom. Our old nature consisted of the following characteristics, **"lovers of themselves, lovers of money, boastful, proud, abusive, disobedient to their parents, ungrateful, unholy** (immoral)**, without love, unforgiving, slanderous, without self control, brutal, not lovers of good, treacherous, rash, conceited, lovers of pleasure rather than lovers of God—having a form of godliness but denying its power"** (II Timothy 3:2-5). Not all of these characteristics are necessarily prevalent in every person's sinful nature at all times, but we are capable of any one of them.

The characteristics of God's Kingdom are impossible if we try to develop them in the strength of our own flesh. This is the reason why we humans have a tendency to ignore them. Mankind has always tried to develop a relationship with God through things, doctrines, rules and regulations that can be accomplished in the strength of our own flesh. It soothes our conscience to do things in the strength of our flesh, but the teachings of Jesus centered in on the heart, on our character. Recall that God is a Spiritual Being and so are we. If our spiritual character is correct, then our desire to follow the laws of God will flow naturally. The development of these spiritual characteristics is the key to pleasing Him.

We are a new creation—having received a new nature through the power of the Holy Spirit (see II Corinthians 5:17). It is no longer I who lives but Christ who lives within me (see Galatians 2:20). It is now the Holy Spirit of God who is to control my thoughts and actions, not the character of my old "self-centered" sinful nature. What I *am* is more critical than what I *do*. Attitude and character are more significant than actions. It is not that we are to try to be Christians in this or that. We are not meant to control our Christianity; our Christianity is meant to control us by the operation of the Holy Spirit. The whole of our life is an expression and proclamation of what we really are.

Study the Scriptures, not to discover what we are to make ourselves become, but to discover what God wants to make us into. He is the potter; I am the clay. I must surrender my being to Him. I require a whole new character from what I was naturally born with. I was born with a self-centered nature. That is the nature that controls my being in the kingdom of the world. The characteristics I develop in this life are geared toward my self-centered nature. Realizing the character of our sinful nature, we begin to understand Paul's proclamation of **"What a wretched man I am!"** (Romans 7:24). We not only need the salvation of our soul because of its sinful nature; we also need to be delivered from what we are. We need to be changed from the inside out. Just as we are dependent on Jesus for the salvation of our souls, we are dependent on Him to deliver us from the characteristics of who we are and to develop in us the characteristics of the Kingdom of God. Jesus is everything and everything is in Jesus.

SPIRITUAL CHARACTERISTIC NUMBER ONE
"Blessed are the poor in spirit, for theirs is the kingdom of heaven" (Matthew 5:3)

POOR IN SPIRIT

This heart characteristic is the key to everything else that follows in the development of our spiritual walk. It deals with the process of emptying us of our old sin nature so we can be filled with the power of God's nature, His Holy Spirit. It is not surprising that Jesus lists this characteristic first, as it is fundamental to the life of a Christian and the Kingdom of Heaven. The development of each of these spiritual characteristics is an on-going, lifelong process. However, the degree to which we develop each one of these spiritual characteristics is dependent on the degree to which we have developed the one that precedes it. For example; if only 20% of our nature has been developed into the character of poor in spirit, then only 20% of our nature will develop in the characteristics of mourning, meekness, hungering and thirsting for righteousness and so on down the right side of the mountain.

The characteristic of being poor in spirit deals with a person's attitude towards self, as we come face to face with God and His Kingdom. This is what brings about true poverty of spirit. It is a characteristic that is despised by the world. The kingdom of this world promotes self-reliance, self-confidence, self-expression, self-exaltation, self-glorification, and self-satisfaction. The world emphasizes personality, natural ability, appearance, family heritage, nationality, natural temperaments, intelligence, wealth, worldly position and authority. The Gospel tears down these worldly characteristics and raises us up to the higher standard that is found in the Kingdom of God. The Kingdom of God focuses on God-reliance, God-confidence, God-expression, God-exaltation, God-glorification, and the desire to satisfy and please God rather than ourselves through obedience to His Word, His will and His standards.

To be poor in spirit does not mean that we should be shy, bashful, weak, or lacking in courage. It is not a matter of suppressing one's true personality in trying to appear humble, to falsely crucify yourself, making great sacrifices like the monks, or retiring from life and its difficulties and responsibilities. We are not to go out of life to be poor in spirit. That certainly was not the life of Jesus. We are talking about something in the realm of the spirit. The Scriptures give us a definition of poor in spirit. **"The sacrifices of God are a broken spirit; a broken and contrite hear, O God, you will not despise"** (Psalm 51:17). **"For this is what the high and lofty One says—he** who lives forever, whose name is holy: I live in a high and holy place, but also with him who is contrite and lowly in spirit, to revive the spirit of the lowly and to revive the heart of the contrite" (Isaiah 57:15).

There are several illustrations in Scripture of those that were poor in spirit. Noah, Gideon, Moses, David, and Isaiah are examples in the Old Testament. In the New Testament we find this statement from Peter: **"When Simon Peter saw this, he fell at Jesus' knees and said, 'Go away from me, Lord; I am a sinful man!'"** (Luke 5:8).

Paul said, **"If anyone else thinks he has reasons to put confidence in the flesh, I have more: circumcised on the eighth day, of the people of Israel, of the tribe of Benjamin, a Hebrew of Hebrews; in regard to the law, a Pharisee; as for zeal, persecuting the church; as for legalistic righteousness, faultless. But whatever was to my profit I now consider loss for the sake of Christ. What is more, I consider everything a loss compared to the surpassing greatness of knowing Christ Jesus my Lord, for whose sake I have lost all things. I consider them rubbish, that I may gain Christ and be found in him, not having a righteousness of my own that comes from the law, but that which is through faith in Christ—the righteousness that comes from God and is by faith"** (Philippians 3:4-9). He also said, **"When I came to you, brothers, I did not come with eloquence or superior wisdom as I proclaimed to you the testimony about God. For I resolved to know nothing while I was with you except Jesus Christ and him crucified. I came to you in weakness and fear, and with much trembling. My message and my preaching were not with wise and persuasive words, but with a demonstration of the Spirit's power, so that your faith might not rest on men's wisdom, but on God's power** (I Corinthians 2:1-5).

Jesus said concerning His actions, **"By myself I can do nothing; I judge only as I hear, and my judgment is just, for I seek not** to please myself but him who sent me" (John 5:30). And **"Don't you believe that I am in the Father, and that the Father is in me? The words I say to you are not just my own. Rather, it is the Father, living in me, who is doing his work"** (John 14:10).

As for each Christian we are in the same spiritual position as Paul who said, **"I have been crucified with Christ and I no longer live, but Christ lives in me. The life I live in the body, I live by faith in the Son of God, who loved me and gave himself for me"** (Galatians 2:20). And, **"Do you not know that your body is a temple of the Holy Spirit, who is in you, whom you received from God? You are not your own; you were bought at a price. Therefore honor God with your body"** (I Corinthians 6:19-20).

The spiritual characteristic **poor in spirit** means:

- We shall not rely upon on our natural birth.
- We shall not rely upon the fact that we belong to certain families.
- We shall not boast that we belong to a certain nation or nationality.
- We shall not build upon natural temperament.
- We shall not believe in and rely upon our natural position in life, or any powers that may have been given to us.
- We shall not rely upon money or the wealth we may have.
- We shall not boast about the education we have received or the college we may have attended.
- We shall not rely upon any gifts like that of natural personality, intelligence or special abilities.
- We shall not rely upon our own morality and conduct and good behavior.

To be poor in spirit is to be delivered from all that which promotes self-sufficiency. It is to know that within the flesh we are nothing (see Romans 7:14 - 8:1), we have nothing, and we must look to God in utter submission to Him and in utter dependence upon His grace and mercy. It is to know what Isaiah meant when he said, **"Woe is me."**

How does one become **poor in spirit**? We do <u>not</u> look at ourselves and begin by trying to do things to ourselves like removing ourselves from society, sacrificing the flesh or suffering some hardship. These things will only make us more conscious of ourselves; therefore, less **poor in spirit**. The way to become poor in spirit is to look to God. The Christian's spiritual character <u>must</u> be developed by the work of the Holy Spirit within us. Our responsibility is to read and study His Word to learn what He expects from us and then to set our face as a flint to walk in obedience. Look to Jesus and view Him as we see Him in the Gospels. As we look at Him we will feel our absolute poverty and emptiness and like the apostles will cry out "Lord, increase my faith."

To be poor in spirit is to know that within the flesh we are empty, hopeless, naked and vile, but <u>He</u> is the all-sufficient one.

Nothing in my hand I bring,

Simply to Thy cross I cling.

SPIRITUAL CHARACTERISTIC NUMBER TWO
"Blessed are those who mourn, for they will be comforted"
(Matthew 5:4)

MOURNING

This characteristic develops in us the truth to see sin in ourselves and in the world as it really is. Christians are to be unlike the people of the world who try to shun **mourning**. Think of all the energy, enthusiasm, and money spent by the world system to blind people and move us away from this spiritual characteristic of mourning over the sin going on in our world today. I have heard it said that the sin of using God's name in vain takes place more than one billion times every day in our country.

As this characteristic of mourning becomes a part of our being, it will cause us to see the horrid, ugly and foul results of all the sin in the world and the consequence of what sin does to people and how it must stab God right in the heart. This characteristic is not as evident in the church as it once was. This could partly have come about as a reaction against false Puritanism, an assumed piety, but the pendulum has now swung too far. There has been a defection from a hatred toward sin in our personal life and the teaching on the doctrine of sin. This is a strong indication of how much influence the world has had on the church. In just about any other area of life, we concentrate on those areas where we are weakest. If we have a health problem, we put in the effort to get it taken care of. If we participate in sports, we spend the most time on those areas where our performance is the poorest.

In addition to being a teacher of the Bible, I own a business that manufactures high-tech aluminum extrusions for the aerospace industry. As I mentioned in the introduction of this book our people meet once a week from the various departments to discuss their activities and review their performance. We spend most of our time discussing those areas where we are weak, where our performance is poor, and how we can improve. We may be excellent in 90% of what we do, but to improve we must do better in the 10% where we are weakest.

This illustrates what Jesus meant when He said we are to examine fruit. I have briefly mentioned its application in a physical way, but the same principle applies to the development of our spiritual walk. Spiritually, mankind's weakness is sin! I don't know why we get so uptight talking about sin. It does not have to be discussed in a negative way. We have a spiritual problem in the fact that we are born with a sinful nature. That is us! That is what we are! Talk about sin! Keep it surfaced, don't try to hide this truth. Otherwise we will not go to God to let Him deal with those areas in our being where we are weak in a sinful way.

God has provided for the forgiveness of our sins through our faith in Jesus Christ through the price He paid for our sins by the shedding of His blood on the cross. However, we are not only dependent on God for the forgiveness of our sins, we are also dependent on Him to deal with the sinful nature that we have. As we share the Gospel with those in the world who are not saved, we must be open and discuss with those who are in the body of Christ, the truth about our sinful nature. After becoming a Christian and discovering the truth about the law of his sinful nature, described in Romans seven, the apostle Paul was grief-stricken about himself. He cried out, **"What a wretched man I am! Who will rescue me from this body of death? Thanks be to God—through Jesus Christ our Lord!** (Romans 7:24-25). There must be a conviction of sin before there can be an experience of true joy.

By necessity, mourning over sin will follow being poor in spirit as we examine ourselves and the life we live. Paul mourned over the sinful condition of his flesh and looked forward to that day when it would be redeemed. **"But we ourselves, who have the first fruits of the Spirit, groan inwardly as we wait eagerly for our adoption as sons, the redemption of our bodies"** (Romans 8:23). **"Now we know that if the earthly tent we live in is destroyed, we have a building from God, an eternal house in heaven, not built by human hands. Meanwhile we groan, longing to be clothed with our heavenly dwelling, because when we are clothed, we will not be found naked. For while we are in this tent, we groan and are burdened, because we do not wish to be unclothed but to be clothed with our heavenly dwelling, so that what is mortal may be swallowed up by life"** (II Corinthians 5:1-4).

This characteristic of mourning applies not only to our own sins, but also to the sins of others and the state of society and the world. When this characteristic is developed, we will mourn over the immorality, unhappiness, suffering, the evil deeds of mankind, wars, and more which are all because of sin. Those in the kingdom of this world have an attitude to 'eat, drink, and be merry' as they want to find ways to escape from thinking about reality.

True happiness and joy can only come after mourning. That is one of the astounding paradoxes of the Christian life. Joy is a fruit of the Spirit! Because of forgiveness of sins, the joy of reconciliation, knowing Heaven will be our home, and the glory that is set before us the Christian receives comfort. The Christian life does not have to be superficial in any sense. The world has only a superficial conception of joy and happiness because they have no true hope. Their only way out is to find a way to escape reality in this life. May we not have such a superficial conception of joy and happiness in the church of Jesus Christ!

SPIRITUAL CHARACTERISTIC NUMBER THREE
"Blessed are the meek, for they will inherit the earth"
(Matthew 5:5)

MEEKNESS

Meekness is often thought of as being similar to the characteristic of **poor in spirit** in that it too is not trusting in any of our own powers and abilities, organizations or institutions. However, it is quite different. The characteristic of meekness is more searching, more difficult, and more humbling than the previous two characteristics that we just examined. To be poor in spirit is to realize our weakness in view of the true Christian mission and what we have to <u>be</u> and have to <u>do</u>. The characteristic of mourning is to see our own sinfulness, which is a part of our true sinful nature, by seeing the sin of our self-centeredness even in our best actions, thoughts and desires. We mourn and cry out "what a wretched man I am."

<u>Meekness</u> is more searching because it is the characteristic that takes us from within ourselves to our relationship with other people. I may be able to take my own personal evaluation and the condemning

of myself, which is the characteristic of being poor in spirit, but when others do it, my tendency is to <u>resent</u> it. Meekness is measured by how we respond when others put the spotlight on us. It will help to understand meekness if we examine the lifestyle of some of God's servants in Scripture. Jesus, Abraham, Moses, David, Stephen, Paul, and Peter, all became servants to others regardless of the cost. They did not rely on their own abilities, taking the things of God into their hands to accomplish His will, but instead submitted their self-will to God, becoming totally dependent on Him.

Jesus took on the form of a servant and submitted to the will of His Father. He did not try to use the political systems of His day to accomplish God's mission. Instead He sacrificed Himself, giving His all for others in meekness—contrary to the world's ways. But that is the way meekness works. As a result, Jesus completely fulfilled God's mission of being the **salt of the earth** and **the light of the world.**

One of the greatest leaders of all time was Moses. In Numbers 12:3 he is described as a meek man. He had been groomed and trained to be the leader of Egypt, and through his position and natural power of authority, he could have tried to accomplish the return of the Israelites to Palestine. Yet God chose to strip and purge Moses of his self-power, position and abilities. The mission of Moses could only be accomplished by the character and power of God. David did not assert himself, though he could have on several occasions, in his relationship to King Saul. The prophet Jeremiah continued to speak a strong unpopular message to the people of Israel regardless of what the people thought or said about him. Stephen spoke up while among those of strong opposition and suffered being stoned to death. Paul suffered persecution on many occasions by speaking the truth.

The characteristic of meekness does <u>not</u> mean that we will be flabby, lacking in strength, firmness, vigor or force. We will <u>not</u> simply be easy-going, nice, weak in personality, or always exhibiting a compromising spirit seeking peace at any price. Examine how Jesus and Paul lived. They knew their missions and set their faces as a flint to accomplish those missions. They defended spiritual truth with great strength, power, and authority, even to the point of becoming martyrs. They may have been weak in their own abilities, but were extremely strong with the spiritual strength of God as they worked to accomplish their mission.

The quality of meekness causes us <u>not</u> to demand anything for ourselves with respect to our relationship with others as we fulfill God's will and purpose in our life. When people talk about us, scorn us, state untruths about us, we are not sensitive toward or concerned about our own interests and rights so that we have to fight back and defend ourselves. It is no longer necessary that we assert ourself, our rights and claims, position or status in life, possessions or privileges in our relationships with others. No longer do we have to go on the defensive in trying to protect ourselves and our opinions in our relationships for the purpose of needing to be right. Our self-life has gone to the cross. It has been crucified. It is no longer I who lives, but Christ who lives in me (see Galatians 2:20).

SPIRITUAL CHARACTERISTIC NUMBER FOUR
"Blessed are those who hunger and thirst for righteousness, for they will be filled" (Matthew 5:6)

TO HUNGER AND THIRST FOR RIGHTEOUSNESS

As we grow spiritually in the Lord, He must cut away our old nature as He develops in us a new nature: A Christ-like nature with Christ-like characteristics. As these first three Christian characteristics we discussed are developed, we see the Lord's perfect sequence in our being emptied of that which is of self—of **our old sinful nature**. We only seek righteousness to the degree that we have been emptied of our old sinful nature. It is only then that we will desire to be filled with God's righteousness and the Lord will develop that desire into a thirst and hunger. The only way to real peace, to real happiness, is to seek righteousness. Righteousness is simply right living before God. **"The law of the Lord is perfect, reviving the soul. The statutes of the Lord are trustworthy, making wise the simple. The precepts of the Lord are right, giving joy to the heart. The commands of the Lord are radiant, giving light to the eyes. The fear of the Lord is pure, enduring forever. The ordinances of the Lord are sure and altogether righteous. They are more precious than gold, than much pure gold; they are sweeter than honey, than honey from the comb. By them is your servant warned; in keeping them there is much reward"** (Psalm19:7-11).

Notice that Jesus did <u>not</u> tell us to hunger and thirst after happiness or blessings. These things are a *result* of seeking righteousness. To hunger and thirst is to have awareness, a consciousness of a deep and desperate need, to the point that we experience pain in our soul. This hunger stays until it is satisfied—the way we long to be home if away and homesick. It is like the inner drive men and women have as they commit themselves for training to be a sports champion. The drive is so desperate, it hurts. It brings pain, suffering and agony because it is an all-out commitment to sacrifice to achieve the desired goal. Jesus' commitment against sin caused Him to resist to the point of shedding blood (see Hebrews 12:4).

Hungering and thirsting for righteousness is the spiritual characteristic which gives a definite sign of our Christianity. It is this nature which distinguished Jesus from all other men who ever lived. If we welcome and desire righteousness, God's Spirit is truly transforming us into His image. We cannot obtain righteousness by our own efforts. Attempting to do so will lead to pride, which has been the downfall of many through the history of Christianity. It leads us to try to do things in the power of the flesh to be righteous, rather than changing the heart and our character as Jesus tells us is necessary for success in the Christian life.

Jesus promised that if we hunger and thirst for righteousness, we <u>will</u> be filled. This will not happen by our efforts, but through God's grace. We will be filled with the anointing and power of the Holy Spirit. If one is emptied of his self-seeking nature and is filled with God's nature, the next three characteristics given by Jesus—**merciful**, **pure in heart** and **peacemaker**—describe those characteristics that will flow naturally as we come down the mountain to minister with the love of God for His Kingdom rather than for selfish reasons.

SPIRITUAL CHARACTERISTIC NUMBER FIVE
"Blessed are the merciful, for they will be shown mercy"
(Matthew 5:7)

MERCIFUL

As these characteristics on the other side of the mountain become a natural part of our being, we will begin to express in a natural way the true character of God by our actions. **Mercy** is a sense of pity <u>plus</u> a desire to relieve the suffering. It is not pity alone, but also includes action. A good example of being merciful is found in the story of the Good Samaritan. Others may have had compassion and pity on the injured man, but they did not do anything about it. They were not merciful. The characteristic of mercy allowed Jesus to see the miserable consequences of sin. It is what drove Him to act and relieve the suffering sin causes both in this life and life after death in Hell. Mercy caused Him to have a deep sense of pity, compassion and sorrow for mankind—and come to die for our salvation.

The characteristic of mercy develops a sacrificial love for mankind, a caring love that inspires a person to do all he or she can to save another from the fiery pits of Hell. We can be so thankful we have a merciful God. He knows the consequences of sin. Mercy caused Him to have pity on mankind and take action to save us. The Bible states: **"For God so loved the world** (mankind) **that he gave his one and only Son** (Jesus Christ)**, that whoever believes in him** (accepts Him in their heart as their Savior) **shall not perish** (spend eternity in Hell) **but have eternal life** (will spend eternity in Heaven). **For God did not send his Son** (Jesus Christ) **into the world to condemn the world, but to save the world through him. Whoever believes in him** (accepts Jesus in their heart as their Savior) **is not condemned, but whoever does not believe stands condemned already because he has not believed in the name of God's one and only Son** (Jesus Christ)**"** (John 3: 16-18).

Mercy differentiates between the sinner and sin. God hates sin, but loves the sinner. Mercy changes our attitude toward others. It causes us to begin to see people as creatures to be pitied—creatures who are slaves to a sinful nature—creatures who are trapped and engulfed in Satan's world system and who are suffering the awful consequences of sin. After He had been beaten and was hanging on the cross being crucified, mercy moved Jesus to say, **"Father, forgive them, for they do not know what they are doing"** (Luke 23:34). It was this characteristic of mercy in His heart that allowed Jesus to see those who persecuted Him as victims of Satan and his world system and still ask for their forgiveness.

His mercy and love for mankind is what drove Jesus to live a sinless life so that He could fulfill His mission and be the perfect sacrifice for the sins of mankind. Our going to Heaven was far more important to Him than His own personal welfare. His mercy is what made possible the whole doctrine of atonement, the Gospel.

SPIRITUAL CHARACTERISTIC NUMBER SIX
"Blessed are the pure in heart, for they will see God"
(Matthew 5:8)

PURE IN HEART

Being pure in heart is having a singleness of mind in bringing glory to God in all things, rather than seeking for our own "self-interest." Christian doctrine emphasizes the heart. Jesus baffled the scholars of His day because He bypassed the intellectual mechanics of the Scriptures and zeroed in on their effect on the heart. He made it clear we must be changed from the inside out; we must receive a new heart. The Pharisees were interested in the outside more than the inside. Externally they may have been clean, but their inward parts were full of wickedness. The Pharisees made the way of life and righteousness a mere matter of conduct, ethics and behavior. Jesus emphasized the heart, not the intellect. The Christian faith is not only a matter of doctrine or understanding or intellect; it is a condition of the heart.

The term **the heart** refers to the center of our being or personality. It includes our mind, will and emotions. It is the total essence of man. The heart is the seat of all our problems. Jesus put it this way, **"For from within, out of men's hearts, come evil thought, sexual immorality, theft, murder, and adultery, greed, malice, deceit, lewdness, envy, slander, arrogance and folly. All these evils come from inside and make a man 'unclean'"** (Mark 7:20-23).

Even if we had a perfect environment, it would not solve man's problems. Remember that it was in Paradise, the Garden of Eden, where man fell. Any problem in life always comes from an unworthy desire in the heart of somebody somewhere. **"The heart is deceitful above all things and beyond cure. Who can understand it?"** (Jeremiah 17:9). To be **pure** is to be without hypocrisy! Hypocrisy may be the worst of all heart problems because it is a lie within our heart that has an attractive cover to hide the truth. It causes us to be dishonest, insincere and to deceive ourselves. A sincere heart is willing to reveal sin and face the truth of its ultimate consequences.

The hypocrite may even claim a share in Christ and His righteousness. He might be involved in religious activity and may appear to outdo the committed Christian. But God looks at the heart; He knows better. Judas confidently sat down with the apostles at Passover as if he was the most welcome, holiest guest of all, yet his heart was evil and he went out and betrayed Christ. We must be sincere in our commitment to Christianity. We must not speak about a personal relationship with Jesus Christ, when in our heart we know it is not true.

David was called a **man after God's own heart** because there was no spirit of deceit in his heart. Yes, he fell into grievous sin, but when his spiritual eyes were opened to his sin, he quickly confessed and repented. The key was the reaction of David's heart. He did not try to excuse or hide his sin. He knew he had done wrong and was ready for God's judgment. Because of his purity of heart, David was quick to fully repent before the Lord. However, he did suffer many terrible consequences in his life because of the sins he had committed. King David is a good example of the awful pain and heartache that sin causes. Because of his repentant heart and confession before God, he was not prevented from spending eternal life in Heaven. However, the pleasure of his sin for a short season brought him nothing but terrible misery for the last 20 years of his life on Earth.

A divided heart has always been a problem for mankind because of our sinful nature. One part of our being wants to know, worship, obey, and please God. But another part wants to do our own thing (remember Romans 7). The characteristic of a pure heart in a person who is spiritually growing is shown as the degree of a divided heart becomes less and less. Psalm 86:11 is one of the best definitions of a pure heart. It states, **"Teach me your way, O Lord, and I will walk in your truth; give me an undivided heart, that I may fear your name."**

Purity carries with it a meaning of "holiness." **"Make every effort to live in peace with all men and to be holy; without holiness no one will see the Lord"** (Hebrews 12:14). This verse is a parallel verse to Matthew 5:8 in that they both speak of seeing God. It is difficult to understand the full meaning of the promise that Jesus gives us in this characteristic; **seeing God**. We know that Moses could only see the glory of God from a distance as He walked away. Jesus said. **"He that has seen me has seen the Father."** We do see God in nature and in the events of history. There is a sense of seeing Him in how we feel when He is near, as we enjoy His presence. Another way we see Him is in our experiences and how the hand of the Lord is involved in our lives. Of course all of these things are nothing compared with what is yet to be. Now we only see through a glass darkly. Then we shall be with Him for an eternity. I believe Scripture does not give us more of a description of God because human terms are inadequate to describe, and our minds are too small and finite to grasp the glory of God.

Pure in Heart! The development of this characteristic is a measure of how much spiritual responsibility we are ready to handle. That is because the more **pure** it is, the more our heart will be merged with God's will. Even when our best effort fails, the willing spirit of a pure heart means success to God.

SPIRITUAL CHARACTERISTIC NUMBER SEVEN
"Blessed are the peacemakers, for they will be called sons of God" (Matthew 5:9)

PEACEMAKERS

Of all the history of mankind, whatever other ambitions a person may have, inner peace is one of the things that he strives most to possess. As members of the Kingdom of God, Christians are the only people that have the way to give mankind the peace that everyone seeks. **"The fruit of the Spirit** (who lives within all who have been born again) **is love, joy, peace, patience, kindness, goodness, faithfulness, gentleness and self-control. Against such things**

there is no law. Those who belong to Christ Jesus have crucified the sinful nature with its passions and desires. Since we live by the Spirit, let us keep in step with the Spirit. Let us not become conceited, provoking and envying each other" (Galatians 5:22-26).

As a peacemaker, Jesus was not a person who kept quiet just to avoid trouble or who tried to appear nice to appease others all the time. Peacemaking does not mean being a person who seeks peace at any price. A peacemaker rather is a person who now has a different view of himself because he is being delivered from concern for self. His interest is focused on bringing inner peace to mankind regardless of personal sacrifice. A peacemaker sees a much bigger and more important purpose in life than gaining his own rights. Jesus was the supreme example of this as He sacrificed His rights and went to the cross to bring a hope of peace to the hearts of all mankind. Other people could sense that He was a peacemaker and could approach Him knowing they would receive understanding and direction that would give them peace in their hearts. This is why people were drawn to Him.

The blessing that is promised to a peacemaker is a great tribute. Jesus said, **"...for they will be called sons of God."** It is like saying, "like Father, like son" for when the characteristic of a peacemaker flows as a natural part of our nature, we will truly be acting like a son of God. This characteristic once again demonstrates how different the Kingdom of God and the Christian life is from the nature of those who are in the kingdom of the world. Any of these characteristics given by Jesus would have been a shock to the Jews living in His time. They thought the coming Messiah would usher in a military and materialistic kingdom like that in the days of King David. The same can be true of us today if we listen to the voice of the world and its drive to build the Great Society. However, Jesus is letting everyone know that His Kingdom, the Kingdom of God, was not of this world. It is a spiritual Kingdom and it will last forever.

There is nothing else in Scripture that so thoroughly condemns the humanistic way of bringing peace as does the Sermon on the Mount. In the kingdom of the world, mankind will always experience international tension, threat of war, unhappiness, turmoil, and discord among people. Human lust, greed, selfishness, and self-centeredness will always prevail. It is a natural part of man's sinful nature. Therefore, mankind's way using political, economic, and social means of bringing peace does not work. There is only one way and that is to go to the heart. That is the theme of all of the teachings of Jesus. We must be made a new person from the inside out.

SOME POINTS TO REMEMBER ABOUT BEING A PEACEMAKER

A peacemaker is one who actively seeks to make peace because he is not concerned about maintaining the "status quo." He is a person who is willing to go out of his way, sacrificing his own self-interest, to produce peace. This requires that his motivation be from a new heart, a pure heart, and that he is no longer sensitive about his rights and privileges. He will not be asking the question "Is this fair to me?" Peacemakers are not touchy or defensive. This characteristic of a Christian means we now have a different view of our old nature. We realize it is wretched and not worth protecting. We are growing in our understanding of what it means to be poor in spirit, to mourn, be meek or humble, and to hunger and thirst after righteousness, those characteristics that deal with the purging or delivering us from our old nature. We are beginning to live out what Jesus meant in His statement, **"For whoever wants to save his life will lose it** (referring to the old life)**, but whoever loses his life for me and for the gospel will save it"** (Mark 8:35, Matthew 10:39, Luke 9:24 and John 12:25). Also **"If anyone would come after me, he must deny himself and take up his cross** (put to death the old self-centered sinful nature) **and follow me"** (Mark 8:34).

121

Do not repeat things that would do harm to someone. A peace-maker understands that the god of this world is controlling others through their old nature when they are offensive and difficult. **"Brothers, do not slander one another. Anyone who speaks against his brother or judges him speaks against the law and judges it"** (James 4:11). As this characteristic grows to become a natural part of our nature we will learn to view any and every situation in light of the Gospel. We will ask ourselves about the implications of each situation, realizing that it is not just us that is involved, but also the Gospel, the Kingdom of God, and the church.

Look at some of the examples of these characteristics that Jesus gives in the second part of His Sermon, especially as they apply to being a peacemaker. **"If someone strikes you on the right check, turn to him the other also. And if someone wants to sue you and take your tunic, let him have your cloak as well. If someone forces you to go one mile, go with him two miles** (Matthew 5:39-41). **"But I tell you: Love your enemies and pray for those who persecute you, that you may be sons of your Father in heaven"** (Matthew 5:44). **"But if you forgive men when they sin against you, your heavenly Father will also forgive you"** (Matthew 6:14). **"Why do you look at the speck of sawdust in your brother's eye and pay no attention to the plank in your own eye? How can you say to your brother, 'Let me take the speck out of your eye,' when all the time there is a plank in your own eye?"** (Matthew 7:3-4).

These seven spiritual characteristics we have examined teach us the unique difference between what is to govern our way of life and that which governs the life of a non-Christian. They show us just how dependent we are on the power of the Holy Spirit within us, and how useless the power of our flesh is in living out the life of Christ. Also remember that as we think about the meaning of these spiritual char-acteristics, they are a mirror for us to look at ourselves, not something that we use to evaluate or judge other people. Also, these spiritual characteristics of the Kingdom of God are <u>not</u> a new moral code or law by which we are saved or become a member of the Kingdom of God. **"It is by grace you have been saved, through faith—and this not from yourselves, it is the gift of God—not by works, so that no one can boast"** (Ephesians 2:8). **"Therefore, there is now no condemnation for those who are in Christ Jesus"** (Romans 8:1). These characteristics are not to be looked at in any way with a condemning spirit. Jesus gave them to us so that we may now know what the character of those who become a member of the Kingdom of God is meant to be.

Although the degree to which these characteristics are developed within our nature is not the criteria for our salvation, they do directly impact how successful we will be in fulfilling God's mission of being the **salt of the earth** and the **light of the world.** Remember as we have already seen that we are salt and light, not because of who we are, but because of the nature of Jesus Christ whose life now lives within us through the power of the Holy Spirit. Paul said, **"I have become its servant by the commission God gave me to present to you the word of God in its fullness—the mystery that has been kept hidden for ages and generations, but is now disclosed to the saints. To them God has chosen to make known among the Gentiles the glorious riches of this mystery, which is Christ in you, the hope of glory"** (Colossians 1:25-27).

The fact that Jesus first lists the characteristics of the Kingdom of God before His proclamation that we are to be the **salt of the earth** and the **light of the world** indicates that the development of these spiritual characteristics is the prerequisite for fulfilling this call. The life of every Christian is a battleground for spiritual warfare. It is the Holy Spirit of God, living within us, guiding and convicting us through the Word of God versus our sinful nature that is being tempted by the enemy. Satan is going to keep us from growing in the spiritual characteristics of God's Kingdom if he can. The Word of

God teaches that his main method of attack will come by tempting us through the things of the world or society.

We are in the world but we are no longer a member of its kingdom. Therefore, we are to separate ourselves from its standards and its characteristics. This is essential if we are going to declare the wonderful deeds of Him who called us out of darkness into the marvelous light of the Kingdom of God. **"Do not be yoked together with unbelievers. For what do righteousness and wickedness have in common? Or what fellowship can light have with darkness? What harmony is there between Christ and Belial? What does a believer have in common with an unbeliever" What agreement is there between the temple of God and idols? For we are the temple of the living God. As God has said: 'I will live with them and walk among them, and I will be their God, and they will be my people.' 'Therefore come out from them and be separate,' says the Lord. 'Touch no unclean thing, and I will receive you. I will be a Father to you, and you will be my sons and daughters,' says the Lord Almighty"** (II Corinthians 6:14-18). **"You are a chosen race, a royal priesthood, a holy nation, God's own people, that you may declare the wonderful deeds of him who called you out of darkness into his marvelous light"** (I Peter 2:9).

"**B**lessed are those who are persecuted because of righteousness, for theirs is the kingdom of heaven**"** (Matthew 5:10). This is the very next verse that follows after Jesus lists the seven spiritual characteristics of those in the Kingdom of God. I believe Jesus put things in this order because He was telling us that as these characteristics become more and more a part of our character, controlling our Christian life, this is how we can expect the world to react. The key to emphasize in this statement is the blessing is promised for those who are **persecuted because of righteousness.** I have found that if you get a group of Christians together, they may well disagree on what it means to be righteous.

The Word of God often deals with the subject of righteousness by pointing out what is unrighteous in the sinful nature of mankind and the ways of the world. Not only does Jesus make it clear in the Sermon on the Mount that righteousness starts in the heart, which is then followed by righteous actions, but so do other Scriptures which point out that the righteous shall live by faith. A righteous Christian is one who is living in the characteristics Jesus has given for the citizens of the Kingdom of God.

It is because the light of Jesus' character begins to shine through our life that we become open to the possibility of being persecuted. Just as the world did not know how to handle the character of Jesus because He dealt with those things of the heart, the same has been true throughout history of His followers. The world hates these characteristics because they don't know how to debate against such positives that deal with the heart. Therefore, their only answer is to try and shoot out this bright light that shows up the darkness in their life. This can happen through either physical or verbal persecution.

Although most Christians have been able to avoid persecution in America, there are growing indications that the safety and ease we have experienced in our country could change in the coming years. Therefore, it is important that we understand some of the things about this comment made by Jesus.

SOME NEGATIVE POINTS

We need to recognize that Jesus does not say that we may be persecuted because we are being objectionable or difficult. We can bring suffering and difficulties upon ourselves that are quite unnecessary because of our self-righteous attitudes. Nor does Jesus say we may be persecuted because we are fanatical or over-zealous. Fanaticism is never commended in the New Testament. This has often led people into difficulties. Peter said, **"If you suffer, it should not be as a murderer or thief or any other kind of criminal, or even as a meddler** (being a busybody in other people's affairs) (I Peter 4:15). Another basis of persecution Jesus does not address is involvement in a cause. There is a difference in being persecuted for righteousness' sake and being persecuted for a cause. The two can be somewhat identical, so we must be careful not to just suffer persecution because we get caught up in a cause and develop a martyr spirit. Jesus also does not say **"blessed are those who are persecuted"** for standing up for certain political principles. It is not wrong to do so if we have that inclination, but politics is not righteousness.

Jesus does not say, **blessed** for being good or noble. In fact the world will generally praise and admire the good and noble. There have been people who have made great sacrifices, given up careers and wealth and maybe even their lives. These people are usually thought of as great heroes and are praised. Some people put the tag on them as great Christians. But Christianity is more than that.

WHAT DID JESUS MEAN?

Practicing righteousness means being like the Lord Jesus Christ. The word "righteousness" has had different meanings for people throughout the history of mankind. We need to rely on God's definition as given to us in His Word. Unfortunately the meaning of righteousness in the religious world too often only has to do with those things that we can do in the power of the flesh. Our actions are important, but because of where Jesus makes this statement I would have to conclude the righteousness He is talking about has more to do with those things of the heart.

Remember that living the way Jesus describes in the Sermon on the Mount through His various illustrations from Matthew 5:21 through chapter 7 requires heart characteristics that are quite different than those that are normal in the make-up of mankind. This must be one of the reasons why Jesus said, **"If the world hates you, keep in mind that it hated me first. If you belonged to the world, it would love you as its own. As it is, you do not belong to the world, but I have chosen you out of the world. That is why the world hates you. Remember the word I spoke to you: 'No servant is greater than his master.' If they persecuted me, they will persecute you also"** (John 15: 18-20). Also in II Timothy 3:12 we read, **"In fact, everyone who wants to live a godly life in Christ Jesus will be persecuted…"**

This is evident as we study the history of the church. From the days of the early church, through the Dark Ages and the Reformation, and in many countries today, Christians are being persecuted. This persecution is not because they are being difficult or over-zealous, but because they seek to live righteous lives.

By whom are the righteous persecuted? Persecution has not only been confined to the world. Some of the most grievous verbal as well as physical persecutions that Christians have experienced have been at the hands of an established church or religious people. The people who persecuted Jesus, the early church, the Reformers, the Puritans, and other Christians down through the ages often thought they were serving God. Formal Christianity has often been the greatest enemy of the pure faith.

WHY THE RIGHTEOUS ARE PERSECUTED

We might ask, why are the righteous persecuted while the good and noble are not? The good and noble are not persecuted because most people feel like the noble are just like themselves. But there is something about the righteousness of Christians that condemns others. This is because it is coming from a changed heart with characteristics that make the good deeds of others look cheap and reveals them to be lacking a true and sincere quality. Christians don't have to condemn others in words; just the righteous way they live is enough to make some people feel uneasy and unhappy. Therefore, they try to find fault with Christians. Being persecuted for righteousness really puts to the test our idea of what it means to be a Christian. Jesus said, **"Woe to you when all men speak well of you, for that is how their fathers treated the false prophets"** (Luke 6:26). We usually think the perfect Christian is the nice, popular person who never offends anybody and is easy to get along with. But the real Christian is a person who is <u>not</u> going to be praised by everybody.

If we try to imitate Jesus with the natural powers of the flesh rather than through the power of the Holy Spirit, the world may praise us, because we will be doing what the natural mind identifies as right. We will be living to the standard that the world thinks is goodness or righteousness. But true righteousness is developing and living the life of Christ, represented by the characteristics Jesus gives us in the Beatitudes: To be poor in spirit in all natural abilities; to mourn for the sins we see in ourselves and in the world; to be meek in our relationships with others; to hunger and thirst for righteousness; to be merciful, which is to have pity for others and to also take action to do something about it; to be pure in heart, without hypocrisy and to be honest about all things; to be a peacemaker. The message of Jesus in the Sermon on the Mount is that we need a changed heart. When we live the characteristics that Jesus lists in the Beatitudes it means we are becoming like Him. It also means we are becoming **salt** and **light** in a dark world. Because light exposes darkness and darkness hates the light, it brings persecution.

REJOICE AND BE GLAD WHEN PERSECUTED

Jesus continues in the next verse by saying, **"Blessed are you when people insult you, persecute you and falsely say all kinds of evil against you because of me. <u>Rejoice and be glad</u>, because great is your reward in heaven, for in the same way they persecuted the prophets who were before you"** (Matthew 5:11-12). The previous statement about persecution was a hard statement for us; this one seems even harder. In the Sermon on the Mount, the Lord gives us two distinct points in how He describes a Christian. One is to look at the Christian as they are, in and of themselves, and the other is to look at their reactions to the various things that happen to them in this life. These two verses in Matthew 5:11-12 about persecution fall into the second way of looking at a Christian, which is their reaction to perse-cution. There are three principles here that the Lord tells of with regard to the Christian.

One: The Christian is **unlike** everyone who is not a Christian. The Gospel creates a clear-cut division and distinction between the Christian and the non-Christian. Those of other religious beliefs, or of no belief at all, prove this by the way they have persecuted Christians at various times in history. There is a light in the Christian's character, as described in Jesus' Sermon on the Mount that penetrates the spiritual darkness of a non-Christian's heart. Therefore, the non-Christian has a tendency to retaliate. They criticize, scorn, falsely speak evil of, speak angrily about, abuse physically—socially—in the work place and maybe in the church.

Two: The Christian's life is controlled and dominated by Jesus Christ, we are loyal to Christ, and our concern is to do everything for His sake. Jesus says it is because we are living for Him that we no longer live like everyone else in the world that live for themselves. This is why Christians are persecuted! We represent Him and the Kingdom of God here on this Earth as His ambassadors. **"Do you not know that your body is a temple of the Holy Spirit, who is in you, whom you have received from God? You are not your own; you were bought at a price"** (I Corinthians 6:19-20).

There have been non-Christians who have been persecuted by others, but it is not for Christ's sake. The persecution we are talking about happens <u>because</u> of our commitment to be controlled by a motive to <u>live for Christ's sake</u>. That is what differentiates us from everyone else. Regardless of how much we may fail in practice, our desire is to live to bring glory to Him. No one was ever persecuted like Jesus and He said, **"Remember the words I spoke to you: 'No servant is greater than his master.' If they persecuted me, they will persecute you also...They will treat you this way because of my name, for they do not know the One who sent me"** (John 15:20-21).

Three: The third principle Jesus brings out in these verses in Matthew 5:11-12 is <u>our life is to be controlled by thoughts of Heaven</u>. This principle is found throughout the New Testament. Hebrews chapter eleven is a great example of this. The Old Testament saints were looking for a city whose builder and maker is God. Nothing that happened to them took their focus off the reward that was to come. How contrary this is to the motives that are in the world, always tempting us with an escape from reality with its pleasures and entertainment, especially avoiding thinking about death and the world to come.

HOW ARE CHRISTIANS TO FACE PERSECUTION

There are many ways in which a Christian may suffer persecution, and the Bible tells us how we are to face that persecution. **One**, the Christian is not to retaliate. Our natural instinct is self-preservation and to try to get even. **Two**, we are not to feel resentment. This is very difficult, but judgment is to be left up to God. **Three**, we should not allow persecution to depress or oppress us. Here again, as with the characteristics in these Beatitudes, we see how impossible it is for us to fulfill these teachings of Jesus by our own efforts. In the natural it is impossible to rejoice and be glad and not react when being persecuted, regardless of what kind of persecution it may be. I have experienced persecution on different occasions because of my commitment. At first I did not have victory! I had to learn that victory can only come through the power of the Holy Spirit living in me. Praise the Lord He did provide the power and the heavy burden in my heart was completely lifted and the fruit of the Spirit ruled once again in my heart.

It is difficult to relate to the subject of physical persecution unless you have personally experienced it. For example, have you ever wondered how the early Christians could have been singing while being fed to the lions? There are other similar examples to be found throughout the history of the church. One thing I have always remembered from reading the book, *The Hiding Place*, which was about Corrie ten Boom's life, was when she asked her father how could they ever stand up under the persecution that appeared to be coming at the hands of the Germans. He answered her question by asking, "Corrie, when do you need your ticket to get on the train?" Of course, the answer is not until you are boarding the train. The point he was trying to help her understand was it is the same with the Lord. We won't need the Lord's strength and He doesn't provide it to handle persecution, either verbal or physical, until the time we need it.

Why would Jesus say we are to rejoice and be glad and how is this possible when facing persecution? We are not to rejoice at the mere fact of persecution. That is something to be regretted. It is not for the purpose of putting ourselves on a pedestal, thinking that we are much better than others. That is how the Pharisees thought. One reason we can rejoice if we are persecuted for "Christ's sake" is because this would be proof of what and who we are. It identifies us with the prophets; God's chosen servants, who are now with Him. Another reason we can rejoice if we have been falsely accused and suffer for "Christ's sake" is because it means that our lives have become more like His. We are being treated as He was, which again is proof that we belong to Him.

Four, we can rejoice because Jesus says, **our reward** in Heaven will be great. He is telling us that our ultimate destiny is fixed. If the world persecutes us, it is just telling us that we do not belong to it. We belong to another Kingdom, which is a good reason to rejoice! According to Scripture, our whole outlook on everything that happens to us should be governed by the realization of who I am, my consciousness of where I am going, and my knowledge of the reward that awaits me when I get there (see II Corinthians 4:17 thru Corinthians 5:10).

The question has been asked, "How is a reward possible since we do not merit Heaven, it is all by grace?" This is true, but because of God's grace and as our Father, He throws other things into the bargain, so to speak, to encourage us with His love and gratitude. Again, look at those described in the eleventh chapter of Hebrews. Faith in the reward to come is what gave these men and women the courage to keep themselves committed to the course of the race they were running. Paul told the Colossians to, **"Set your minds on things above, not on earthly things. For you died, and your life is now hidden with Christ in God. When Christ, who is your life, appears, then you also will appear with him in glory. Put to death, therefore, whatever belongs to your earthly nature: sexual immorality,** impurity, lust, evil desires and greed, which is idolatry…You used to walk in these ways, in the life you once lived. But now you must rid yourselves of all such things as these: anger, rage, malice, slander, and filthy language from your lips. Do not lie to each other, since you have taken off your old self with its practices and have put on the new self, which is being renewed in knowledge in the image of its Creator" (Colossians 3:2-10).

What is to be our reward? The Bible does not tell us a great deal about it. It is so glorious and wonderful that human language falls exceedingly short of being able to describe its glory. We do know our bodies will be changed. There will be no sickness or disease, and no sorrow as all tears are wiped away. No separation, no unhappiness for even a second. It will be unmixed joy and glory, holiness, and purity and wonder! That is the destiny that awaits us! Therefore, Jesus is saying, rather than resenting and wanting to hit back if persecuted, or being depressed by it, let it make you realize all the more of what is waiting for you. You have joy unspeakable and glory waiting for you. All that is in the now is but temporary and passing; regardless of what happens to you it cannot affect what is waiting for you. In these truths you can rejoice and be exceedingly glad. This is why Paul said, **"For to me, to live is Christ and to die is gain"** (Philippians 1:21).

After speaking about how we are to react to persecution Jesus then follows with this statement, **"You are the salt of the earth. But if the salt loses its saltiness, how can it be made salty again? It is no longer good for anything, except to be thrown out and trampled by men. You are the light of the world. A city on a hill cannot be hidden. Neither do people light a lamp and put it under a bowl. Instead they put it on its stand, and it gives light to everyone in the house. In the same way, let your light shine before men, that they may see your good deeds and praise your Father in heaven"** (Matthew 5:13-16).

Being **the salt of the earth** and **the light of the world** is our fundamental mission statement as Christians. This mission is so important to Jesus that He declared that to lose our <u>saltiness</u> would be to render ourselves Kingdom rejects. This battle we are involved in is serious business.

Having concluded our examination of God's special calling for America and the fundamentals of how He expects us to live in a world that does not truly know Him, we are now ready to examine the nature and method of Satan's attack against us, and how we should respond.

CHAPTER NINE

In these last days of the Church Age <u>what geographical area</u> on Earth do you think would be Satan's major spiritual battleground? If we know this, that is the key to knowing where Satan's major spiritual battleground will be in these last days because Satan has always tried to sabotage any work of God by developing a scheme alongside any spiritual development of God to counter-attack, undermine, and attempt to destroy God's purpose. We know this is a fact as both history and Scripture confirm it! **"Be self-controlled and alert. Your enemy the devil prowls around like a roaring lion looking for someone to devour. Resist him, standing firm in the faith…"** (I Peter 5:8-9a).

It is a well-known fact that America has been the world's center of Christianity for the last three hundred years. This means that if we accept what the Scriptures teach about Satan, the major thrust of his spiritual activity in these last days is going to be here in our country. Therefore, we must conclude that as Satan sees his time is growing short he is going to attempt to destroy every good thing with which God has blessed our country, especially our Christian values. It also means that many of the prophetic warnings given to us in Scripture about the last days apply to America as much as or more so than any-where else.

America has indeed become a major spiritual war zone in these last days of the Church Age. We are being hit daily in every way imaginable to bend and compromise biblical standards. Many Christians readily admit they <u>do not understand</u> the root cause of the rapid breakdown in our society's moral fiber or the methods by which the enemy has conducted such a successful spiritual warfare against our country. Never in the history of mankind has the sinful nature of Christians been subject to such heavy temptations as that of our mass communication system to mix and become contaminated by the world. The heavy contamination by the world is why our function as salt has lost its saltiness.

In this last generation this spiritual warfare of contamination has taken its toll on the effectiveness of the body of Christ to fulfill our mission to be salt and light. The 'new moral' standards developed in our country in this generation have influenced the Christian community much more than we have influenced the world. We have become more tolerant and indifferent to many of the sins in the world. In this generation people have begun to feel free to openly display and even promote their sins, not only by their lifestyle but also through the media that is available to everyone. This was not the case throughout most of the history of America.

"Finally, be strong in the Lord and in his mighty power. Put on the full armor of God so that you can take your stand against the devil's schemes. For our struggle is not against flesh and blood, but against the rulers, against the authorities, against the powers of this dark world and against the spiritual forces of evil in the heavenly realms. Therefore put on the full armor of God, so that when the day of evil comes, you may be able to stand your ground, and after you have done everything, to stand" (Ephesians 6:10-13).

SPIRITUAL TRUTH

God and His people have always had a spiritual enemy and any work of God involves great spiritual battles. The Bible calls our enemy Satan or the Devil. The fact that he is out to destroy God's calling for Christians in our country is not unique. He has always worked to undermine and sabotage God's purpose. God's spiritual enemy does not remain idle. His tactics are ruthless and deadly. He always plays hardball. He never calls for a spiritual cease-fire! He is going to wage spiritual warfare anywhere God's light is shining.

Satan caused Adam and Eve to fall persuading them to disobey the one command God had given them. You would have thought that to obey only one command would not have been that difficult. In the days of Noah he caused lawlessness and wickedness to become so terrible that God had no choice but to cleanse the Earth by a flood. As you travel through the Old Testament you will find that he was successful in constantly developing the spirit of rebellion and permissiveness in Israel. Even though God warned them, they still turned against His standards in disobedience. When God Himself came to Earth in the person of Jesus Christ, Satan had so deceived most of the Israelites they not only didn't recognize Him, they crucified Him.

Satan's warfare against God's people continued after the church began. In the first 300 years of church history, Satan's attacks against Christians, working primarily through the Roman government, were so harsh that an estimated three million Christians were persecuted for their faith by every cruel act of torture imaginable. They were hunted down and thrown to wild animals, torn to pieces, beheaded, burned, crucified and buried alive.

Satan's attacks on the church continued during the Dark Ages and the Middle Ages. His attacks were so severe during this period of time God prepared a place of near obscurity to protect the church and His Word. The church operated mostly in secret, through the underground, during this period of time. After Martin Luther posted his "95 theses" on the church door in Wittenberg, Germany on October 31, 1517, the Reformation began and the Gospel of Jesus Christ began to be openly preached. Satan, however, continued his attacks against Christians during the Reformation wars when thousands of Christians were brutally massacred for their faith in Jesus Christ.

No doubt you have heard about some of these terrible historical events. In France, during the year 1557, Pope Pius called for an extermination of all believers that were not members of the Roman Catholic Church. On August 24, 1572, 70,000 Christians were massacred in what is known as the "St. Bartholomew's Day Massacre." The Spanish Inquisition left over 100,000 people dead and 1,500,000 were banished from the country. Between 1566 and 1598, over 100,000 Christians were slaughtered in the Netherlands. In the country of Bohemia 3,200,000 Christians were exterminated during the Reformation Wars. That was 80% of the population. Persecution of the church continues. Historian David Barrett estimates that more than 45 million Christians were martyred during the 20th century. 13,300,000 since 1950!

America has largely enjoyed freedom from religious persecution. And our nation remains the center of Christian witness for the world. Therefore, from what the Scriptures teach us and from what history has confirmed to be true, it is easy to see why Satan launched an all-out spiritual attack against our country. He is doing everything he can to change every law or standard in our country that is based on Christian standards. The body of Christ in America must be aware and understand this. There is no doubt that we are living in the time of his attack. Prophetic Scriptures warn us that this would happen in these last days as Satan sees that his time is running short. He has set out to destroy God's standards that were established in God's end-time geographical base in this world. History illustrates the reality of the spiritual warfare against Christians in this world. I briefly reviewed the history of persecution because I want you to see just how ruthless and wicked our adversary Satan really is.

PERSECUTION AND DECEPTION

The Bible teaches that Satan has always used two distinct methods when attacking God's people: **Persecution and deception!** They both have the same goal—to keep God's people from fulfilling their mission of being the **salt of the earth** and the **light of the world** in this dark and evil world. Persecution is easy to detect; deception is not. We can see how severely Satan uses the method of persecution to attack Christians. He uses deception just as much if not more, but it is much harder to detect.

Persecution is an attack against the body that will cause physical harm. Satan's objective in using persecution is to get us to deny our relationship with God to avoid the persecution. Look at the lives of the Apostles, who were almost all martyred for their faith. Consider this thought from someone who recently experienced persecution and was asked why God had allowed him to be persecuted: *"Not only would He not kill our enemies for us, but He would empower us to love them while they killed us."* Another missionary, Jim Elliot, killed in 1956 by headhunters in Ecuador stated, *"He is no fool who gives what he cannot keep to gain what he cannot lose."*

DECEPTION

Both persecution and deception are dangerous and destructive. However, deception has been the primary method of attack against Christians in America. The same was true for Israel throughout most of its history. Deception is an attack through our mind tempting our sinful nature (using the lust of the eyes, the lust of the flesh, and the pride of life) to disobey God's Word. It corrupts the heart. This is my definition of deception: *Seducing or deceiving spirits tempt God's people to trade the truth of God's Word to accept something that is contrary to the Word of God. They try to make something wrong seem innocent. To perform their acts of seduction they attempt to make their enticements irresistible. They try to make the difference between black and white seem like a shade of gray.*

If we do not know the Word of God and diligently seek righteousness, and hate every evil way, we will become susceptible to deceiving spirits, for this is one of the greatest dangers in the last days. Scripture is clear that deception will be a primary method in which Satan will attack Christians in these last days. Paul states, **"The Spirit clearly says that in later times some will abandon the faith and follow deceiving spirits..."** (I Timothy 4:1). Deception is an insidious and dangerous weapon. It often goes undetected by its very nature. DECEPTION BREEDS COMPROMISE WHICH LEADS TO DISOBEDIENCE AND SPIRITUAL DEFEAT! The only way you can determine the use of deception is by an examination of the fruit. As we look at the fruit produced by our society in this last generation keep in mind that, **"The fruit of the Spirit is love, joy, peace, patience, kindness, goodness, faithfulness, gentleness and self-control. Against such things there is no law. Those who belong to Christ Jesus have crucified the sinful nature with its passions and desires. Since we live by the Spirit, let us keep in step with the Spirit. Let us not become conceited, provoking and envying each other"** (Galatians 5:22-26).

Through persecution, some 70,000,000 Christians have been killed over the last 2000 years (Source: World Christian Encyclopedia Global Diagram 6). But Satan's use of deception is just as ruthless, wicked and severe, and has impacted every believer. It brought down Eve, then Adam as well as leaders like Samson, King Saul, King David, Solomon and many more. It is destroying the Christian moral standards of the American people today. Many Christian leaders and church members have fallen into sin through deception. Sexual sins and the breakup of marriages are at epidemic levels. Addiction to pornography has also become a national epidemic among Christian men and women alike. Deception is causing divorce, immorality, dishonesty and greed to run rampant within the church.

By the time today's adolescents graduate from high school, they will have spent 15,000 hours watching television, compared with 12,000 hours spent in the classroom. They are exposed to over 14,000 sexual references per year on television. Only 165 of these references deal with birth control, self-control, abstinence, or risk of pregnancy. A very high percentage of all TV shows now include sexual content, an increase from about half of all shows just ten years ago! **"See to it that no one takes you captive through hollow and <u>deceptive</u> philosophy, which depends on human tradition and the basic principles of this world rather than on Christ"** (Colossians 2:8).

One of the strongest influences the world has had on the Christian community has been to get us to become self-centered. A fruit of spiritual deception is to change our standards to serve our self-interest, self-satisfaction and self-gratification over and above our willingness to seek God's will and His standards first. We may say that we are standing against the tide, but the truth of the matter is we are simply a few decades behind the world's acceptance of many of our society's 'new' moral standards. This has caused Christians to be more tolerant of and more indifferent to many of the sins described in the Bible that are now commonplace in our culture. What was permissible by worldly standards in American society twenty or thirty years ago is now largely acceptable to Christians. Finding a Christian who has a <u>fear of sinning</u> is rare these days.

FRUIT REVEALS DECEPTION

In this past generation, we Americans have changed the standards and guidelines that the majority of the American people lived by for years. We have changed the way we think, raise our families, run our public schools, run our government, set our moral standards, and establish our social order. America's 'new' moral code says, "If you can get away with it, then it is all right." This has resulted in moral actions, which were "unthinkable" thirty-to-forty years ago, to become "commonplace." Personal accountability, respect for authority and self-control have become an antiquated way of thinking. Nothing, it seems, is indecent or repugnant. Rules and boundaries are resisted and fought against. Very little deserves to be honored and respected. We are told that everyone should be tolerant of the 'new' moral standards.

Even our government leaders began to pass legislation that has allowed and promoted immoral causes and ungodly standards on issues they never before would have considered. Passing out condoms in schools, for example, sanctions promiscuity and promotes sexual immorality. Prayer was made illegal in all public schools. A law was passed that has allowed the murder of over forty-five million innocent babies through abortion.

A report that covered a recent 30 year period of our country's 'new' moral standards revealed that during this 30 years our society produced the following fruit. Crime increased by 500%! Illegitimate births increased by 400%! Three times the number of children were living in single-parent homes. The teenage suicide rate tripled. The divorce rate doubled. Over 40 million babies during this thirty-year period were murdered through abortion. It became okay to openly teach homosexuality as an acceptable lifestyle in our public schools. The entertainment industry discovered it could display sexual permissiveness and violence with very little resistance. Child molestation and incest became a national disaster and the police state that only 25% of the cases are reported. Our children began to gun down their peers and teachers at school. Every day the newspapers are crowded with reports of robbery, murder, hate, greed, violence and other horrors.

In American society today, the most fundamental means of preserving social order—the commitment to family—has been shattered. Sexual immorality and the divorce rate have skyrocketed to epidemic levels, even among Christians. Greed and unethical conduct have tainted such professions as doctors, bankers, lawyers, politicians, educators, corporate leaders, spiritual leaders, and others that have historically represented the pillars of our society. Our great American cities, once the principle evidence of a mighty, industrial nation, have been turned into a stalking ground for crime, violence, sexual perversion, and the distribution of drugs. The <u>character</u> of many Americans has also been transformed through sexual immorality and a lifestyle devoted to self-gratification. Our public schools, once the showpiece of a young democracy, have surrendered to drug abuse, sex, and criminal violence. Our great republic form of government has turned from the Scriptural principles that formed the foundation of our country by passing laws that actively undermine the truth.

This attack on our children is also being carried out in our public schools. A school principal was recently quoted as saying, *"The law requires a public school facility to be used to teach sexual perversion and call it, 'an alternate lifestyle.' If someone is offended, that's OK. The school can condone sexual promiscuity by dispensing condoms and call it, 'safe sex' If someone is offended, that's OK. The school can present the merits of killing an unborn baby as a 'viable means of birth control.' If someone is offended, no problem. The school can designate a school day as, 'Earth Day' involving students in activities to worship religiously and praise the goddess, Mother Earth and call it 'ecology.' The school can use literature, videos and presentations in the classroom that depict people with strong, traditional Christian convictions as, "simple minded" and "ignorant" and call it, 'enlightenment.' It is OK if anyone is offended in these situations, but to offend someone by saying a public prayer is a violation of Federal Law."*

Humanistic thinking has captured public education. Humanism is a religion that sets man up to be his own god. You can no longer find textbooks in our public schools that clearly teach the Christian influence in our country's development. However, nearly every textbook has the religion of humanism running through its pages. Secular humanists know that if they can control what our young people are taught—what they see, hear, think and believe—then they can determine our society's philosophical standards. This is definitely one of the reasons why our Christian heritage, which burned brightly for many generations, has been extinguished so quickly. We are seeing come true what Abraham Lincoln said: *"That the philosophy of the classroom today will be the philosophy of the government tomorrow."*

What our country's 'new' moral code has done in just one generation to the discipline problems in our public schools was reported by a survey completed by Gospel Films. Although this survey was done several years ago it is still a report that makes a valuable statement. In the year of 1940 the seven major discipline problems in our schools were: Talking in class: Chewing gum: Making noise: Running in the halls: Cutting in line: Improper clothing: Littering. One generation later in the year of 1983 the seven major discipline problems were: Rape: Robbery: Assault: Burglary: Arson: Bombing: Murder.

A high school student that loves the Lord recently wrote this prayer.

> *Now I sit me down in school, where praying is against the rule.*
> *For this great nation under God, finds mention of Him very odd.*
> *If Scripture now the class recites, it violates the Bill of Rights.*
> *And anytime my head I bow, becomes a federal matter now.*
> *Our hair can be purple or orange or green, that's no offense, it's the freedom scene.*
> *The law is specific, the law is precise, prayers spoken aloud are a serious vice.*
> *For praying in a public hall, might offend someone with no faith at all.*
> *In silence alone we must meditate, God's name is prohibited by the State.*
> *We're allowed to cuss and dress like freaks, and pierce our noses, tongues and cheeks.*
> *They've outlawed guns; but first the Bible, to quote the Good Book makes me liable.*

We can elect a pregnant Senior Queen, and the unwed daddy,
our Senior King.

It's "inappropriate" to teach right from wrong, we're taught
that such "judgments" do not belong.

We can get our condoms and birth controls, study witchcraft,
vampires and totem poles.

But the Ten Commandments are not allowed, no Word of God
must reach this crowd.

It's scary here, I must confess, when chaos reigns, the school's a
mess.

So Lord, this silent plea I make: Should I be shot, my soul to
take.

Dr. James Dobson, Founder and President of Focus on the Family, and Gary L. Bauer, President of the Family Research Council (and who served as President Reagan's Domestic Policy Advisor) wrote a book titled *Children at Risk*. This book details the battle in our society for the hearts and minds of our kids. Every parent and grandparent needs this kind of information and more. Speaking about our culture, they write: *"The same twisted philosophy that permits us to kill infants through abortion with impunity is now prevalent throughout the western world. This new way of thinking has produced a* <u>*society that is extremely dangerous to minds and bodies of children*</u> (emphasis added).

At the arrival of adolescence, teenagers are subject to the pressure and wrath of their peers, making them prime targets for brainwashing with the mind-bending process at which television and movies constantly hammer away at moral values and principles. Any form of self-discipline or restraint is usually ridiculed by friends and acquaintances. This develops a lot of pressure for conformity, until finally, many of our youth trade in their freedom for slavery and domination. Their behavior has been warped by the enormous social pressures coming through society. This opens the doors of temptation which carry many names: alcohol, marijuana, hard drugs, pornography, gambling, homosexual experimentation, premarital sex and more.

It should be clear that one of our jobs as parents must be to keep these temptation doors closed, locked and barred to adolescents. It is frightening today to see that these doors are not only unlocked for many of our youth—they are wide open. It is no wonder that the kids who want to remain chaste are often made to feel like prudes and freaks.

With the heartache and illness the loose humanistic standards are now causing for the families of our society, one would think responsible adults would be united in a campaign in opposition. But normally the contrary is found to be true."

Dr. Dobson goes on to point out how human-centered value systems (which is what the religion of humanism teaches) have come to dominate our thinking; they have scorched our land, spreading like wildfire with disastrous consequences. Does it concern you that the moral standard by which the American people have lived by for years have deteriorated much more in this last generation than in all of the previous years combined since we became a nation? It is not pleasant to consider these truths. I would rather hear about positives than negative. But when you are in a battle, you cannot afford to hide your head in the sand or you will soon face defeat. It is extremely important to be honest with whatever the facts and fruit may reveal. The spiritual foundation of our country is being torn apart and yet the majority of the people, including Christians, do not seem to be that concerned. They ignore the scoreboard! In fact there is a cry for greater freedom to feed our sinful natures. That is deception.

FULFILLING OUR MISSION STATEMENT

We need to look no further than ourselves to find the real reason behind the corruption and violence in our nation. As Pogo said, "We have met the enemy, and he is us!" The body of Christ has lost much of its light and the function of being salt—God's mission statement for every Christian. We have allowed society to exchange our commitment to righteousness for a spirit of tolerance towards the ways of the world. The freedom people have these days to openly talk about and display the most blatant of sins, flaunting them before the public's eyes, is a sad commentary on Christians being the salt of the earth.

The principle of Jesus' teaching about salt is that if Christians assimilate anything other than the purity of God's Word by mixing with the impurities of the world, we will become contaminated and lose our saltiness or influence. Our influence in and on society is dependent upon our being distinct and separate from, not identical to the world. Herein lies the problem for Christians in our society. This is the reason for the bitter harvest of suffering and defeat so many Christians have experienced this past generation. **"But you have planted wickedness, you have reaped evil, you have eaten the fruit of deception. Because you have depended on your own strength..."** (Hosea 10:13).

The fruit of our society, as well as those of the Christian community, compared to the teaching of Jesus Christ and the Word of God, is not a pretty picture. However, we cannot blame the people of the world for the heavy toll of suffering and pain that the American people have suffered over this past generation. The people of the world will naturally do what the standards of the society in which they live allow. This is what we should expect as they don't know better. They live in darkness. They are part of the kingdom of the world. But we do know better and that is why Jesus declared that it is our responsibility to be the salt and the light.

It was so important to Jesus that we preserve the good that He declared for us to lose our saltiness is to render ourselves Kingdom rejects. It seems that very few Christians today are committed to our mission to be salt and light. We have been deceived by the influence of the world to be more interested and focused on "me, myself and I." Maybe you have been caught in the web of deception?

CHAPTER TEN

It was in the Garden of Eden that sin first entered God's creation. In chapter five where I discussed the kingdom of the world I briefly reviewed the fall of Adam and Eve while discussing our sinful nature. I am going to look further at their fall in this chapter to help us understand the enemy's use of deception. The same temptations we face and the choices we make every day are displayed for us in this tragic story. Satan has not changed his method of attack on the child of God. He has used the same basic pattern of deception throughout the history of mankind that he used against Adam and Eve.

As the story of Adam and Eve begins to unfold in the book of Genesis, we notice at first, everything was good. There is no sign or hint of rebellion. **"God saw all that He had made, and it was very good. And there was evening, and there was morning—the sixth day"** (Genesis 1:31). There was no opposition present. It was a lovely picture of fellowship between God and His creatures, with God providing the perfect setting for man. God and man walked together in happy communion. The Bible presents this scene as a blessed picture of love and peace.

God's Word to Adam and Eve at that time to obey and express their love was short and simple. **"The Lord God took the man and put him in the Garden of Eden to work it and take care of it. And the Lord God commanded the man, "You are free to eat from any tree in the garden; but you must not eat from the tree of the knowledge of good and evil, for when you eat of it you will surely die"** (Genesis 2:15-17). Just the one command to keep! You would not think that would be difficult.

There was sweet fellowship in the Garden of Eden between God and Adam and Eve. Satan knew if he could only cause Adam and Eve to step out and become independent of this one command, to not eat from the tree of the knowledge of good and evil, it would break the bonds of that fellowship and God would lose something which was most precious to Him. Satan cared nothing for the suffering that would follow. This has been his objective throughout the history of mankind and it is still his objective today.

Satan employed several tactics in his temptation to accomplish his goal in the Garden of Eden. He would love to remove the third chapter of Genesis from the Bible, for here we see his plan and how he uses the method of deception. His methods are still the same to this day as he tempts the child of God. **"Now the serpent** (the animal Satan spoke through) **was more crafty than any of the wild animals the Lord God had made. He said to the woman, "Did God really say, 'You must not eat from any tree in the Garden'?"** The **woman said to the serpent, "We may eat fruit from the trees in the garden, but God did say, 'You must not eat from the tree that is in the middle of the garden, and you must not touch it, or you will die.'" "You will not surely die,"** the serpent said to the woman. **"For God knows that when you eat of it your eyes will be opened, and you will be like God, knowing good and evil." When the woman saw that the fruit of the tree was good for food and pleasing to the eye, and was also desirable for gaining wisdom, she took some and ate it. She also gave some to her husband, who was with her, and he ate it"** (Genesis 3:1-6).

Satan's technique of temptation to bring deception into the heart and mind of Adam and Eve is described in these verses. His **first** attack technique was to implant thoughts of doubt and then, if those were not dealt with properly, outright denial of the meaning of God's Word (Genesis 3:1-4).

We have to be extremely careful in our day to stay alert and be self-controlled because of the ease for our enemy to influence us through so many avenues of the world. Daily, hourly, we are confronted with spiritual issues in our everyday lives that challenge the standards of God that are given in Scripture. Count on the enemy to raise doubts in your mind concerning the meaning and importance of following God's Word. It is a good policy, indeed the only safe policy, to check everything out with the Word of God because our spiritual enemy will use anything and everything that is available to him to draw us away from the Bible and its truths.

If we are not careful, and stay alert, we begin to reason and rationalize the situation in our mind. If we do, there will be a strong temptation to serve whatever pleases us and our desires rather than having a concern to be obedient to what is taught in God's Word. Our subconscious plays tricks on us. We begin to think: *This can't really make that much difference to God,* or *God's Word really doesn't mean that does it?* If we allow this process to take hold of our heart and mind, Satan's next step will be to cause the doubt to become an outright denial. *No, God understands, He doesn't mind. He wants me to have what I think is best for me.*

If we accept this position and ignore God's Word, as Adam and Eve did, we break our communion with God, and like them will suffer a spiritual defeat. Not only that, but the next time when a similar situation occurs, it will be a lot easier for Satan to get us to fall again. Before long our conscience becomes seared and no longer are we convicted to follow that particular standard found in God's Word. We may even speak out about how it is meaningless and that to think otherwise is being judgmental. Doubt comes first, then denial. This is how Satan's temptations work through deception.

Please note that I am not talking about the times when we make a mistake and fall; spiritually we all have our weaknesses and do make mistakes. And of course, we all start our Christian life in the Kingdom of God as babies. But it is God's desire that we grow and mature to be open to His Word and the working of His Holy Spirit. As we do, we will come under conviction as the Lord reveals His Word to us. We have fallen into deception when the enemy brings us to a point that the Holy Spirit can no longer bring about conviction in our hearts concerning something that is addressed in the Word of God. Also remember that Satan's use of deception will not necessarily be something that will happen immediately; it may be the changing of our thinking or values over an extended period of time.

Satan's **second** attack technique was to deceive Adam and Eve to elevate themselves, *to be like God,* so that they could make their own decisions about right and wrong (see Genesis 3:5).

"When the woman (Eve) **saw that the fruit of the tree was good for food** (lust of the flesh) **and pleasing to the eye** (lust of the eyes)**, and also desirable for gaining wisdom** (pride of life)**, she took some and ate it"** (Genesis 3:6). When the Lord saw what Eve had done, He said to her, **"...What is this you have done?" The woman said, "The serpent deceived me, and I ate"** (Genesis 3:13). It was through the use of deception that God's enemy caused her to disobey.

"For all that is in the world, the lust of the flesh and the lust of the eyes and the pride of life, is not of the Father but is of the world. And the world passes away, and the lust of it; but he who does the will of God abides for ever" (I John 2:16-17 RSV). Mankind has been subject to yielding to these three parts that make up our sinful nature ever since Adam and Eve fell.

Satan deceived Eve to rebel against God's spoken Word by tempting her to be independent and use human wisdom and reasoning to decide right and wrong, "knowing good and evil." If we do not follow the Word of God to establish our standards, by default we will accept the standards of the society in which we live. We know this by an examination of the history of mankind. It is unbelievable how cruel, violent, and evil mankind has been. It is no different today.

However, this should not be true for those who have been reborn spiritually into the Kingdom of God. We look to God's Word to establish our standards of good and evil. We are no longer a member of the kingdom of the world. But this also means, as I Peter 5:8 warns us, that we must be alert and self-controlled because Satan is going to tempt our sinful nature, using the attack technique of deception, to cause us to elevate ourselves to be like God and make our own decisions regarding a certain right and wrong. The Devil prowls around like a roaring lion looking for someone to devour. He succeeds when we begin to accept the standards of the society in which we are living.

Another important point to learn from Satan's attack on Adam and Eve is how freely he used the name of God. That is one of his major traps when attacking God's children through deception. He didn't ask Eve to deny God or to quit walking with God, in fact he told her that following his advice would make her like God. He knew it was important for her to follow God. He just encouraged her to step out and disregard God's Word. He caused her to doubt that God was really serious about the one command He had given them.... **"You must not eat fruit from the tree that is in the middle of the garden...or you will die"** (Genesis 3:3). He attacks us using the same method.

SATAN'S TEMPTATION OF JESUS

Another graphic illustration of how Satan uses deception is found in the way he tried to trap and deceive Jesus. Satan did not tempt Jesus with the obvious vices of the world. He didn't tempt Jesus to deny God or to quit being religious. He tempted Jesus with self-serving attractions. He wanted Jesus to step out on His own, to become independent and make His own decisions about right and wrong, rather than follow the principles of God's Word.

His **first** temptation of Jesus was with the <u>lust of the flesh</u>. **"Then Jesus was led by the Spirit into the desert to be tempted by the devil. After fasting forty days and forty nights, he was hungry.**

The tempter came to him and said, "If you are the Son of God, tell these stones to become bread." Jesus answered, "It is written: 'Man does not live on bread alone, but on every word that comes from the mouth of God'" (Matthew 4:1-4).

God was not going to deprive Jesus of food, but it was to be provided according to God's timing and will, not Satan's. Jesus knew He was not to perform a miracle to serve His own self-desires, even if it would help prove who He was.

The **second** temptation was the pride of life. "Then the devil took him to the holy city and had him stand on the highest point of the temple. "If you are the Son God," he said, "throw yourself down. For it is written: "'He will command his angels concerning you, and they will lift you up in their hands, so that you will not strike your foot against a stone.'" Jesus answered, "It is also written: 'Do not put the Lord your God to the test'" (Matthew 4:5-7).

This time Satan tempted Jesus to be proud of the fact He was a child of God by tempting Him to perform a miracle to serve His own self-interest. He tempted Him to do a foolish thing to prove God would save Him. Jesus again responded to the temptation by quoting Scripture.

The **third** temptation was through the lust of the eyes. "The devil led him up to a high place and showed him in an instant all the kingdoms of the world. And he said to him, "I will give you all their authority and splendor, for it has been given to me, and I can give it to anyone I want to. So if you worship me, it will all be yours." Jesus answered, "It is written: 'Worship the Lord your God and serve Him only'" (Luke 4:5-8).

Notice that all of the kingdoms of the world (society) had been given to Satan, a fact which Jesus did not deny. What a heavy temptation—to be offered all the authority and splendor of the things of the world! We have difficulty in not bowing to this temptation when offered far less than what was offered to Jesus. Satan again tempted

Jesus' self-life—something that would serve His personal being.

When attacking through deception, Satan's temptations may use the name of God or something that appears to be a godly cause. Notice how freely Satan used the name of God and even quoted Scripture when tempting Adam and Eve and Jesus. This may be the case when he attacks us through deception. If the inner motivation is to serve the desires of our flesh or promote something for our ego, **be on guard.**

Another good example of Satan tempting Jesus came through a friend. It is found in Matthew 16. Jesus had asked His disciples the question, **"But what about you?" he asked. "Who do you say I am?" Simon Peter answered, "You are the Christ, the Son of the living God." Jesus replied, "...this was not revealed to you by man, but by my Father in heaven"** (Matthew 16:15-17). Peter had received a revelation from God. Notice what happened immediately following this revelation.

"From that time on Jesus began to explain to His disciples that He must go to Jerusalem and suffer many things at the hands of the elders, chief priests and teachers of the law, and that he must be killed and on the third day be raised to life. Peter took him aside and began to rebuke him, "Never, Lord!" he said. "This shall never happen to you!" Jesus turned and said to Peter, "Out of my sight, Satan! You are a stumbling block to me; you do not have in mind the things of God, but the things of men" (Matthew 16:21-23).

Peter receives a revelation from God. Then in the very next scene he states the desire of Satan. Why? The motivating force was self-preservation for Jesus over and above the will of God. This time Satan tempted Jesus through someone He loved to seek His self interest. Jesus knew the will of God and, therefore, let Peter know that his thoughts of self-preservation on this occasion were from the enemy.

At various times we have all fallen victim to deception in one way or another in our Christian walk. When we do it can cause a multitude of personal problems, pressures and conflicts for Christians and requires that we understand another important biblical principle—that of repentance. We must turn from that which we were deceived about, and confess it to the Lord. Without repentance, our position of living in victory through the power of the Holy Spirit is seriously affected.

TWO MAJOR WAR FRONTS

Have you ever stopped to consider that America is actually engaged in two major war fronts? You probably still remember where you were on the morning of September 11, 2001 when millions of Americans huddled around their television or radio confused and shocked as disbelief spread across the nation and the world. Terrorists had attacked America and we were at war. The impossible happened that day and we are still faced with the threats of future attacks by an enemy committed to tearing apart the fabric of our country. Most people agree with the fact that our country has entered into a major war against terrorism; an enemy that has no borders, no conventional military, and no specific nationality—an enemy with no face.

There is another war being waged in our country that every Christian also needs to be aware of and understand. It is a spiritual war with our spiritual adversary, Satan. Satan is out to destroy the spiritual heritage of our country and all the good with which God has blessed America. The difference between the attacks we experienced on September 11, 2001 and the second warfare of deception I am discussing, is that the terrorist attack was obvious and abrupt. It was swift and sharp—piercing the heart of Americans. The country united and we immediately took action! This second attack has slowly been taking place during the last forty-to-fifty years and even Christians do not stand united in this warfare.

How many Christians do you know that talk about or even understand our country's second war front of spiritual deception? Both wars have the same objective, to tear apart the fabric of our nation and destroy the foundation upon which America was built.

SPIRITUAL ATTACK AGAINST AMERICA

With what the Lord has taught me and all of the research and study that I have done for the books, booklets and newsletters that I have written (see website www.christianlifeoutreach.org), I can tell you without hesitation and with complete confidence that we are now living in a crucial period of time. It is a period when America is under a vicious spiritual attack from God's enemy, Satan. Prophetic Scriptures warn that this is going to happen in the last days as Satan sees that his time is running short. He is going to fight hard to the end. He has set out to destroy God's standards that were established in God's end-time geographical base in this world. His success in this spiritual warfare of deception, which has escalated in our country in the last 50-60 years, has been overwhelming.

This second warfare began in earnest after World War II—after we became the greatest superpower in the history of mankind. That is when the moral standards which had bound our nation and our people together for generations began to unravel. Any American willing to face reality must admit that in the 1950s we began to experience a period of heavy spiritual warfare and it has continued to escalate. Deception has been the root of the enemy's spiritual attacks. Since deception is only determined by examining fruit, I think that we can safely say that America has been overcome by an epidemic of the spiritual heart disease of deception.

We can readily see the effect of this spiritual warfare on American society. But Satan's main opponent is not society at large but rather the body of Jesus Christ. He is always scheming to dilute our saltiness, keeping us from preserving the good, and dimming our light in a dark world. The fruit of Christians in this last generation reveals that the enemy's spiritual warfare has also had a dramatic effect on us. Before I continue there is an important point that I want you to clearly understand. I am not bringing up the effects of this spiritual warfare to be critical or to point a finger. We all have failed at one time or another. I certainly don't know how much this warfare may have influenced you. I don't know how many spiritual mistakes you may have made. Regardless of how the enemy may have deceived you in the past, we are all in this spiritual warfare together. We need each other to stand against the enemy together! As Dr. James Dobson pointed out, *"With the heartache and illness the loose humanistic standards are now causing for the families of our society, one would think responsible adults would be united in a campaign in opposition. But normally the contrary is found to be true."*

One of the objectives of Campaign Save Christian America and this book is to give the body of Christ a sound and solid Scriptural foundation on how the enemy is conducting his spiritual warfare of deception in these last days with so much success. Prophetic Scriptures, which I review later, give us the details of how Satan has implemented his attack in these end-times. Having this knowledge about the enemy's attacks will help equip us to know how to stand firm and develop a corrective action plan to help preserve God's special calling for Christians in America during these last days.

CHAPTER ELEVEN

Spiritually, deception is a terrible thing. It is extremely difficult to discern deception in these days, especially in America, because Satan has so many weapons at his disposal. And because we have been the world's center of Christianity, he is using all of his weapons to tempt Christians at every turn to determine right and wrong with their own reasoning power rather than using and obeying God's Word. This is why we need all the insight we can gain on this subject.

DECEPTION ILLUSTRATED THROUGH THE STORY OF AN EAGLE

The eagle is an amazing specimen of God's creation. This bird is mentioned over 30 times in Scripture. Eagles are swift, having been clocked at 120 to 150 miles per hour in flight. Their powerful seven-foot wing span allows them to soar and glide effortlessly at heights up to one-half mile, and the aerodynamics of their wing construction permits flight even in winds of hurricane force.

The eagle's eye has two fovea (areas of acute vision) which gives them the ability to spot a rabbit two miles away. Their great depth perception allows them to dive accurately at speeds up to 200 miles per hour. They have 270-degree peripheral vision. Their two sets of eyelids permit closing one, which is clear, which protects the eyes from dust and wind during flight.

The eagle's decisive appearance is different from other birds, due to a bony protrusion which extends outward over the eyelid, and is not found in most other fowl. A stern and decisive appearance, along with its other unique characteristics, gives the eagle a "royal" pose. Its grandeur and grace have been revered and esteemed for centuries. The eagle has been chosen as the official symbol of some of the greatest countries and leaders including the Romans, Charlemagne, Napoleon, and of course the United States.

Picture this monarch of the sky perched high on a mountain ledge overlooking a valley below with a beautiful stream, trees and mountains in the background. This majestic eagle has a clear view of the entire area below him as he sits basking in the morning sun. After bathing in the sun for awhile, enjoying his domain on this particular morning, the eagle launches himself into the air. He sails over the green valley and swoops down toward the stream, heading for his favorite fishing spot to catch his breakfast.

When he arrives at the stream's bank his keen eyes notice there is a slight change near the area where he normally fishes. There, near the shore, close to his fishing spot, is a large rock, about two or three feet in diameter and two feet high. It is something new. The eagle knows this rock has never been there before. Therefore, to him it appeared dangerous.

The eagle flies right on by his fishing spot without stopping, sailing to a nearby tree, and perching on a limb so he can observe the area. He wants to determine if this new and strange object might be harmful. He sits there for better than an hour, his keen eyes looking up and down the stream. In time he can tell there is no activity around; he sees no danger, so he sails down and lands on the rock.

Next to the rock, not by the stream, but in the nearby grass is a large, beautiful fish. Fish are one of an eagle's favorite foods. He is quickly drawn to the fish, but he is puzzled. If the fish had been on the shore near the stream, that would have been normal. But there it is on the grass, several feet from the shore—that is puzzling. The eagle is suspicious. Things don't seem right to him. His sharp eyes scan every grassy area around, all the nearby bushes, and the shore of the mountain stream. There seems to be no danger. He jumps off the rock, clutches the fish in his claws and is about to fly away when he notices another fish lying nearby in the grass. Then he sees another! There are three beautiful, plump fish. The wilderness is caring for his needs this morning in a most amazing way!

On the other side of the stream, however, a wise trapper is hiding in a thick clump of bushes watching every move the eagle makes. This trapper has been promised a large sum of money to capture an eagle alive. And he knows the wise eagle will require him to use his best and most crafty skills.

The eagle ate well that day. The next day, after his morning sunbath, he returned to his favorite fishing spot. The rock was still there. He sailed to the nearby tree to observe the area—this time for only a few minutes. He was more quickly satisfied there was no danger. The eagle flew to the rock and after landing, found the supply of fish had been miraculously renewed. This was unbelievable! Mother Nature was surely providing for him in a beautiful way. Eating these fish would give him more time to sit on his perch and soar through the heavens, viewing his lovely mountain and valley domain.

After several days had passed, the eagle was becoming conditioned. Now each morning he would fly directly to the rock. He had found that each day the supply of fish was being replenished. After landing, he would jump down, grab a fish, jump back on the rock and sit there to eat and enjoy his breakfast. When finished, he would again jump down; clutch another fish in his claws and fly off, taking the second fish to his nest high on a cliff for a meal later in the day. The eagle loved it! This was saving him better than half of every day which could be used for soaring through the sky and perching high in the cliffs, his two favorite pastimes.

Several days passed and the eagle had developed a frame of mind of acceptance. The trapper was now ready for his next move. He made a strong hoop like a fish net about four feet in diameter. He attached to the hoop a long handle with a curved bow. The next night he went to the mountain stream where he had placed the rock and carefully dug the long handle into the ground, positioning it at an angle. The hoop hovered about three feet above the rock, yet the bow in the handle kept the net fairly level over the rock. Then, as he had been doing every night, he spread fish out in the nearby grass.

The next morning, the eagle sat perched on his high cliff lookout as usual, enjoying the beauty of the mountains, forest and stream below. In about an hour, he lifted off his perch and began what was becoming a leisurely flight to his favorite spot. The eagle's acceptance that Mother Nature was providing his food without any effort on his part was beginning to develop in him a dull and sluggish nature. As the eagle drew near to the rock, he was suddenly puzzled and annoyed. There was an odd structure erected above the rock. He checked his flight and began to soar in circles. He flew fairly high, around and around, trying to make out the strange object. He could see the fish were there as usual. After 20 to 30 minutes of flight, there wasn't any evidence of danger in the bushes near the rock, so he descended to a nearby tree top where he landed. There he spent over an hour in complete silence, observing. His keen eyes kept watch for any strange movement and he listened for any unusual sound. There was nothing!

Far off, however, a good 200 yards away, hidden in the thick bushes, was the motionless trapper, patiently watching every move the eagle made. After sitting in the tree top for over an hour, the eagle could sense no danger, so he believed it was safe to investigate. He flew down to the shore, landing away from the net. He found a fish in the grass, ate it, grabbed another in his claws, and flew back to his nest. He had not determined that the strange object over the rock was harmless, but it appeared so.

That afternoon as the eagle was soaring through the sky, he couldn't erase from his mind that new object over the rock. He had to know if it was going to interfere with the beautiful way his food had been provided the last couple of weeks. He flew back to the rock and after circling several times, landed on the handle of the net. Nothing happened! The structure appeared to be harmless. There were still a couple of fish near the rock under the net. He hopped down to test this strange structure. He reached out with his beak and claw clutching one of the fish and then quickly hopped back. The object didn't move.

For the next few days the eagle proceeded with caution. With each visit he surveyed the area closely, making sure there was nothing else new. He would move quickly, devouring one fish and carrying a second off to his nest, all the time staying away from the rock. As the days passed, he regained his confidence that all was well. He was overjoyed that his food was still miraculously being provided. Once again he began to get a fish and perch on the rock, which was directly under the net, to eat his banquet.

The trapper was now ready. Before dawn the next morning, he made some important changes in the arrangement of the net. He tied a strong cord to the rim of the hoop. He ran the cord down to the ground in front of the rock, under a small root, and then ran the cord into the nearby thick bushes. To test the cord, he pulled on it, bending the rim of the net down until it covered the rock. The trapper satisfied himself all was ready. He baited the trap with the usual fish. Then he moved into the nearby thicket where he had run the cord to wait in silent anticipation.

Right on time, the eagle came the next morning. The trapper watched. The eagle, now full of confidence, had no hesitation. Though wise, he had been deceived into accepting this strange structure and free fish every day as a part of the established order. He landed on the sand near the rock, grabbed a large fish and perched on the stone under the net to enjoy his meal. At that very moment, the eagle sensed there was a slight movement in the nearby thicket. His muscles tightened! He was ready to spring into the safety of the air, but before he could move, the four-foot hoop with the net attached came down over him with a vicious swish.

There was an intense battle—the eagle against the net. Beating his wings, tearing at the net with his beak and claws, he fought for his freedom. He strained with every ounce of energy, but the eagle was helpless. He was entangled in the mesh of the trap. The mighty and glorious monarch of the sky had fallen to defeat <u>through deception</u>.

The story of the eagle demonstrates several principles of deception that we should be aware of. From this story we can learn some of the aspects of dangers that draw us into being deceived. Most deceptive traps are hidden, but there will usually be visible evidence of their presence. Spiritually, we are warned not to believe every spirit, but to try the spirits. **"Dear friends, do not believe every spirit, but test the spirits to see whether they are from God, because many false prophets** (teachers) **have gone out into the world"** (I John 4:1). The most reliable way to test the spirits, even if we think it is something we have received from the Lord, is to search the Scriptures. What we believe and accept must be in compliance with the spiritual principles and teachings found in God's Word. This should be done with prayer and a time of waiting to make sure that our emotions are no longer a part of any decision we make. Remember we still have the sinful nature that we are born with, which is self-centered. As Jesus used the Word of God to combat those temptations He had from the enemy (see Matthew 4:1-11), we are to follow His example and do the same thing.

The eagle trusted what he saw with his eyes. He ignored his instinct. Adam and Eve were first lured into deception by what they saw with their eyes—the lust of the eyes—rather than listening to the word they had from God. The eagle was drawn to the trap through an appeal to one of his basic needs—food. The deadly temptations of Satan always include an appeal—lust of the flesh—to one of our basic needs such as food, material possessions, security, acceptance, money, power, beauty, and sex drive. These things are not wrong in and of themselves, but satisfying these needs outside of God's plan is always wrong.

The eagle had inner warnings of the hidden dangers, but his desires caused him to go against his wisdom. God provides us with warnings and insights of spiritual danger. Like Jesus, we must by faith believe and follow His Word instead of our wants and desires. It was the eagle's pride—the pride of life—that made him believe he had all things under control regardless of the new surroundings. This is what caused the eagle to fall victim to the hidden cost of getting something for nothing. He gained his provision of food every day without labor, but it cost him his natural instinct to be alert and self-controlled. He became dull and sluggish, and it eventually cost him his freedom.

It is easy for us to let our guard down and accept a watered down biblical standard. One of Satan's most successful attacks of deception in this last generation is how he has changed our attitude toward the Bible and our failure to take it seriously. This is what happened to Adam and Eve. It is certainly the opposite of the attitude that Jesus had. There was nothing more important to Jesus than the way He approached the Scriptures. The same should be true in the life of a Christian. The Bible is our textbook, our only source. It is our only authority. We cannot rely solely upon subjective experiences because there are evil spirits as well as good spirits. The Bible warns there are deceiving spirits which can cause us to have counterfeit experiences. The Scriptures teach this will especially be true in the last days, the time in which we now live.

A current example of this is the way the church is dangerously handling and teaching the matter of the relationship between law and grace. To say that because we are under grace we therefore have nothing at all to do with law and can forget it, is definitely not the teaching of the Scriptures nor the attitude of Jesus. We are not under the law as a means for our salvation, but that does not mean that we are to ignore it. We are no longer under the law in a sense that it condemns us, but we are meant to use it as our guide in living out our life on this Earth as members of the Kingdom of God. **"The law of the Lord is perfect, reviving the soul. The statutes of the Lord are trustworthy, making wise the simple. The precepts of the Lord are right, giving joy to the heart. The commands of the Lord are radiant, giving light to the eyes. The fear of the Lord is pure, enduring forever. The ordinances of the Lord are sure and altogether righteous. They are more precious than gold, than much pure gold; they are sweeter than honey, than honey from the comb. By them is your servant warned; in keeping them there is great reward"** (Psalm 19:7-11).

Christ kept the law; He lived the law. His teachings in the Sermon on the Mount emphasize our righteousness must exceed that of the scribes and Pharisees. Jesus Himself said that He had not come to abolish the law, but that every jot and tittle has to be fulfilled and perfected. That is something that we often forget. Jesus said, **"Do not think that I have come to abolish the Law or the Prophets; I have not come to abolish them but to fulfill them. I tell you the truth, until heaven and earth disappear, not the smallest letter, not the least stroke of a pen, will by any means disappear from the Law until everything is accomplished. Anyone who breaks one of the least of these commandments and teaches others to do the same will be called least in the kingdom of heaven, but whoever practices and teaches these commands will be called great in the kingdom of heaven. For I tell you that unless your righteousness surpasses that of the Pharisees and the teachers of the law, you will certainly not enter the kingdom of heaven"** (Matthew 5:17-20).

It is our spiritual pride and false confidence that tells us we can enjoy the pleasures and sins of the world, and not be hurt spiritually, or get caught in its consequences. One thing for sure, as proven over this last generation, it will definitely contaminate the purity of our being the **salt of the earth** and it will dim our being the **light of the world**.

The eagle became conditioned to his surroundings through the lust of the flesh, lust of the eyes and pride of life because he was interested in satisfying his self-desire for food. Though these new surroundings in its life were contrary to the laws of nature, the eagle soon accepted these new standards because they pleased him and would allow him more time for pleasure. In like manner, God's Word warns us that our spiritual enemy, Satan, will attempt to deceive us into accepting or changing biblical standards through "self-serving" traps, just as he deceived Eve. Throughout the history of mankind Satan has proven to be a master in tempting God's people with the pleasure and advantages of sin without revealing the spiritual defeats and the hurt and pain in our life that we will suffer as well as many others.

I am going to also illustrate Satan's use of deception through the personal testimony of my brother, Dr. Charles Fraley. My brother had a special calling of God on his life, but was led into deception by the enemy, even though he was a dedicated Christian.

DR. CHARLES FRALEY'S TESTIMONY

I was raised on a small farm near Greenville, Ohio in a family of 13 children. I was number 12. My parents were godly people, sincerely dedicated to serving the Lord Jesus Christ. Precept and example trained their 13 children. Many who knew my mother testified that she lived an exemplary Christian life—much like the outstanding women of the Bible as talked about in Proverbs 31.

Growing up, I had a strong desire to know the Lord. When I was about 7, I joined the church and was baptized in a local creek, thinking this might help me go to Heaven. At age 11, I heard and understood the Gospel of Jesus Christ for the first time. I came under conviction for three days and nights until I finally made a decision to accept Jesus as Lord and Savior.

Upon graduating from high school, I entered the Navy. Our country was in the Korean War and I was sure I would be drafted. This was a real time of testing for me in that I found myself to be one of the few committed Christians in the military. However, the Lord provided an inner strength where it really did not bother me to live by God's biblical standards.

While in the Navy, the Lord gave me a great desire to know Him better through His Word. I had a lot of spare time while on ship duty and was able to spend most of those hours learning the Word of God. As a normal practice in the morning, I would rise two hours before wakeup call to pray, study the Word and memorize Scripture. By the time my four-year tour of duty was over, I had memorized over eight hundred verses, word perfect, and would review about 150 of them every day from morning to night.

It was during my four years of military service that I had a unique, or what would be called "supernatural," experience that led me to commit my life to work in the service of our Lord Jesus Christ. The presence of God surrounded me one day as I was reading Hebrews 13:5. The Lord spoke this verse to my spirit. It said: **"Let your conversation be without covetousness; and be content with such things as you have: for He hath said, I will never leave thee, nor forsake thee"** (KJV). That caused me to commit my life into the Lord's hands for His service and give up any of my own plans.

AFTER THE MILITARY

After military service, I felt led to enter Bible College in Nyack, New York, being supported by the GI Bill. It was there that I met, Marlene, the girl I would one day marry.

A few months after entering Bible College, while praying one evening, I asked God what He wanted me to do with my life. As yet I had not really received any clear directive. My prayer was quickly followed by a vision. Before telling you about this vision, I should make a comment about visions. According to the Bible it is not unscriptural for the Lord to direct Christians through a vision or dream. However, any vision must be tested to be sure it is of the Lord by examining its fruit and whether it fits all of the spiritual principles found in the Word of God. The vision I had was a very clear picture. I saw a man standing over the ocean with one foot in Africa and the other foot in America. The man was dressed in doctor's clothing wearing doctor's gear. The man was saying, *"Come over and help, come over and help."* I later learned that this call was somewhat similar to the Macedonian call that the Apostle Paul had experienced. As I sought the Lord for the meaning of this vision, the Spirit of the Lord rose up in my being in a very strong way. The Spirit convicted me that I was to become a doctor and go to Africa to help the poor and needy in the Lord's service.

At that time I had never thought about being a doctor. I was not even familiar with what was involved in becoming a doctor. Growing up on a small farm in the southwestern part of Ohio, I had never been academically inclined. My career plans were to be a farmer. The Lord blessed me with the faith to step out and transfer to Taylor University, a Christian liberal arts university, in Upland, Indiana where I entered pre-medical school. In the three years of pre-med at Taylor, I was blessed with all A's in my classes except for one B in Physical Education and a B in Literature.

After completing pre-med, I went to medical school for four years at Ohio State University from which I graduated. I next served one year of internship and four years of surgical residency at Saint Elisabeth Hospital in Youngstown, Ohio. I took and passed the National Exams of the American Board of Surgery and became a fully Board Certified General Surgeon. I had spent 13 years preparing myself so I could be obedient to the Lord's call to go to Africa as a medical missionary doctor.

However, during this 13 year extended period of preparation, I somehow had slipped in my spiritual walk with the Lord and lost my commitment to go to Africa. I had allowed thoughts to come into my mind such as the rationalization that I could just as well serve the Lord and practice medicine here in the states. That would enable me, along with my wife Marlene and the two children we now had, to enjoy all the benefits I had found were available to doctors in this country. Besides, I thought, if I ever did go to Africa it would be good to have some practical experience beforehand. Several doctor friends and other Christians agreed with me.

The truth is I had gradually fallen into *deception,* though I had not realized it. How did that happen? It is actually hard to say. It seemed to develop over a period of time in a very subtle way and just infiltrated my mind. I justified it with the idea that, even though I was going to practice medicine in this country, I would still be willing to go over-seas when the Lord showed me that I should. But I was really rationalizing at that point because I had already received a direct leading from the Lord to go to Africa.

MEDICAL PRACTICE

I started a medical practice in the area where I grew up. My practice grew each year and I was soon earning a net income of $300,000.00 to $400,000.00 per year, and that was in the early 1970s. I had my own airplane and the nicest Buick one could buy. Our family had a nice home in town. I bought the 100-acre family farm where most of my brothers and sisters had grown up and fixed it up very nicely with tractors, a pick-up truck, animals and horses. I was able to buy about everything anyone in my family wanted and it was all paid for.

My medical practice was very successful; however, there was one major thing wrong spiritually. By having a practice here in the States, I was out of the Lord's will and His direction for my life. I was walking in direct disobedience to the Lord's original call, which was to go to the mission field. The enemy had drawn me into *deception*! I had fallen prey to the influence of the world and did not know it had happened.

GREATER DECEPTION

The worst was yet to come! By being out of the Lord's will for my life, this first *deception* opened the door for me to fall into an even greater *deception*. It happened about four years after I started my medical practice. I got involved in a situation, and in consideration of others, I do not believe I should share the details, but it was definitely sinful. It had the potential of devastating not only me but destroying everything I had, including my family. Of course that is what Satan wanted! He had *deceived* me and I could not see it! As Eve was *deceived* to eat the fruit from the garden, I can also say: *"The enemy deceived me."*

A LESSON TO BE LEARNED

At this point I am going to digress for a minute because there is an important lesson to be learned from my experience of *deception* for anyone who claims to be a Christian. Although God is very merciful and long suffering, there comes a time when He expects us to clean up our lives and follow the straight and narrow—the sooner the better! Otherwise, He will have to do it for us, which may require our walking through some very deep valleys that we will not like.

As a physician for many years, I have often had to deal with and assist Christians with personal problems, including pastors and Christian leaders. These are usually problems they do not want to share with other people. Often it is these personal problems that are the secret sins that trip us up in our Christian life. It takes a humble and sincere Christian to admit he has a problem and seek help. This is partly because many Christians are too proud to admit they may have a spiritual problem, or because their problems are of such a nature that they just don't want to talk about them. When God says that we are to come out of the ways of the world and be separate, He really means just that and for a good reason. **"What agreement is there between the temple of God and idols? For we are the temple of the living God. As God has said; "I will live with them and walk among them, and I will be their God, and they will be my people." "Therefore come out from them and be separate, says the Lord. Touch no unclean thing, and I will receive you." "I will be a Father to you, and you will be my sons and daughters, says the Lord Almighty." Since we have these promises, dear friends, let us purify ourselves from everything that contaminates body and spirit, perfecting holiness out of reverence for God"** (II Corinthians 6:16-7:1). (Author's comment: Notice that this last verse states, **"purify ourselves from everything that contaminates body and spirit."** Remember that contamination is what makes salt useless.)

SPIRITUAL DEFEAT

I had been *deceived* by the enemy and fell prey to the many attractions and cares of the world. It brought about a major spiritual defeat in my life and I did not realize it was happening. To deliver me from this *deception,* the Lord had to open my spiritual eyes before I could see the condition of my heart. When He did and I realized I was walking in disobedience, after having committed myself to the Lord's service, I was devastated. From my youth I had always had such a strong desire and commitment to serve the Lord. Being overcome and failing to go to Africa and do the Lord's revealed will for my life literally crushed my heart.

I could not believe I had gotten so far out of the Lord's will. But it happened! I had been active in church during this time. I had studied the Word of God and spent time in prayer, but my disobedience to a direct command from the Lord had allowed the enemy to *deceive* me. After realizing I had fallen into *deception,* I began to seek the Lord with all the strength I had and with a true heart of repentance. I sought the Lord for a new filling of the Holy Spirit and the power to walk with Him according to His will as I had once experienced. I put forth every ounce of my being seeking God for *seven* months, studying the Word, meditating, praying and worshiping Him in a state of repentance. I also sought the Lord wanting to know <u>why so many Christians seemed to be living such defeated lives</u>.

At the end of this seven-month period of seeking the Lord, my family and I went on a two-week vacation to Florida. I had decided to spend this time fasting and praying—seeking the Lord—still in a spirit of repentance for my disobedience of being overcome by the ways of the world. I was determined not to stop until I knew beyond a shadow of a doubt that the anointing and fullness of the Holy Spirit had once again been released in my being. Midway through the second week of our vacation, I awoke one night and knew the presence of the Lord was in the room with me in a special way. I began to have visions similar to the one where the Lord had called me to become a doctor.

The first vision I had was that of a large head of a "beast"—very fat looking—hovering over America. It was swallowing up Christians in our country almost at will. The Spirit of the Lord showed me the meaning of this vision. This "beast" represented the power of materialism and pleasure in our country. It was swallowing up Christians by spiritually *deceiving* and then overcoming them through the influence of the materialistic and pleasure-seeking lifestyles that had developed in our society. Those Christians who were spiritually being overcome were not aware of what was happening.

I was convicted this is what the enemy had used to tempt, *deceive* and then conquer me in my spiritual walk. It had pulled me away and caused my disobedience in not going to the mission field. The Lord showed me that the enemy, working through the powerful temptations of materialism and pleasure, had caused most Christians

173

in America to lose their spiritual power. It was why so many had become apathetic towards the deterioration of the biblical standards in our country. And why many Christian families were experiencing major spiritual defeats, causing thousands to suffer hurt and pain.

I was shown that it has been the tremendous temptation of materialism and pleasure in our society that Satan has used to spiritually attack and destroy America's Christian foundation and biblically based moral standards, the guidelines that the majority of our people have lived by for years. I want to make it clear the Lord did not show me that it is wrong to have material things or enjoy good wholesome pleasure. What the Spirit of the Lord revealed to me through this vision of a head of a "beast" over America, was how the enemy is using our society to create an abnormal desire for material things and pleasure. He knows that if Christians become over-committed to the everyday affairs of life and use them to serve ourselves over our service to God, we will lose our spiritual discernment. It will cause us to no longer function as **the salt of the earth** and **the light in the world** which we are called to be. In these days of great prosperity we are so busy with our everyday affairs many of us cannot see that we are in the middle of a spiritual warfare that has produced very self-centered, self-serving people. The focus of God's warning through this vision of the head of a beast is with the attitude of the heart. The commitment of Christians has become greater in satisfying their everyday wants in life over and above their commitment to obey the standards of God. This is the sin that is taking us out from under the hedge of God's protection and is quenching the power of the Holy Spirit in our lives. It is the same problem that Jesus warns will happen to us, as it did in the days of Noah (see Luke 17:26-30). It has become a powerful *deceptive* snare in our culture with its ability to heavily influence our lives.

Satan used *deception* to get Eve, then Adam, to sin in the Garden of Eden. Just as Satan bombarded the mind of Eve to disobey

God's Word, Satan is attacking the minds of Christians today, day in and day out, with worldly, ungodly and unscriptural ideas and principles. One of his most powerful tools to accomplish this is through the media—television, radio, movies, the press, Internet, etc., which often acts like a false teacher to influence us to disobey the Word of God. The power of the media to implant the standards of the world into our minds is a method of attack the Christian community has never had to contend with until the last 50 or 60 years.

That first vision of a beast hovering over America, attacking Christians, was confirmed to me by the Holy Spirit by giving me several other visions of Jesus Christ. The Scriptures tell us the Holy Spirit always testifies of Jesus. In these visions I was shown how Jesus was willing to pay a tremendous price by going to the cross for the salvation of mankind. He was a disciplined person who had set His face as a flint and would not let anything deter Him from His call and purpose. I was shown the tremendous love that Jesus has for mankind and that He was standing at the door of my heart knocking, wanting to come in and re-establish the Lord's will in my life.

All of these visions had a powerful and profound impact on me. Through these visions the Holy Spirit was showing me what had caused my *deception,* and how Jesus did not deserve the kind of treatment that I had given Him with all that He had sacrificed for me. I could now see how I had become neglectful, disobedient and unfaithful. Through *deception* the enemy definitely had me on a path of falling away from living a biblically-based Christian life.

Since the time of these visions, I have walked with a certain holy fear in my life that has helped me stay in the Lord's will and follow His commandments. I count it a great privilege to do so. It actually resulted in my following through with the Lord's first directive to go and serve the people in Africa, which has been very joyful. My wife and I first went to Tanzania for a year and afterwards to Kenya where we served for 29 years. I recently was required to retire from the mission field as I had reached the mandatory retirement age of 70.

The spiritual teachings about *deception* and our responsibilities in living the normal Christian life which came from the visions the Lord gave me, must be taken very seriously. The Word of God backs them up. If you are not alert and ready—have become slothful in your commitment—you could be in for a big surprise as the events of these last days unfold. Not only that, you may already be caught in the web of *deception*. The majority of Christians in America are not prepared to stand against the spiritual attacks of *deception* that are taking place daily to control the hearts and minds of the American people.

There is no greater privilege on this Earth, or in Heaven, than to know and serve our Lord Jesus Christ who loved us and gave His life for us. He paid a tremendous price for our salvation and has every right to expect that we would seriously consider seeking to fulfill the directive given to us in Romans 12:1-2. It reads, **"Therefore, I urge you, brothers, in view of God's mercy, to offer your bodies as living sacrifices, holy and pleasing to God—which is your spiritual worship. Do not conform any longer to the pattern of this world, but be transformed by the renewing of your mind. Then you will be able to test and approve what God's will is—his good, pleasing and perfect will."** As this Scripture states, this is only reasonable and makes perfect sense.

DR. FRALEY'S MINISTRY

This concludes my brother's testimony, but before I move on I do want to add a brief word about how the Lord used him in Africa after his repentance and restoration.

Dr. Charles Fraley, M.D., and his wife, Marlene, R.N., served the Lord on the mission field in Africa for about 30 years. He became the Medical Coordinator & Executive Director of a large health ministry in the country of Kenya with a list of responsibilities that was almost endless. He and his wife shared the love of Christ as he oversaw five hospitals and established over fifty health centers and dispensaries throughout the entire country.

Dr. Fraley delivered supplies, checked on patients, performed surgery, as well as assisting in administration, the teaching of the staff and encouraging each facility. His duties required him to spend many days away from home traveling over dirt, rock, and sand roads or paths. He also faced risk, traveling among the African tribes and wild animals, which posed life threatening danger at times. In addition, when he traveled out into the bush country, he lived as the natives eating their food, and sometimes sleeping in his vehicle or under the stars.

My brother and his wife were involved in building a new hospital (located in Kenya) and establishing a school of nursing on one of the largest mission stations of its kind in the world—the African Inland Mission Station in Kijabe, Kenya. The hospital provides one of the highest qualities of health care of any mission hospital, not only in Kenya, but throughout East Africa. The quality of training he and his staff have developed at the nursing school is as good as any in western civilization. All staff members in this health ministry must profess Jesus as Lord and Savior, and maintain high Christian standards.

Dr. and Mrs. Fraley also assisted and worked with the Kenyan government in obtaining licenses for many of the long and short-term missionary doctors and nurses coming into the country. He participated with missionaries from different mission organizations in Bible study and prayer groups for their spiritual growth. He was the attending physician for many of the missionaries of all denominations that came into the country, and sat on the Board of Mission for Essential Drugs for over 10 years, an organization he helped establish in order to get medicines at cost for Mission Health Services. He served as Board Member and Vice Treasurer of the Christian Health

Association of Kenya (CHAK) for over 10 years. This organization was developed to serve all of the Protestant Health Services in Kenya, consisting of over 260 health units.

The President of Kenya asked the health ministries that my brother directed to take over a major health center in a remote area of the country among the poor people there. He agreed to do this, not only to meet the desperate health needs of these people, but it would provide a great opportunity to share the love and salvation of our Lord Jesus Christ. All of the 57 health units under his direction minister to the poor and needy in remote areas.

I have barely touched the surface of all that happened for the Lord over the years on the mission field through the ministry of Dr. Fraley and his wife, Marlene, as well as others with whom they worked. God has blessed them to lead a team of godly and committed Christians to work through in developing these many ministries. All of the glory, praise, and honor, must go to the Lord. As you can see, there is more work to be done than there are hours in a day. Only the power and anointing of the Holy Spirit could have given a man the strength to accomplish all that he accomplished.

My brother and his wife are among those godly servants who forsook their material possessions, family ties, pleasures, home and country to follow the call of our Lord Jesus—to serve wherever He leads—helping the poor and needy of the world. They are not seen on TV nor do you hear much about them, as they were not in the public eye. They labored selflessly, day in and day out, to share the love and salvation of our Lord Jesus Christ, and reach out to the needs of the sick, hurting, and needy people of this world. Their ministry was built on solid rock. They stood the test of time in their obedience and faithfulness.

MANY OTHERS

There are many others in our country, including several of our nation's spiritual leaders, who have experienced similar spiritual defeats of deception as my brother because of the power our world has to tempt Christians. If you have not become a victim, you no doubt know some who have. Satan has been able to set many traps of deception in these last days through the many things offered in our society. He is attacking us with all of the elements at his disposal because we are the world's center of Christianity. Our history confirms that we have a special calling of God. When you consider that we live under the influence of a society that has the means to produce so many material things, a highly skilled professional advertising business and communication system to continuously tempt us to buy, even right in our own home, beautiful shopping malls, no down payment, ability to buy on credit and so on, it is not difficult to see why we are attracted to many of his traps that are of the world. His traps are not only very enticing; at times they seem to be irresistible.

We are being tempted at every turn today to be like God and determine right and wrong through our own reasoning power. We are being hit daily in every way imaginable to bend and compromise biblical standards. We are living in the middle of a spiritual war zone. **"Be self-controlled and alert. Your enemy, the devil, prowls around like a roaring lion looking for someone to devour"** (I Peter 5:8).

A few years ago when the world shouted, "God is dead," in my arrogance I scoffed at those who were making this statement. Of course the statement is not true, but rather than scoff I should have tried to find out why the world was making such a proclamation. Now I can see that it was because the world could no longer see that there is much difference in the moral standards of Christians compared to the moral standards of non-Christians. They saw that many Christians were experiencing the same defeats in their lives as the people of the world were experiencing. They began to shout "God is dead" because they could no longer see God's standards being lived out in our lives. Although the world does not know about the two spiritual functions for Christians to be the **salt of the earth** and the **light of the world,** our fruit is the way they evaluate the success of the Christian community. This is what the enemy's attack of spiritual warfare has done to the body of Christ in America. To often our actions reveal that we have fallen into a deceptive trap like the frog that was put into a pan of cold water? The water was then slowly heated so that the frog didn't notice the water becoming warm. As the water continues to heat to a boil, the frog is gradually overcome and never legitimately tries to escape. He didn't become alarmed because the change was not sudden. Therefore, he paid little attention to what was happening. The results were that he became a casualty to his environment by being overcome by deception.

In the days of Noah, God warned of a coming catastrophe. Noah tried to warn the people of his day, but his words fell on deaf ears. God warned Lot before He rained down fire and sulfur from Heaven and destroyed the people of Sodom. God has also warned the people in our day. His warnings have come mainly through His Word, the Bible, as well as several Christian leaders in our country who have said they have a major concern that America is racing toward God's judgment—Dr. Billy Graham, David Wilkerson, Dr. Henry Blackaby, James Robison, Pat Robertson, Tommy Barnett, the late Larry Burkett, Bill McCartney—to name a few.

Sexual sins, the dissolution of families, greed, dishonesty, and the deterioration of other moral standards are some of the fruit in our society, and in the church, that have brought about a major concern that we may fall under God's hand of discipline or judgment. The fruit is the result of spiritual deception. However, one of God's most significant Bible warnings concerning spiritual deception in these last days came from Jesus. It deals with a different type of deception—the same deception that caused my brother to fall out of God's will.

Jesus warned, **"Just as it was in the days of Noah, so also will it be in the days of the Son of Man. People were eating, drinking, marrying and being given in marriage up to the day Noah entered the ark. Then the flood came and destroyed them all. It was the same in the days of Lot. People were eating and drinking, buying and selling, planting and building. But the day Lot left Sodom, fire and sulfur rained down from heaven and destroyed**

them all. It will be just like this on the day the Son of Man is revealed" (Luke 17:26-30).

There is something missing in this passage of Scripture from Luke concerning the times of Noah and Lot that I want you to notice! Jesus doesn't mention the many evil gross sins that were taking place in Noah's day or Lot's day, which is what we usually hear about when those days are mentioned. Also Jesus does not say anything about the many gross sins now taking place in our day. In fact, not one of the things He mentions is a sin. They are the everyday normal things people do in living this life: drinking, eating, marrying, buying, selling, planting and building. It is important to recognize this fact to properly understand the full meaning of this prophecy.

The Old Testament Scriptures state that in the days of Noah and Lot lawlessness, permissiveness and rebellion were running rampant. This was the reason God destroyed both of those societies. Yet, when comparing our day to those days of Noah and Lot, Jesus does not make one comment about this fact. His comparison is with the buying, selling, eating, drinking, marrying, planting, and building. He only talks about the everyday normal affairs of life! WHY?

The answer to this question takes us to the very core of the spiritual deception now taking place in our country. It helps explain why the moral values of our society have deteriorated so quickly. Everyone knows about the many gross sins. Jesus did not have to mention them. We hear about and read about them every day. David Wilkerson, Pastor of Times Square Church in New York City and one of our country's spiritual leaders stated, *"I was listening to a special radio program in a large eastern city, where the people on the street were being interviewed about the moral condition of America. The question was asked, 'Do you believe America has lost its moral integrity?' Almost all who were interviewed said basically the same thing. 'America is going to hell in a hand basket!' 'We no longer care if scoundrels run our country, as long as we prosper.' 'Anything goes now; we are in the last days of our society—we are modern Rome going into collapse!' 'Morality and purity have been sold out to pleasure and prosperity.' 'Sodom had no porno, no Internet sex, no abortion, no filthy television polluting that society, so how can America expect to go on without being held accountable?'"*

In this warning from God that compares our day to the days of Noah and Lot, I see God pouring out His love to the majority of the people—people like you and me—the average person on the street, rather than the minority who are involved in gross sins. We are the Lord's main concern in this warning. We are those who go about doing those things that people do in the normal way of living their life—the buying, selling, building, marrying, and so forth.

Why are we, the average citizens, Jesus' main concern in His warning about our times, rather than those people who are involved in the many gross sins taking place? Looking ahead, God gave us this prophetic warning about the last days because He could see that one of the greatest concerns about the people living in our day would be their <u>over-commitment</u> to these everyday affairs of life—the buying, selling, building, and so on. What we are doing is not a sin in and of itself. Our sin is the commitment of our heart to these self-serving affairs of everyday life, over and above our commitment to live by the standards of God. This is what happened in the days of Noah and it is happening today! Our everyday affairs have become more important to us than our seeking to understand and obey God's standards.

This is exactly what has happened to us in America! The influence of the worldly ways of our society in which we live has become so strong; it has changed the attitude of the majority of Christians towards their everyday affairs. This is what happened to my brother, taking him out of God's will for his life. You and I are the people who can help put a stop to our society's morality falling apart at the seams. We are the people who can make a difference. But rather than doing anything about it, Jesus saw that the majority of Christians in our day would become so wrapped up in their everyday lives—our own little world so to speak—the buying, selling, building, planting, marrying—that we would ignore all of the warning signs and the fruit that our society would produce.

The signs are everywhere that our nation is on the brink of a great chastening from the hand of God. Our nation has been blessed by God far above most nations throughout history. The Bible says that God will hold us accountable for the deterioration of our society's moral standards. Luke 12:48b states, **"From everyone who has been given much, much will be demanded; and from the one who has been entrusted with much, much more will be asked."** The Scriptures teach God disciplines or brings judgment, gives a good spiritual spanking, on those He has blessed if they become misguided and careless in their style of living. It is His way of correcting those He loves. **"My son, do not make light of the Lord's discipline, and do not lose heart when he rebukes you, because the Lord disciplines those he loves, and he punishes everyone he accepts as a son. Endure hardship as discipline; God is treating you as sons. For what son is not disciplined by his father?"** (Hebrews 12:6-7).

Just as in the days of Noah, people are doing very little to prepare themselves—to build their spiritual ark—which is the only way we are going to fulfill God's special calling for Christians in America and keep His hand of judgment from falling. What Jesus has warned us about are the symptoms of deceptive spiritual warfare that has produced very self-centered, self-serving people—including Christians. This condition caused the Lord more concern than the many gross sins the minority of the people were involved in. He was more concerned with the heart attitude He saw in the majority. The focus of the heart was a problem in

Noah's day and He warns it will be a problem in our day. That is why He lists the things that have to do with our everyday affairs even though not one of them is a sin.

The everyday affairs of life caused the downfall of the people in the days of Noah and Lot, and Jesus has warned us that the same kind of deception will cause our downfall. We have become so pre-occupied with these everyday affairs of life that serve our-selves—the buying, selling, building, eating, planting, and mar-rying—that our hearts have grown cold towards a dedicated commitment to live by biblical standards. The worldly media has deceived us and caused us to lose our ability to know right from wrong concerning our commitment to these everyday things.

Also, as Jesus said it would be as it was in the days of Noah, preoccupation with these things has caused us to lose our discernment in interpreting the signs of the times. This too has become a major deceptive snare in our society because of the overpowering ability our society has to influence our commitment to these everyday affairs of life. Jesus warned that even the elect (Christians) would be deceived in our day if that were possible. **"For false Christs and false prophets will appear and perform signs and miracles to deceive the elect—if that were possible. So be on guard; I have told you everything ahead of time"** (Mark 13:22-23. Also see Matthew 24:24).

One question that you may ask is: Why does Jesus include the institution of marriage in His warning about these everyday affairs of life? Actually marriage is an excellent example of how far off track we have gotten. Look at the way He mentions marriage, **"... marrying and being given in marriage..."** This speaks to the way our society has lost its commitment to the marriage vows. People feel so free to marry again and again—even though God says, **"I hate divorce"** (Malachi 2:16). God obviously knows the hurt and pain that accompanies divorce and the devastating effects it has on children.

Divorce and remarriage has become a plague in our society resulting in what sociologists call "serial monogamy."

The basic institution of marriage is highly honored by the Lord. It was at a wedding that Jesus performed His first miracle. But the attitude that many have developed in our day about the sanctity of marriage is a good reflection of how far off we have gotten in handling the other affairs of everyday life.

The moral standards of permissiveness and lawlessness deteriorated to the point of being completely out of control in the days of Noah and Lot. But Jesus says there was a greater concern. It was the heart attitude of the people to serve themselves above what is normal. I think this was because it applied to practically everyone; whereas all of the terrible evil would not have. It is an attitude that causes people not to believe—pay any attention to—taking seriously the standards of God. What the people were doing was not sinful, but the commitment of their heart to these self-serving things drew them away from their commitment to walk according to the standards of God and to His will for their life. This also prevented them from seeing the signs of the times. They became blind in Noah's day, deceived by the attitude and commitment of their heart.

The truth of this prophecy is a tough issue to discuss because I do not want to discount the blessings of God. But the spirit of merchandizing has captured the heart of most Americans, creating an over-commitment to our everyday affairs. As my brother shared in his testimony, the Lord gave him a vision of a beast over our country, overcoming Christians almost at will through the deceptive tools of materialism and pleasure.

God chose to put these words of warning from Jesus in the Bible to warn us about our day, and the truth of this prophecy is being fulfilled in America. God is faithful. It was important to Him that we know the kind of spiritual deceptive warfare the enemy would throw at Christians in these end-times. These words of Jesus describe the essence of what the enemy is using to keep you and me from standing up for and living by God's moral standards. Many Christians have fallen into deception and become victims of his attacks. But the Scriptures warn us about his tactics—we have just failed to heed those warnings that are so needed today.

CHAPTER THIRTEEN

In the next few chapters, as we examine what the Scripture says about end time prophecy, much of what you are going to read will probably challenge what you have heard all your life. As I told you at the beginning of the book, this is a very different approach than is commonly taken. But as we have shown in this book, what the church is doing isn't working! Please read what I have to say carefully and prayerfully. Compare what the Scriptures actually say with the interpretations you have heard before. I believe that one of the greatest assets Satan has in attacking the church is our ignorance of the Bible—and to overcome that, we must discern what the Bible teaches instead of relying on traditions and what we've always been taught.

There are basic biblical truths that Christians in America need to keep in the forefront of our minds as we live out our life in this world. We are no longer members of the spiritual kingdom of the world. We live in the world but we are now members of the Kingdom of God. The Word of God has many warnings telling us that we must constantly be alert and self-controlled concerning the methods and tactics of how Satan is executing or implementing his spiritual attacks. The nation of Israel and its people also had a special calling from God. In the last days before the Lord's first coming, the enemy had deceived the people to where most of them had completely fallen away from the Word of God and their calling. This happened in the very country where God's presence had been the strongest. That is how the enemy works! His hardest attacks of deception are going to be in the area where God's people are the strongest, especially if they have a special calling from God.

Is the body of Christ in America repeating history? The fruit of our nation in this last generation reveals that we too, are falling away from our calling in these last days before <u>the Lord's second coming</u>. And like Israel it is happening in the area of the world where God's presence has been the strongest.

SPIRITUAL ATTACK

My research and study into this issue began in the spring of 1971. At that time, after my wife and I were obedient to the leading of the Lord to take six children, He began to open my eyes to the tremendous increase in the spiritual warfare the enemy was waging against the biblical values in America. I even wrote a book on this topic in 1975. Now more than 30 years later, these truths are more clear than they were then. The fruit produced in our country this past generation now confirms what I shared in this book. The root cause of this spiritual warfare is the core message of my corrective action plan for Campaign Save Christian America. Remember these key core facts.

One: The spiritual development of America reveals that we have a special calling from God in these last days. <u>Other than the nation of Israel, there has never been another country in the history of mankind in which God has intervened as He has in the spiritual development of America.</u>

Two: It is always a wise thing to review fundamentals in any endeavor when there is a problem and things are deteriorating as our fruit reveals. This principle is true in business, sports, personal relationships, etc. and it is true in our commitment to the basic truths of Christianity.

Three: It is important to develop an understanding of what is causing the problem. As we saw in the past few chapters, the history of God's people reveals that Satan has always used either persecution or deception against them. The Bible has warned us about his use of deception in these last days and that the way he will deploy his methods and tactics of deception will primarily be through the kingdom of the world, or society, and its systems.

Four: Satan has <u>executed</u> his method of deception against the fundamentals of Christianity in America through a plan that has been very successful in this last generation. Identifying his plan of implementation is a crucial part of my corrective action plan. It is the part that will open your eyes to the root cause of Satan's success in his spiritual warfare against the people in our country. This is the part that will set you free—bring deliverance—from the bondage of the spiritual chains that hold so many Christians in America captive to the kingdom of the world and its standards.

SPIRITUAL WARFARE NOT PHYSICAL

The root cause of the spiritual warfare in which we are engaged in America is not dealing with something physical, but spiritual. Our battle is not against flesh and blood but against the spiritual forces of evil (see Ephesians 6:10-13). My interest is not the saving of America as a physical entity in the kingdom of the world, but about <u>saving the mission of Christianity in America</u>. I am a patriotic person, I love our country and am grateful for the freedom which our forefathers secured and developed for the people of America. However, the great political freedom we have enjoyed will not survive long after the enemy has deceived the body of Christ into taking a detour from the path of righteousness.

I don't know what will happen to the values of the people in the world as time goes by in America; however I do know that God's call for His people is to remain faithful to biblical values. The means through which the enemy has gotten us off the path is a truth that <u>must</u> be revealed because it is the root cause of the enemy's success that is causing so much defeat in the body of Christ.

AMERICA IN BIBLE PROPHECY

Have you ever wondered why America, the greatest super-power in the history of mankind and the center of Christianity in these last days, is not mentioned in Bible prophecy about the end-times? I found the key for <u>understanding the root cause</u> of the spiritual warfare now taking place in America is knowing America's place in prophetic Scriptures. Therefore, knowing America's place in Bible prophecy is vital to responding to the enemy's attacks.

The results of my study and research revealed that America actually does play a major role in Bible prophecy about the last days. Because my approach is so new and may be somewhat over-whelming, I have had the meaning of what I share about the end-time prophetic Scriptures completely checked out with Greek scholars. Not one scholar has disagreed with what I found; none of them viewed it as without a valid basis. When you read these words as to what the Greek means, do not reject them until you have compared what I say to what the Bible says. These comments are especially important to what I share about Revelation chapter 13. This point not only applies to what I share about these verses but also to what others teach about Revelation 13. I give you a meaning for every descriptive word or phrase of these prophetic words that prophetically describe America in Revelation 13. I cannot find where anyone has ever done that to substantiate their interpretation.

DISCOVERING AMERICA IN BIBLE PROPHECY

Revelation chapter 13 is key to understanding spiritual warfare in these last days. It is called the "last days" spiritual warfare chapter. Knowing the moral values in our country have deteriorated so rapidly; knowing the fact that America is the center of Christianity in these last days; the truth that Scriptures teach and history proves that Satan has always viciously attacked anything that God has raised up; I had to research and study to see if America fit into this end-time "spiritual warfare" prophecy recorded in Revelation chapter 13. This chapter is about what is called in prophetic language, a "beast." These thoughts plus my brother's experience of spiritual defeat and having a vision of a "beast" hovering over America defeating Christians through deception, added to the strength of my closely examining this warfare chapter about the last days.

One way to know if a prophecy is true is to put it to a test. No one can be harmed by investigation, because whether the investigation leads to truth or falsehood, the investigator reaps a reward for undertaking the search. If the investigation leads to truth, the investigator would have missed it if the effort had not been made. If the investigation leads to falsehood, the investigator has been strengthened from the experience because knowing what we believe, and why, gives us a more sound and sure faith.

If you find that what I found through my research to be somewhat overwhelming remember that is not an unusual response to Bible prophecy. That has been the experience of God's people throughout their history concerning the fulfillment of prophecy. Recall the Israelites and their refusal to accept Jesus as the Messiah, even though He fulfilled over 500 Bible prophecies. Their minds were closed! They were looking for an earthly king and kingdom. The message of Jesus was about the spiritual Kingdom of Heaven, so the majority rejected Him and His message.

INTRODUCTION TO SATAN'S END-TIME BATTLE PLAN

Before giving you a summary of Revelation chapter 13, I need to review some important truths given to us in Revelation chapter 12. It is a lead-in chapter to 13.

The scene changes in Revelation chapter 12 from the previous chapters. Chapter 12 gives us an overview of some of the major events in God's plan for the salvation of mankind and God's plan to protect the race of Israel after the birth of the Savior. After the destruction of their country in the first century by the Roman Army, God dispersed the people of Israel for nearly 2000 years throughout the world, yet they have kept their identity as a race.

You need to keep in mind that prophetic verses are not written in the normal way the rest of the Scripture is written. The Lord must shower us with His wisdom to understand their meaning. Even if we think we understand, we must research and seek the Lord for confirmation, and see that all things fit and are consistent with other Scriptures. The twelfth chapter opens with the appearance of a great wonder in the sky, **"A great and wondrous sign appeared in the heaven; a woman clothed with the sun, with the moon under her feet and a crown of twelve stars on her head"** (Revelation 12:1). The woman symbolizes God's people here on Earth. She wears luminous clothing—the sun and the moon, or that element of God's creation that controls the functioning of the natural elements on the Earth. The woman is the nation of Israel and the twelve stars, the twelve tribes of Israel.

"She (the woman) **was pregnant and cried out in pain as she was about to give birth"** (Revelation 12:2). This verse speaks of the purpose God had intended for the nation of Israel from the time of Abraham, which was to give birth to the Son of God—Jesus (see Galatians 3:16-29). The Old Testament chronicles these birth pains, which lasted for 2000 years.

"Then another sign appeared in heaven: an enormous red dragon with seven heads and ten horns and seven crowns on his heads" (Revelation 12:3). We are told in verse 9 of this chapter that the dragon is the Devil or Satan. At this point in history in God's dealing with mankind, according to the first phrase in this verse the dragon or Satan still had access to Heaven. The symbolic language of **"seven heads and ten horns and seven crowns on his heads"** speaks of an earthly power or authority. Combining Satan together with an earthly power is typical since Satan's kingdom is of this world. The Roman

Empire fulfills the identity of this earthly power. I explain the meaning of the phrase **"seven heads and ten horns and seven crowns on his heads"** in my discussion of chapter 13.

"His tail swept a third of the stars out of the sky and flung them to the earth. The dragon stood in front of the woman who was about to give birth, so that he might devour her child the moment it was born" (Revelation 12:4). It appears the first part of this verse is referring to that time when Satan lost his position in Heaven and one third of the angels were cast out with him. God put this fact in John's prophecy at this point to show the power of Satan's army. The second part of this verse is referring to the fact that Satan was aware of Jesus' birth and stood ready to kill Him at the first opportunity, which would have stopped God's plan for the redemption of mankind. We are told in the Bible that such an attempt was made when Satan motivated King Herod to give orders to kill all of the boys in Bethlehem two years old and under. This event was also prophesied by the Prophet Jeremiah (see Jeremiah 31:18) and we are told in Matthew 2:18 specifically that this event fulfilled Jeremiah's prophecy.

"She (the woman or Israel) **gave birth to a son, a male child, who will rule all the nations with an iron scepter. And her child was snatched** (the word "caught" is a more accurate English rendering of the Greek) **up to God and his throne"** (Revelation 12:5). Of course Jesus was the male child to whom Israel gave birth. He returned to Heaven after living here on Earth for about 33-1/2 years. Notice that John doesn't just say Jesus returned to Heaven, but that He returned to the <u>throne</u> of God, which indicates His deity.

Verse 6 states, **"The woman** (people of Israel) **fled into the desert to a place prepared for her by God, where she might be taken care of for 1260 days"** (Revelation 12:6). A major historical event happened to the people of Israel within the generation after the ascension of Jesus. The Romans dispersed them throughout the world, but they were protected by God and kept their identity as a race for nearly 2000 years. Then in the 1900s, as the last days of the church age were drawing near, the race that descended from Abraham was re-established in their homeland, the land of Palestine. (I will explain the meaning of the 1260 days later in this chapter.)

"And there was war in heaven, Michael and his angels fought against the dragon, and the dragon and his angels fought back. But he was not strong enough, and they lost their place in heaven. The great dragon was hurled down—that ancient serpent called the devil or Satan, who leads the whole world astray. He was hurled to the earth, and his angels with him" (Revelation 12:7-9). After the resurrection of Jesus there was a war in Heaven between the arch-angel Michael and his angels, and Satan and his angels. Satan and his angels were not strong enough. They lost the war and lost their place in Heaven after which they were hurled down to Earth. Notice that the place of this battle was in Heaven and that the battle included both Satan and his angels.

I certainly do not understand all that takes place in the spiritual realm other than what Scripture tells me. We know that in the beginning, Satan was present in the Garden of Eden and he has been very active on Earth throughout the history of mankind. But according to these verses he and his angels still had a place in Heaven until the death and resurrection of Jesus. But after this battle, Satan and his angels lost their place in Heaven, wherever that place in Heaven may have been, and they were permanently hurled to the Earth. We learn from the next verse when this event took place.

"Then I heard a loud voice in heaven say: "Now have come the salvation and the power and the kingdom of our God, and the authority of his Christ. For the accuser of our brothers, who accuses them before our God day and night, has been hurled down. They overcame him by the blood of the Lamb and by the word of their testimony; they did not love their lives so much as to shrink from death." (Revelation 12:10-11).

The word <u>now</u> in this verse is the key because it tells the time when these things of God came into existence. Ephesians 1:18-23 tells us exactly when the time was that the word <u>now</u> is referring. **"I pray also that the eyes of your heart may be enlightened in order that you may know the hope to which he has called you, the riches of his glorious inheritance in the saints, and his incomparable great power for us who believe. That power is like the working of his mighty strength, which he exerted in Christ when he raised him from the dead and seated him at his right hand** (at His throne as stated earlier in Revelation verse 5) **in the heavenly realms, far above all rule and authority, power and dominion, and every title that can be given, not only in the present age but also in the one to come"** (Ephesians 1:18-21). The salvation of mankind came through the blood of the Lamb on the cross. The power of the Kingdom of God and the authority of Christ came when God raised Jesus from the grave and seated Him at His right hand. It was at the time when Jesus was crucified and rose from the dead that victory was won, and Satan and his angels were hurled down to Earth and the power and authority of Jesus came into being.

Because of the salvation, power and authority of Jesus, John makes another major and important fact known in Revelation 12:12 that <u>we seldom hear talked about or taught</u>. **"Therefore rejoice you heavens and you who dwell in them! But woe to the earth and the sea, because the devil has gone down to you! He is filled with fury, because he knows that his time is short."** <u>This is one of the most powerful warnings about Satan to the people of God that is found in Scripture</u>. **"...woe to the earth and the sea, because the devil has gone down to you! He is filled with fury, because he knows that his time is short."** The balance of Revelation chapter 12 describes the protection afforded to the woman (Israel) after the birth of the male child (Jesus) after Satan and his angels had been hurled down to Earth.

"When the dragon (Satan) **saw that he had been hurled to the earth, he pursued the woman** (people of Israel) **who had given birth to the male child** (Jesus). **The woman** (people of Israel) **was given the two wings of a great eagle, so that she might fly to the place prepared for her in the desert, where she would be taken care of for a time, times and half a time, out of the serpent's** (Satan's) **reach"** (Revelation 12:13-14). In my research I discovered that the phrase time, times and half a time was used by Jewish scribes to refer to an unknown troublesome period of time that lingers—and lingers—and lingers. According to Jewish history, when John wrote this book, they had no way by their calendar to determine or express an extended period of time. Recall in verse 6 it states, **"The woman fled into the desert to a place prepared for her by God, where she might be taken care of for 1,260 days."** 1,260 days is a figurative reference to the same unknown period of time that God would protect the nation of Israel from Satan. In verse 14 John uses this phrase that was Jewish custom, time, times, and half a time for the same period. The Jewish calendar consisted of 12 equal months, each with 30 days corresponding to the approximate cycle of the moon. Therefore, 1,260 days would be one year, two years and one half of a year. Of course we know their dispersion lasted for over 1800 years, but as John prophesied God protected them and their national identity. One of the things that I found in my research is that when used in prophecy, numbers are often used symbolically rather than literally, which is different than the way they are usually used in regular Scripture. Therefore, the meaning of the number rather than the actual count of the number is what is important.

If you are wondering about the Jewish 30 day month, which doesn't quite add up to a year, at the end of every 2 or 3 years they would add an extension to the Jewish calendar at the end of the 12th month. The extension was called the month of Adar II. This was done to make up the additional days needed to align the length of the

Jewish year with the solar year or a complete cycle of the Earth around the sun. We do the same thing but in a different way. We have 12 months that are not all equal in the same number of days to give us 365 days a year, yet every 4th year we still have what we call a leap year giving us a year of 366 days to get in line with the solar years.

The next two verses finish what John began in verses 13-14 about God protecting the people of Israel. **"Then from his mouth the serpent spewed water like a river, to overtake the woman and sweep her away with the torrent. But the earth helped the woman by opening its mouth and swallowing the river that the dragon had spewed out of his mouth"** (Revelation 12:15-16). In 70 AD, the Roman army destroyed Jerusalem, which began the time, times and half a time or symbolically the 1260 days. We now can see that it refers to the Diaspora, over 1800 years of dispersal of the Jewish people throughout the world. Many Jews fled to Italy and Spain, some as far away as China and some to Ethiopia. Scattered elements settled in Europe, however, Spain was the center of Jewish life until 1492. During the Spanish Inquisition, they were expelled from Spain after a century of persecution by the then ruling Catholic Church. From Spain they moved to Europe where most of them settled in the countries of Germany, Russia, and Poland. They lived in districts of a city or territories out in the country, which were occupied only by Jewish people. This continued until the Nazi massacres of the 1930s and 1940s, when as many as two-fifths of the Jewish people on Earth lost their lives.

The persecution of the Jews provoked many of them to begin to search for a way to return to their homeland during the 19th and 20th centuries. Their return culminated with the creation of the State of Israel when the United Nations recognized the new nation on May 14, 1948. Through the many years of dispersion and persecution since 70 AD, God fulfilled His promise to Abraham and preserved Abraham's descendants. This second restoration of the Jewish people's return to

Palestine was prophesied by Isaiah11:11-12, by Jeremiah16:14-15 and by Ezekiel 11:16-17. Since May 14, 1948 the Jewish people have continued to battle for their homeland. They have won every war miraculously! The small land of Palestine and the nation of Israel is constantly front page news today.

Seeing that the woman, the people of Israel, was dispersed throughout the world where God was protecting them as a race, Satan went off to make war against her offspring, which is the body of Christ or Christians. **"Then the dragon** (Satan) **was enraged at the woman and went off to make war against the rest of her offspring—those who obey God's commandments <u>and hold to the testimony of Jesus</u>"** (Revelation 12:17). For nearly two thousand years, Satan has attacked Christians through relentless persecution and deception. As we already saw, nearly 70 million Christians have been killed since the church began. Over 43 million of these Christians were killed in the last 100 years. Spiritual warfare is for real. It is not a game.

The pronouncements **"…woe to the earth and the sea, because the devil has gone down to you! He is filled with fury, because he knows that his time is short"** and **"went off to make war against the rest of her offspring—those who obey God's commandments and hold to the testimony of Jesus"** have certainly been true prophecies about the church. Having finished chapter 12, we are now ready to turn to Revelation chapter 13 and the prophecy about the "beast" and the "spiritual warfare" during the last days of the Church Age.

CHAPTER FOURTEEN

I am going to set a proposition before you. Consider the following: Both Scripture and history tell us that spiritual warfare is for real. Satan was hurled to the Earth and we are warned he furiously makes war against Christians. The history of the church over the last 2000 years confirms this truth. America was founded on Christian values. God intervened on different occasions in our country's spiritual development to establish a special calling for Christians in America. As a result, America became the world's center of Christianity. Satan has always raised up a scheme to destroy anything God has raised up (I don't know all of the reasons why God has allowed Satan to experience the success that he has in this world, except that one reason might be to show us how totally dependent we must be on Jesus regardless of what happens). Two unique things happened in the history of our country in this last generation; one is that we became the greatest superpower in the history of mankind; the second is that even though there are now over 250,000 churches in America our moral values have deteriorated more in this generation than in all of the previous years combined since the beginning of our country.

My proposition is this: Knowing these things, wouldn't you agree with me that we should at least consider the possibility of America somehow fitting into this "spiritual warfare" prophecy about the last days? Is it possible that as a nation our government has become the "beast" or superpower that is prophesied in Revelation 13 that overcomes the testimony of Christians in these last days? There is a sure way to find out. It is to put this possibility to a sound and solid Scriptural test. No one should object to an open and fair test.

Before I begin this test I found there are basic guidelines one should use when interpreting prophetic Scripture.

1. There is no higher authority for understanding God's Word than to refer to other Scripture where a similar word or phrase is used. This is what Jesus would often do. This is the most important guideline to follow because you are going to the source of that inspiration. No author of a book in the Bible writing about a similar topic will contradict another author. If an interpretation holds for one passage, it will hold for another passage.

2. In order to understand a passage or word it is often necessary to research and study the original language in which it was written. The Old Testament was written mostly in Hebrew and the New Testament in Greek. Difficult words or phrases in Scripture often require learning what that word or phrase would have meant to the Hebrew or Greek author who wrote it. This is especially true with prophetic words and phrases. For this reason I acquired the help of Greek scholars with advanced degrees in the language.

3. Historical evidence either confirms that a prophecy has already been fulfilled, or that it is yet to be fulfilled. Prophesies are statements about future events and either they have happened as foretold or they haven't. Through proper research the evidence must be conclusive.

4. Words used in prophecy must be examined differently than when the same word is used to explain a happening. A word in prophecy may have a symbolic meaning rather than a specific meaning. You will see this as we proceed.

The first principle in developing the understanding of prophecy must be followed by the others. To do otherwise may lead to mistaken interpretation. To move the interpretation of Bible prophecy outside the realm of speculation and conjecture, we must start with a thorough reading and comparison of Scripture with Scripture. One other thing I want you to be aware of is that I believe the Word of God is absolutely accurate. We may not always understand everything it says, but I was not interested in trying to come up with some kind of truth unless it could be documented accurately with Scripture.

It is hard to find a description of anything in the Bible that is as detailed and exact as these verses that describe the "beast" in Revelation 13. Evidently God did not want any mistake made as to its identity. There are many different views taught today on the meaning and identity of this "beast" in Revelation13, however, not once could I find where anyone stated they ran <u>a Scriptural test on each word and phrase</u> in this chapter that would accurately confirm their view or theory on the identity of this "beast."

There is another point I want you to be aware of as I talk about America in Bible prophecy. <u>I am referring to the spiritual influence in our country that is now having the most effect and success.</u> **Is it Christians and the Kingdom of God, or is it our enemy and his kingdom–the world?** In the early years of America and up until the last 50 years or so, it was obviously the standards of God that had the most influence, but that all started to change after World War II. We became the greatest superpower in the history of mankind and began to develop what is called the "great society." True spiritual influence is expressed through the flesh—by actions—which can be evaluated by looking at the fruit being produced.

IDENTIFYING THE BEAST OF REVELATION 13

John prophesies, **"And the dragon** (Satan) **stood on the shore of the sea. And I saw a beast coming out of the sea. He had ten horns and seven heads, with ten crowns on his horns, and on each**

head a blasphemous name" (Revelation13:1). Anyone who wants to identify this "beast" should be able to explain in detail exactly how each of these words are being fulfilled in what they claim to be its identity. Although these prophetic words seem difficult, if not impossible, to decipher they are actually a blessing from the Lord to keep us from all of the different ideas that we may want to come up with as to the identity of this "beast." It is wonderful how the Lord protects the mind of mankind through His Word because of our nature to wonder off in so many different doctrinal directions.

A careful reading of this verse reveals there are <u>seven distinct descriptive characteristics or happenings</u> that we need to test to determine the identity of this "beast" or superpower. I think you would agree with me, that if I can demonstrate that since World War II we began fulfilling all that John prophesies about this "beast" in Revelation chapter 13, the enemy has come up with <u>a sly and deceptive method</u> to overcome and keep Christians in America from fulfilling our mission to be the **salt of the earth** and the **light of the world** in these last days.

The seven descriptive words and phrases about the "beast" in this verse are: **1. "The dragon (Satan) stood on the shore of the sea." 2. "Beast." 3. "Coming out of the sea." 4. "Ten horns." 5. "Seven heads." 6. "Ten crowns on his horns." 7. "On each head a blasphemous name."**

Test number one: "Shore of the sea." We are told in the last verse of Revelation 12 that Satan went to war against Christians. Since Revelation 13 is prophesying about the spiritual warfare in the last days, this reference to an ocean beach could be speaking about the movement of those who testify of Jesus from the Old World moving to the New World, which is America. In the New World, the Great Awakening led to the American Revolution and the founding of a new nation, whose government was grounded on Christian principles. As this new nation became the geographic center of Christianity during the modern era, Satan would make it one of his main battlegrounds for his relentless attack against the church. Giving a reference point of standing on the shore of the sea to describe the location of where this "beast" would rise up is the first test that must be met. We pass this first test.

Test number two: The "beast." Before testing any of the other words or phrases that John uses to describe this "beast," the actual meaning of this word "beast" as it is used in prophecy should be made absolutely clear. Remember that the highest authority anyone can use to determine the meaning of a word in Scripture is to use the inspired Word of God itself.

We are fortunate because in the case of the word "beast" the prophet Daniel speaks of "beasts" in chapter seven of Daniel, and is told the meaning by an angel. I would recommend that you read all of chapter seven in Daniel; I will only quote the highlights that will help determine the meaning of this word "beast" when used in prophecy.

"In the first year of Belshazzar king of Babylon, Daniel had a dream, and visions passed through his mind as he was lying on his bed. He wrote down the substance of his dream. Daniel said: "In my vision at night I looked, and there before me were the four winds of heaven churning up the great sea. Four great beasts, each different from the others, came up out of the sea" (Daniel 7:1-3). **"I, Daniel, was troubled in spirit, and the visions that passed through my mind disturbed me. I approached one of those standing there and asked him the true meaning of all this. So he told me and gave me the interpretation of these things: The four great beasts are four kingdoms that will rise from the earth"** (Daniel 7:15-17).

This passage from Daniel shows that from the interpretation given to him when the word "beast" appears in prophetic Scripture it refers to a powerful governmental authority—a kingdom, an empire, or what we today call a superpower. In other parts of the book of Daniel the four "beasts" he saw in his vision are described as the superpowers of Babylon, Media-Persia, Greece under Alexander the Great, and the Roman Empire. In the first part of chapter seven he also makes use of wild animals to help describe three of these "beasts;" a lion, bear and leopard. I mentioned this fact because John uses all three of these animals in Revelation 13:2 to help describe the "beast" he saw, indicating the Revelation 13 "beast" is the greatest superpower in the history of mankind, which America has become in this last generation.

Daniel used the word "beast" to describe the superpowers he saw in his vision and John uses this word in the same way to describe the superpower that would rise up in the area of those who give testimony of Jesus Christ in the last days. America passes the test of being called a "beast" in a prophetic sense because we are and have been the superpower on the world stage in these last days.

Before I continue the test, there is another issue that I should address. It is a common teaching among some Christians that the word "beast" in Revelation 13 refers to a man. I had to check this out because of what I found in the book of Daniel as to how he used this word "beast." I surprisingly discovered that some translations of the Bible refer to the "beast" in Revelation 13 as a man and some translations as an entity or government superpower. For example, the King James and New International Version (the version I use most of the time), use the masculine gender pronoun of "he," "his," and "him" when referring to the "beast" in Revelation 13, which would indicate the "beast" could be referring to a man. The Revised Standard Version, Philips Translation and other Bible translations use the neuter gender pronouns "it," and "its" when referring to the "beast" in Revelation 13, which would indicate the "beast" is referring to a superpower instead, just as it is used in Daniel.

This certainly raised a question! Why would some translations translate the pronoun one way and others another way? To make sure I was getting the correct information I acquired help from a seminary professor who has his doctorate in the Greek language. Both translations could not be right! Were the pronouns "he," "his," and "him" correct, which would indicate the "beast" would be referring to a man; or were the pronouns "it," and "its" correct, which would indicate the "beast" is referring to a governmental superpower?

The Greek word *"onpiov"* is the <u>noun</u> translated "beast" in Revelation 13. This Greek word in English is the word *"therion."* The Greek word *"avrov"* is the <u>pronoun</u> throughout Revelation 13 that is used to make reference to the "beast." To be grammatically correct a <u>pronoun</u> must always be of the <u>same gender as the noun</u> to which it refers. If the original Greek word used for "beast" is <u>masculine gender</u> then the pronouns "he," "his," and "him" are the correct translation. If the original Greek word used for "beast" is <u>neuter gender</u> then the pronouns "it" and "its" are the correct translation.

The Greek word used for "beast" in Revelation 13 is <u>neuter</u> gender, which means those translations that use the pronoun "he," "his," and "him" are incorrect, and those translations that use the pronouns "it" and "its" are the correct translations. This is not a hypothetical answer, but a grammatical fact. Publishers of the Bible agree on this point that, to use the pronouns "he," "his," and "him," which is to use the masculine gender when referring to the word "beast" in Revelation 13, is an incorrect translation of the pronoun to be used (see Zondervan Publishing House, *Greek-English New Testament,* Grand Rapids, MI 1975, p. 751).

Let me repeat: the Greek word for "beast" is neuter gender. This means the proper rendering of John's writing is to use the pronouns "it" and "its." This also means that it is more probable that John, like Daniel, is using the word "beast" to refer to some superpower rather than to a man. Interpreting John's use of the prophetic word "beast" to mean a superpower is also consistent with the first guideline that one should resort to, in our case Daniel, as the most authoritive means to the understanding of God's prophetic Word, which is to use other Scripture.

Test number three: "coming out of the sea." This phrase also appears in Daniel, and so the angel's interpretation of Daniel's vision can also be used to understand John's vision. Daniel writes, **"Four great beasts, each different from the others, came up out of the sea"** (Daniel 7:3). Daniel's four beasts (Daniel 1:1-7) refer to the succession of great world powers which shaped Israel's history before the time of Christ. The lion represents Babylon, a nation which conquered Egypt in 606 BC and achieved political prominence in the Middle East. The bear stands for the Media-Persian Empire. The Media-Persians conquered the Babylonians in about 539 BC, and ruled until 331 BC when Alexander the Great defeated them (Daniel 8:21). The leopard represents the Greek Empire under Alexander, which splintered into four separate kingdoms as Daniel prophesied it would (Daniel 8:8, 22). The last of these four kingdoms continued until 31 BC, when as Daniel prophesied (Daniel 8:9-12, 23-25), the Roman Empire rose to power.

From this historical review, one may infer that the phrase **"coming out of the sea"** has to do with an empire or nation that is culturally and ethnically diverse. In Daniel's account, a succession of ethnic peoples from different geographic bases conquered one another, bringing together people from the continents of Africa, Asia, and Europe into a great mixture of customs, cultures, and languages. As a nation of immigrants, the United States fits this prophetic description of **"coming out of the sea."** Europeans and Africans joined indigenous peoples of North America during the colonial period, followed by waves of immigrants from all parts of the Earth in the 19th and 20th centuries. Together, these peoples make up the American Nation.

America is known as a "Nation of Nations." The peopling of America is one of the great dramas in all human history. Over the years a massive stream of humanity crossed every ocean and continent to reach the United States. They came speaking many languages and representing most every nationality, race, and religion. Today, there are more people of Irish ancestry in the United States than in Ireland, more Jews than in Israel, more blacks than in most African countries. There are more people of Polish ancestry in Detroit than in most of the leading cities in Poland, and more than twice as many people of Italian ancestry in New York as there are in Venice.

The setting in which the history of all these people unfolded is no less impressive than the numbers and varieties of the peoples themselves. The United States is the largest cultural-linguistic unit in the world. The distance from San Francisco to Boston is the same as from Madrid to Moscow. Yet, we have one primary language, one set of federal laws, and one economy. This same area in Europe is fragmented into a multitude of nations, languages, and competing military and political blocs.

The "melting pot" was once a popular image of American assimilation, (though is now a largely disdained concept). The largest single ethnic strain is of European ancestry, the region of the old Roman Empire. Daniel prophesied in chapter 7 that there would be another power, a little or new country, that would rise up out of the people of the old Roman Empire and that it would become stronger than any of the other powers—that it would become a superpower. He even states that this new power would defeat three of the powers out of the old Roman Empire as it developed, which we did: England, France and Spain.

Daniel prophesied of superpowers that had an effect on the history of Israel. Therefore he would not have prophesied of any other superpower after the Roman Empire until Israel once again became a nation (after World War II), which was when we gained superpower status. America fits the descriptive characteristic of the "beast" or superpower of **"coming out of the sea."** We pass this test.

Test number four: "Ten horns." Understanding the biblical use of the prophetic phrase *"ten horns"* requires an interpretation of *"ten,"* a number, and *"horns,"* a word used in prophecy to indicate a nation of power but not of superpower status.

Many of the numbers used in Scripture have symbolic meaning in addition to their numerical value. Bible scholars have produced entire books on these meanings. From their study it can be stated that *"ten"* denotes all-encompassing, orderliness, and completeness. Examples of Bible uses of ten include the Ten Commandments, the ten virgins, and the ten plagues. And though in these examples ten is used to mean an exact count, when a numerical number is used in prophecy it is often used in a symbolic way to carry the meaning of the number, rather than the actual count. For example in Revelation 12:3, John uses the phrase *"ten horns"* to describe the Roman Empire, although historically, the Romans controlled more than two dozen other nations. The use of the number *"ten"* was also used in a symbolic way to mean an all encompassing number in the book of Daniel (see Daniel 7:20 and 24).

The second word in this descriptive phrase about the "beast" is *"horns."* Throughout the Bible, the word *"horns"* was used to indicate power and authority. In the book of Daniel, the word *"horns"* represented nations, and since John is also describing a superpower as was Daniel, I would have to think he too is using the word *"horns"* to represent nations. These would be nations with power and influence, but less power and influence than a "beast" or superpower. To describe this superpower in Revelation 13 of having *"ten horns"* would suggest that it has quite a bit of influence over several other powerful nations.

The United States is a power of superpower status. There are other powerful nations (horns) in the world today. Several nations in the United Nations, for example, can be said to be powerful within a particular sphere of influence. Japan and Germany are economic powers; Russia is still a military power. France and England are former colonial powers that continue to hold political influence over other nations. But only the United States can claim to be a superpower. It exercises a certain amount of influence over all these lesser powers, economic, military, and political.

I am familiar with another interpretation of *"ten horns"* that says the horns represent the European nations allied in the European Union (EU). However, for this interpretation to hold true the EU would have to also meet all of the other descriptive words and phrases given in Revelation chapter 13 that describes this end-time super-power. I have never seen anyone even try to apply a test like I am doing for another interpretation. It is possible that there may be several other possibilities of interpretation for one or two of these descriptive words and phrases that characterize this "beast" or super-power. But that is not enough! To have a valid interpretation it must fit every word and phrase that the Lord has given us. That is why each one of these descriptions is there, so that we can know without having to guess, which has led to many different interpretations. America passes the test of meeting the description of having *"ten horns."*

Test number five: "Seven Heads." The explanation of the descriptive phrase *"seven heads"* is fairly simple. <u>The word *seven* throughout Scripture is a word used to represent something that is complete.</u> There are several examples in the Bible to illustrate this meaning. God completed the creation of the universe in *seven* days. Joshua was commanded to march around the city of Jericho for *seven* days. On the *seventh* day the priests and the army marched around the city *seven* times and when this was completed the wall around Jericho fell and the Lord gave Joshua and the Israelites the city of Jericho. Another example occurred in II Kings chapter 5 when Elisha told the military captain, Naaman, to go and dip himself in the Jordan River and he would be healed. The number of times he was to dip himself was *seven* times before he would be healed. Like the number *ten,* the number *seven* is used in this descriptive prophetic phrase for its symbolic meaning of completeness, not for an exact number count.

The meaning of the word *heads* simply indicates *leadership*. For John to prophesy that this "beast" or superpower would have *seven heads* would be stating that its leadership would be complete in all areas of world affairs. It would dominate or be the leader—be number one—in commerce, industrial output, output of goods and services, agriculture, military might, political power, economic power, and so on.

Seven heads is not referring to seven aspects of leadership, it is describing the fact that this superpower in the last days would enjoy superiority or be complete in all areas of international influence. Since World War II we have developed the position in world affairs that would allow John to make this prophecy about us. We pass the test of this descriptive characteristic of the last days superpower.

Test number six: "Ten crowns on his horns." Of all the identifying descriptive characteristics that Scripture gives about the "beast" or superpower in Revelation 13, this one of having **"ten crowns on his horns"** is the most unique. It is a very demanding and exact characteristic. It is extremely meaningful because it is so difficult for any superpower to pass the test. The word *"crown"* (or *"diadem"* as some versions read) was a distinctive mark of royalty among the early Greeks and Romans. The word refers to political position. If a country or nation is being discussed and the word *crown* or *diadem* is used, you can know that something was being said about its political position.

When I earlier discussed the phrase *ten horns* we saw in the book of Daniel that the word *horns* is used in prophecy to refer to nations or countries. To add the word *crowns* with the descriptive word *horns* indicates this prophecy is making a statement about the political position of these *horns* or nations that the superpower in Revelation 13 influences. I will break down this descriptive phrase that describes a very unique characteristic of the "beast." *Ten* means all-encompassing, *crowns* means political position, and *horns* makes reference to various countries. This superpower has "**ten crowns on his horns**," which is a prophetic way of describing how it could politically control various countries around the world, but it does not. The **crown is on the horn**, meaning political control is resting upon each individual country. When John writes that the crowns were positioned on the horns, he is saying that each country has its own governing political body. This indicates that the nations under the superpower's influence retain political autonomy.

If the superpower described in Revelation 13:1 politically controlled other countries then Scripture would have used the phrase *ten crowns on his head,* reflecting **the beast's political leadership**. It would not have placed the *crowns on the horns*. Notice how the Roman Empire in Revelation 12:3 is prophetically described. The *crowns* (political control) are on the *heads* (under Rome's control) not on the *horns* (individual countries under Roman rule were not allowed to have their own political governing bodies).

I don't know of any other superpower in the history of mankind that has ever met this distinctive characteristic except the United States. For example we defeated both Japan and Germany in World War II, yet we allowed each country to retain its own political autonomy. We have not tried to rule them politically from Washington D.C. In fact we have helped rebuild the countries we have conquered. This imagery of crowns and horns, of politics and nations, is a telling description of America's relationship with other countries. America's influence stretches across the globe. Missionaries journeying to the remotest parts of the Earth have found that American brand names, television programs, and popular music have preceded them. The United States maintains more military bases and foreign embassies than any other nation, and its technological, industrial, and commercial influence pull even more of the world's peoples into its grasp. Yet none of these people owe allegiance to the American flag. Few of those under American influence are actually citizens of the United States.

How aptly John's phrase of crowns and horns describes American influence; the nations are heavily influenced by American culture and commerce, but not ruled by American law and government. We pass this very unique test.

Test number seven: "On each head a blasphemous name." In order to appreciate the significance of this phrase, *"on each head a blasphemous name,"* it is necessary to understand the word blasphemy. Without a proper understanding of this sin, it would be difficult to comprehend how it relates to the heads or aspects of the beasts' leadership.

Throughout the Old Testament, blasphemy was one of the gravest sins a person could commit. To blaspheme is to make light of, or sport of the name and sovereignty of God. In the New Testament, the Greek word used for blasphemy means to injure one's reputation. The Scriptures are very strict in teaching that the holy name of God is extremely sacred. To misuse His name in any way, either in normal conversation or in any way that is not marked with a sense of awe and majesty, is viewed as blasphemy. Blasphemy injures or diminishes the truth of God's holiness and who He really is.

A way that might help us understand the word blasphemy is to think about what happened prior to the crucifixion of Christ. Although Jesus was true deity the Jewish leaders did not accept Him as such, therefore the high priests, elders, and teachers condemned Jesus to death for what they claimed was blasphemy. The seriousness of this sin is shown by the fact that it was punishable by death. So when Jesus acknowledged his deity, these religious leaders claimed he had misused the name of God. This was blasphemy to them.

The blasphemous name on each head that John speaks of in describing the superpower of Revelation 13 means that the leadership of our government would misuse the sacred name of God after it became the superpower in the world. John indicates that in each area of leadership, each head, this last days superpower will use the sacred name of God irreverently in carrying out unrighteous acts. That is more serious than most people realize today.

As applied to the United States, this would mean that our government promotes a worldly cause but claims an association with the name of God. This is, in fact, what has happened in this last generation as our government began to pass laws that promote sin. A few examples would be the promotion of sexual promiscuity in schools by passing out condoms, sponsoring the destruction of millions of unborn babies through abortion, outlawing even the reference of God in schools or praying out loud. There are many actions that our leadership has taken during this last generation that have injured the name of God.

Undoubtedly, many of our nation's founders submitted to the Lord's direction. But on our way to worldwide superiority in the last generation, we have abandoned the godly principles of our founding fathers. Other governments and other peoples engage in wicked activities. But no other nation claims to have God's blessing while its people commit such great evil. We easily pass the seventh test of Revelation 13:1 that the Lord gave to identify this superpower in the last days. If this verse had been written in contemporary English, and the symbols were replaced with their contemporary explanation, it might read something like this:

And I saw a world superpower develop in a new country made up of people of many nationalities. It influenced many other powerful nations throughout the world; it held a position of leadership in every area of world affairs, although it did not try to politically rule other countries, they were allowed to govern themselves. It used the name of God freely and irreverently in many of its worldly activities.

The following is a quick reference to the words and phrases in verse one that characterizes the superpower of Revelation 13.

BEAST ....Empire or superpower.

OUT OF THE SEA ....A nation comprised of peoples with diverse cultural and ethnic background.

NUMERAL TEN ....Denotes all encompassing, orderliness and completeness.

HORNS ....Nations with significant power, authority and influence, but not a superpower.

NUMERAL SEVEN ....Complete or full.

HEADS. ....Leadership.

CROWNS OR DIADEM ......A distinct mark of royalty or political position.

BLASPHEMY ....To diminish or injure the sacred sovereign of who God is by misusing His holy name.

CHAPTER FIFTEEN

"The beast I saw resembled a leopard, but had feet like those of a bear and a mouth like that of a lion. The dragon gave the beast his power and his throne and great authority" (Revelation 13:2). As John continues to describe this last days superpower, he uses animals as Daniel did. Daniel characterizes three different world powers with three different animals. He used a lion to describe the Babylonian Empire's power, but it also adds the element of pride, for which the Babylonians were noted. He used the bear for the Media-Persian Empire, which symbolized its brute force. He used a leopard for the Greek Empire of Alexander the Great, which symbolized its military power and quickness. John, however, uses all three of these animals to describe the superpower of the last days indicating how great a superpower it becomes in comparison to others in the history of mankind.

"The dragon gave the beast his power and his throne and great authority." We saw in Revelation 12:9 that the dragon is none other than Satan himself. What does it mean for Satan to give this superpower his power, throne and great authority? If you will recall, we studied the Kingdom that Satan rules in chapter 5; it is the king-dom of the world or society. There are several verses of Scripture that confirm this; a couple are: **"In their case the god of this world has blinded the minds of the unbelievers...** (II Corinthians 4:4 RSV). **"We know that we are children of God, and that the whole world is under the control of the evil one** (Satan)" (I John 5:19).

We learn from the book of Job that Satan's authority over the world is limited by God's providential guidelines. Satan has his limits. But on the whole, God's Word is clear that the systems and things developed by unregenerate man that make up society are controlled by or under the influence of Satan and are often used as his elements to attack God's people in spiritual warfare. This is why we are told not to be friends of the world (James 4:4), not to love the world (I John 2:15), to keep ourselves from being spotted by the world (James 1:27), to put on the whole armor of God so we can take our stand against the powers of this dark world (Ephesians 6:10-12), and to no longer conform to the pattern of this world, but to have our mind renewed then we will be able to test and approve what God's will is (Romans 12:2). Jesus even acknowledged Satan's authority over the world when Satan tempted Him. **"The devil led him** (Jesus) **up to a high place and showed him in an instant all the kingdoms of the world. And he said to him, 'I will give you all their authority and splendor, for it has been given to me, and I can give it to anyone I want to. So if you worship me, it will all be yours"** (Luke 4:5-7). Satan claimed to have authority over the world, or society and Jesus did not dispute his claim.

It is as we understand Satan's position of power and authority in the societies of this world that we will understand John's statement in Revelation 13:2 about Satan giving this superpower his authority over the world. For Satan to give a superpower his power and authority over his throne of the world, would allow that superpower to gain for itself the number one position in those elements that make up a society: economics, military strength, politics, industry, agriculture, production of goods and services, entertainment and so on.

It was after World War II that the United States emerged as the most prosperous and mighty of all nations. Historical records prove it was primarily the outcome of this war that made us the greatest superpower in the history of mankind. World War II left the nations of Europe and the Pacific Rim in shambles. Many people not only lost their homes, they lost their means of livelihood as well. The fighting destroyed factories, businesses, power plants, roads, bridges, rail lines and much more. Germany, England, France, Japan, Russia and many other nations lost much of their industrial capacity. The infrastructure needed for economic productivity was wiped out by the war.

Consequently, the economic strength of these nations experienced a severe setback. England's financial and political power, for example, never returned to the previous status quo. It went from being an industrial power with globe-encircling interests to a more internally-focused nation with a moderate role in today's international affairs. While the European and Pacific powers crawled out from under the rubble of World War II, the United States was on its way to economic supremacy. World War II actually enhanced America's economic position.

None of the major fighting occurred on American soil, so we emerged as the only major world power with its industrial and agricultural output intact. This brought the development of a lifestyle for the people in our country that was unimaginable before the war. Production by American factories after the war continued at a steady clip as we were in a unique position to furnish our wartime allies and enemies with many of the products and services they needed. This allowed the average United States worker to have a steady job with a good income. Few countries in the industrial world could boast higher pay, more extensive fringe benefits, or better working conditions.

During the years after World War II, American products achieved worldwide reputation. We were the "great society" emerging. American companies captured first place in the production of automobiles, machine tools, electronic equipment, and many other vital industries. The output of our land with rich quality agricultural goods was unsurpassed. We provided the major share of the goods and services needed around the world in the generation that followed World War II. This created an impressive trade surplus. Year after year following the war, Americans sold far more overseas than they bought, and billions of excess dollars from around the world poured into the U.S. economy.

As a result, the American standard of living shot up beyond belief. The average American family claimed vast worldly possessions that were unprecedented in the history of mankind. With less that 7% of the world's population, we accumulated half of the world's wealth and consumed a full third of the world's resources each year. From a material standpoint, Americans lived better than virtually all people throughout the world. This was not our position before World War II.

After World War II the American lifestyle became the envy of people everywhere as Americans routinely enjoyed products and services completely out of reach for people in other lands. Those categorized as poor in America would have been in the upper class in many countries. Our country emerged as the greatest political, military, industrial, and economic power ever to exist on the face of the Earth. We, indeed, had received the throne of the world as John prophesied. This was soon proven as many countries aligned themselves with the United States Government. The entire world was awestruck by the way the United States demonstrated its great power and ended the war with the dropping of the atomic bomb.

It is important to note, that I am not saying there was anything wrong with the way our economy flourished after World War II. I would not pass judgment on that. I have given you a brief review of our economic development, because it does relate to the materialistic lifestyle and the spiritual warfare that has caused much spiritual defeat for Christians in this last generation. This is not to say that I am not thankful for the many conveniences, services, opportunities and freedoms we have in America. But these blessings make it easy to become attached to the material things. After the Lord's warning to my wife and me in the early 1970s about the spiritual warfare our country would be experiencing we have been cautious to tread lightly with prayer and waiting on the Lord to eliminate our making emotional rather than wise decisions. The temptations of the enemy's traps coming from the standards of the world can be overwhelming.

I have been successful in my business career. However, the Lord did put my wife and me to a test that would expose the degree of our attachment to the things of the world. To be obedient to the Lord's guidance for our family it became necessary for us to give up my successful career and our material possessions. We were led by the Lord to remove our children from the humanistic philosophy that was being taught in the public school system and put them under Christian teachers and a Christian environment, which would be consistent with their training environment at home. This principle is strongly taught in the Word of God by what the Lord taught the people of Israel. The actual verse the Lord used to confirm this directive to us was **"Blessed is the man who does not walk in the counsel of the wicked or stand in the way of sinners or sit in the seat of mockers. But his delight is in the law of the Lord, and on his law he mediates day and night"** (Psalms 1:1-2). If it is true that adults should not to be taught by people of the world, it is even more important for children. We are to train our children in the way they should go, so that when they are old they will not turn from it (see Proverbs 22:6).

To obey the Lord's leading required selling the new house that we built for our expanded family on 15 acres of land with woods, a small running stream, an acre garden, and plenty of room for the kids to roam. It had become a favorite place for many of the church's activities. We had an auction, packed up our remaining things and the kids in two U-Haul trucks, and like a caravan began our journey of over 2,000 miles across our country to Phoenix, Arizona, the place the Lord had directed us to move. In Phoenix we found an excellent Christian High School and a Christian grade school. Although our financial status became very tight for the next several years we kept the children in Christian schools. In 1974 my wife and I founded Paradise Valley Christian School (K thru 8), which today is one of the major Christian schools in the Phoenix area (visit web site www. paradisevalleychirstian.org).

The Lord has been faithful to our obedience. We now have 54 in our family including children and spouses, grandchildren, and great grandchildren. Every one of them, except those that are still too young has made a commitment to serve the Lord. Our family testimony is that we have not experienced the normal drug, alcohol, or divorce problems in a society where this has become common even in Christian families. We are very close and the family spends holidays and vacations together.

A MAJOR IDENTIFYING EVENT

John continues his prophecy about this superpower in the next verse by prophesying about a major event in the history of this superpower's development—recovery from a mortal wound. **"One of the heads of the beast (superpower) seemed to have had a fatal wound, but the fatal wound had been healed. The whole world was astonished and followed the beast"** (Revelation 13:3). John says four things about this monumental event in the history of this superpower. They are:

1. One of the heads of the "beast" (one area of the superpowers' leadership) receives what appears to be a fatal wound. One aspect of its superiority is nearly wiped out. Understand that only *one of the heads of the beast seemed to have had a fatal wound,* not all seven. Remember in verse one of Revelation 13 John said this superpower had *seven* heads—complete leadership in all areas of worldly influence. We discussed the meaning of this descriptive phrase in the last chapter. In verse 3 it is made clear that one, and only one, of these seven heads receives what appears to be a fatal wound. John does not tell us in this verse which head suffered the wound and then recovered.

He does, however, provide the answer in verse 14. The second half of Revelation 13:4 reads, **"…in honor of the beast who was wounded by the sword and yet lived."** In biblical times this phrase indicated military action. The wound was to this superpower's military head, or leadership, and it appeared to be a fatal wound.

2. The second point John makes about what seemed to be a fatal wound to what we learned to be this superpower's military leadership is this wound is healed. This aspect of the superpower's leadership recovers from the blow it suffered.

3. The world is amazed at this recovery. The recovery is dramatic, awesome, and inexplicable. That is exactly what happened in World War II. We won wars on two fronts, the Pacific and European, in about 3-1/2 years. We ended the war with the dropping of the atomic bomb.

4. After the wound heals, the world follows this superpower as the whole world is astonished at its recovery. After World War II many nations aligned themselves with our government and came under our influence. Our recovery catapulted our position of leadership in the world as never before. The leadership of the superpower grows as a direct result of its recovery from the near-fatal blow.

REVIEWING MILITARY HISTORY

For the American Government to be the "beast" or superpower referred to in Revelation 13, something in our country's past must match the description of a mortal military wound. If we have become this superpower, then our military capability must have been severely wounded and we emerged on the world stage in such a dramatic turn of events that the other nations of the world were astonished. Is there a historical event involving the United States military that led to the development of our nation becoming the world's greatest superpower?

The event *could not* have occurred within the last generation because we had already become a superpower by that time. And this event must have occurred within the last hundred years because at the time of the Civil War, Americans fought with themselves to decide whether there would even be an America. That narrows it down to the wound and the recovery occurring sometime during the first half of the twentieth century.

Both World War I and II were watershed events for the United States. However, World War I saw our foreign policy geared toward our hemisphere. We limited our international influence to Central America and the Caribbean. It was during World War II that we became a power with globe-encircling interests. Our influence in Africa, Asia, Europe, and the Middle East continued to grow and expand during the Cold War.

History uncovers an unnerving realization of how close the event that led to our involvement in World War II matches John's prophecy of this end-time beast receiving a mortal wound to its military leadership. The event that led us into the war happened on December 7, 1941—the "day that will live in infamy." Few people today would at first equate Pearl Harbor with this prophecy, a mortal wounding of our military leadership. It was something horrible that occurred, but a mortal wound? Because of its significance, in attempting to see if we fit all of the prophetic descriptions given about this last days superpower, let me review with you the attack on Pearl Harbor.

A BRIEF HISTORY OF THE ATTACK ON PEARL HARBOR

Historians, statesmen and journalists throughout the world refer to this attack as one of the greatest turning points in world history. At the time, world leaders viewed this event as a mortal wound to our military leadership. Prior to this time, America had been reluctant to get involved in the war in Europe and Asia. But the attack on Pearl Harbor jarred the United States into astonishing activity. It was the catalytic event of the century. As U.S. soldiers marched off to war, victory gardens sprang up, recycling bins appeared, and gas-rationing cards were used. Factories that produced autos were converted to produce airplanes, jeeps and tanks.

The Japanese attack on Pearl Harbor was so sudden, so spectacular, so devastating. It was even more than that—it was one of the turning points in modern world history. U.S. Congress convened a joint committee to investigate the event and filled forty volumes with its findings. The Second World War set into motion forces that changed the way Americans work, play, build families, and conduct their lives. The war transformed our land from a provincial, isolationist country to a superpower, a technological hothouse of incredible economic, political, and military power. The duties of men and women in America were changed forever.

To understand what happened at Pearl Harbor, and what led up to it, I recommend one source above all others: the book, *At Dawn We Slept,* by Gordon W. Prange. It is considered the finest historical work available on the topic of the Japanese attack on Pearl Harbor. Historians and publishers have praised this book as a "masterpiece" and as "authoritative," "unparalleled," "definitive," and "impossible to forget."

Prange was uniquely qualified for the task of writing this book. He was educated at the University of Iowa and the University of Berlin. Later, he taught history at the University of Maryland. From October 1946 to June 1951, Prange was chief of General Douglas MacArthur's G-2 Historical Section located at General HQ, Far East Command, Tokyo.

From his historical training and firsthand knowledge, Prange knew more about the attack on Pearl Harbor than any other person. He interviewed virtually every surviving Japanese officer who took part in the Pearl Harbor operation, as well as every pertinent source on the U.S. side. His 873-page history of the attack is based on 37 years of research. His work is acclaimed worldwide and is an invaluable reference. His book was used as a major source of information in making the movie about the attack on Pearl Harbor, *"Tora! Tora! Tora!"*

Military historians agree that when the Japanese attacked Pearl Harbor the United States suffered the greatest defeat any nation had ever endured at the beginning of a war. It is easily one of the most significant naval operations in twentieth-century military history. At the time, ships represented the ultimate technological achievement. It is difficult to exaggerate the importance of naval power prior to the aviation age. Battleships were the mightiest weapons of war, and luxury liners represented the epitome of western culture. When a great ship sank—*the Lusitania, the Bismarck,* or *the Titanic*—people listened to the details in amazement. These events inspired legends, ballads and movies. Sinking ships were cataclysmic events akin to natural disasters like earthquakes and hurricanes. At Pearl Harbor, the United States had twenty-two ships either sunk or damaged in a matter of hours.

PRELUDE TO THE ATTACK ON PEARL HARBOR

In the spring of 1940, a large segment of America's Pacific Fleet had been stationed at Pearl Harbor. It was the world's greatest aggregation of warships—a million tons of fighting steel. But United States influence in the Pacific irritated the Japanese. While the European nations fought each other in the 1930s, the island nation of Japan did not want to miss this golden opportunity to expand its empire in Southeast Asia. Japan feared that our huge naval program in the Pacific threatened their ambitious plan of conquest.

So in December 1940, Admiral lsoroku Yamamoto, Commander-in-Chief of Japan's combined naval fleet, convinced the Japanese Imperial Council to make use of their aircraft carriers to launch a surprise attack against America's Pacific Fleet at Pearl Harbor. He reasoned that for Japan to achieve political supremacy in the Pacific, it would have to neutralize America's military capacity at Pearl Harbor.

Yamamoto's plan was to catch us sleeping—literally. He knew that just as a weaker judo expert can toss a stronger opponent by catching him off balance, Japan would have to seize the initiative for the island nation to defeat the United States. By striking a fatal blow to the U.S. Pacific Fleet in one bold attack, Yamamoto hoped to gain the military edge in the Pacific for a year. He and his advisors concluded that if Japan had the military advantage for a year they could win a war in the Pacific against the United States.

Yamamoto's plan had merit! The mass majority of the people in America were completely caught off guard. A statement made on February 19, 1941, by Congressman Charles I. Faddis of Pennsylvania can best sum up the United States' perspective prior to the attack on Pearl Harbor. He declared: *"The Japanese are not going to risk a fight with a first class nation. They are unprepared to do so, and no one knows better than they do. They will not dare to get into a position where they must face the American Navy in open battle. Their Navy is not strong enough and their homeland is too vulnerable."*

It took a year of intense preparation for the Japanese naval forces to be ready. All of the planning had to be done in the strictest secrecy. If the attack did not catch the United States by surprise it would fail. Japanese military planners had several problems to solve before they could launch an attack. They had to design and build special torpedoes capable of operating in the shallow waters of Pearl Harbor; produce new armor-piercing shells that could be delivered by planes from low altitudes; select and train the pilots on how to fly in low and attack an area like Pearl Harbor; organize a naval task force and teach the personnel how to refuel the ships in the rough seas of the Pacific Ocean—the route selected to avoid detection to assure a complete surprise. The Pearl Harbor plan was the most highly classified, closely guarded, best-kept secret of World War II prior to the

Manhattan Project (development and dropping of the atomic bomb).

At 6 o'clock on the morning of November 26, 1941, the Japanese strike force weighed anchor. Twelve days later, just before dawn on December 7, they reached the launching point for their attack: 230 miles due north of the island of Oahu, Hawaii. The Japanese task force of 33 warships, including six aircraft carriers, had successfully sailed on a northern route through rough waters and dense fog to avoid detection by American ships and surveillance aircraft.

DAY OF INFAMY

The attack came with startling swiftness that Sunday morning. On every Japanese carrier, the scene was the same. The engines sputtered to life, up fluttered the signal flag, then down again as one by one the aircraft roared down the flight decks drowning the cheers and yells from the crews. Plane after plane rose in the sky, flashing in the early morning sun that peeked over the horizon. This airborne armada consisted of 353 planes. It represented the largest concentration of air power in the history of warfare. On the island of Oahu, American sailors were unaware of the tremendous fighting force that would send many of them to a watery grave.

Perfect timing was essential. The Japanese knew full well that if anything went wrong, the entire surprise attack would collapse. They were dead on course. Their mission: destruction of the U.S. Pacific Fleet stationed at Pearl Harbor and all of the nearby American Air Force installations.

It was 7:40 AM when the first Japanese pilots sighted Oahu's coastline. The element of surprise belonged to the Japanese. As the first wave of planes approached Pearl Harbor, they deployed into three groups. They first struck our air bases so our fighter planes could not get airborne to counterattack their bombing of Pearl Harbor. They hit Hickam Air Force Base, Wheeler Field, Bellows Field, Kaneohe Naval Base and the Naval Air Station at Ford Island.

Japanese pilots flew in at treetop level bringing massive destruction to our air bases. Hangars were burned, barracks were razed, and hundreds of men were killed. A total of 341 U.S. planes were destroyed or damaged on the ground that Sunday morning. Since the air bases were so close together, the attacks all came at the same time. Everything happened at once.

But the assault on the airfields was only the beginning of the Pearl Harbor drama. In the harbor were 96 warships of the United States Pacific Fleet. Included were 8 cruisers, 29 destroyers, 5 submarines, assorted mine craft and 8 U.S. battleships: the *West Virginia, Arizona, Oklahoma, Nevada, Tennessee, Pennsylvania, California and Maryland.*

At approximately 8:10 AM the battleship *USS Arizona* exploded, having been hit by a 1,760-pound armor-piercing bomb that slammed through her deck and ignited the main fuel tank. In less than nine minutes, she sank with 1,177 of her crew. The *USS Oklahoma,* hit by several torpedoes, rolled completely over, trapping over 400 men inside. The *California* and *West Virginia* sank at their moorings, while the *Utah,* which had been converted to a training ship, capsized with more than 50 of her crew. The *Maryland, Pennsylvania, and Tennessee,* all suffered significant damage. The *Nevada* attempted to run out to sea but took several hits and had to be beached to avoid sinking and blocking the harbor entrance.

As the Japanese dive-bombers rocked the harbor, the mammoth gray ships along Battleship Row, writhing from the explosions of bombs and torpedoes, burned at their moorings, sending billows of black smoke into the morning skies over the island of Oahu. The Japanese dealt crippling blows to ship after ship. Most of the damage was done in the first fifteen minutes. Mitsuo Fuchida, the Japanese commander who led the first formation of planes (who became a Christian after the war), later wrote: *The harbor was still asleep in the morning mist.*

The attack on Pearl Harbor ended at about 9:45 AM. In less than two hours the Japanese had immobilized most of our air strength at Oahu, and nearly eliminated their chief objective, the U.S. Pacific Fleet. The once-mighty U.S. military fortress at Oahu had been pulverized. As the drone of enemy formations disappeared over the horizon heading back to their carriers, they left behind a scene of horrible chaos—cackling flames, moaning men, and hissing steam. Half submerged ships were strewn about the harbor, tilting at crazy angles. Wreckage floated across the oily surface of the water as bodies washed ashore.

As the billows of black smoke over Oahu began to clear, United States forces assessed the damage. Twenty-two ships, including eight battleships, were sunk or heavily damaged and more than 340 American aircraft had been destroyed. Japanese losses totaled 29 aircraft destroyed and 74 damaged. America had suffered one of the greatest defeats any nation ever endured right at the beginning of a war. The Japanese secured mastery of the Far East in a couple of hours. In Germany, news of the defeat tempted Hitler to declare war on the United States.

THE FATAL WOUND IS HEALED

The attack seemed fatal, but it energized the fighting spirit of Americans as nothing else could have done. The United States jumped to its feet, despite the wound that had cut the heart out of its military, to become the most fearsome warrior the world had ever known. During the next three and a half years, we forged a war machine that conquered enemy forces on two different fronts in the European and Asian theaters. America was transformed from a provincial, regional power to a technological, military, and political titan stretching across both hemispheres and this changed forever the American way of life.

Former President George Bush journeyed to Hawaii on December 7, 1991, to revisit Pearl Harbor on the 50th Anniversary of the Japanese attack. The years have slipped by quickly, and most Americans have all but forgotten the scars of the attack on Pearl Harbor. However, the stark horror and grim reminder of defeat that Sunday morning which caught our country in the fierce vortex of history will live forever through the Arizona Memorial, dedicated on Memorial Day, 1962.

USS Arizona[1]

A single 1760-pound armor-piercing action bomb sank the battleship Arizona. The bomb penetrated through six decks of steel and exploded in the main aviation fuel tank. A tremendous internal chain reaction followed. The force of the explosion was so great it raised the bow of the ship completely out of the water, and split her right behind the number one gun turret. The Arizona sank in less than nine minutes. Out of her crew of 1,543 men, 1,177 lost their lives in those few awful minutes.

USS Arizona[1]

Today, the *USS Arizona* rests peacefully in an upright position under 38 feet of water at the bottom of Pearl Harbor. Oil still rises from her rusting hull and the 1100 men still entombed there provide a silent but eloquent witness to the fury of defeat on Pearl Harbor Day.

Arizona Memorial Spans Sunken USS Arizona[1]

I was astounded to discover the theme used for building this memorial reflects the prophecy given by John in Revelation 13:3 when he said: **"One of the heads of the beast seemed to have had a fatal wound, but the fatal wound had been healed."** This memorial was structurally designed with a sag in the middle to express our initial defeat—a wound to our military—but stands strong at the ends to express our recovery and victory—the wound was healed.

Arizona Memorial Design Theme[1]

After World War II, our country emerged as the greatest political, military, industrial, and economic power ever to exist on the face of the Earth. We received the throne of the world as John prophesied. Many countries soon aligned themselves with the United States Government. The entire world was awestruck by the way we demonstrated our great power and ended the war with the dropping of the atomic bomb. The fatal wound had indeed been healed. America perfectly fits the prophecy of Revelation 13:3 regarding the beast.

---

[1]Photographs of the USS Arizona and the USS Arizona Memorial are assumed to be in the public domain. These images were reproduced for educational purposes. An unsuccessful attempt was made by the author to discover the identity of the photographers in order to credit them for their work.

CHAPTER SIXTEEN

At this point I am going to move on to the first part of Revelation 13:7, then we'll come back to review verses 4-6 and 8-10 together. **"Also it** (the beast or superpower) **was allowed to make war on the saints and to conquer** (overcome) **them"** (Revelation 13:7a RSV).

The word *conquer* in this verse brings to mind the defeat of one army by another. This is, in fact, a good illustration because the word means to overcome, defeat, or subdue, not to obliterate or eliminate. For example we conquered both Germany and Japan, but we did not eliminate them from the globe. John is prophesying the society of this superpower will have the power to overcome Christians and keep them from walking in the power of the Holy Spirit—the power source that is necessary for us to live the victorious Christian life.

Verse 7 is referring to what happens to the spiritual state of the majority of Christians living under the influence of this superpower's society. Recall Dr. Billy Graham said that according to his research, over 90% of the Christians in America are now living defeated spiritual lives. And our review of the fruit being produced by the body of Christ confirms that we are fulfilling the prophecy of John in this verse.

It is not only important for us to see that we are fulfilling this prophecy; we also need to understand how <u>the enemy has developed the degree of lawlessness that now prevails in our society</u>. I want to discuss that in this chapter. Our society is definitely influencing and affecting the spiritual walk of most Christians, which has caused us to lose sight of what it means to lead a committed spiritual life. We may know what to say in Christian circles to make it seem as if we are devoted, but our actions, our fruit, broadcast our weakness to the world.

"I pray also that the eyes of your heart may be enlightened in order that you may know the hope to which he has called you, the riches of his glorious inheritance in the saints, and his incomparably great power for us who believe" (Ephesians 1:18-19). His incomparably great power for us who believe! What is this great power? It is the Holy Spirit which we receive at our spiritual birth. How can we tell if we are walking in the power of the Holy Spirit? The same principle applies: it is by an examination of our fruit and our character. **"But the fruit of the Spirit is love, joy, peace, patience, kindness, goodness, faithfulness, gentleness and self-control. Against such things there is no law. Those who belong to Christ Jesus have crucified the sinful nature with its passions and desires. Since we live by the Spirit, let us keep in step with the Spirit"** (Galatians 5:22-25).

Walking in the power of the Holy Spirit is not the demonstration of the gifts of the Spirit, which some teach. The gifts of the Holy Spirit will demonstrate power because the Holy Spirit is power. But gifts do not reflect if we are personally walking in the power of the Holy Spirit. A gift is a gift and should be considered as such. Paul spent considerable time trying to explain this point in I Corinthians chapters 12, 13, and 14. He said he did not want the Corinthians to be ignorant about the meaning of spiritual gifts (see I Corinthians 12:1). They had the gifts, but as you read through the two books in the Bible to the Corinthians they certainly were not having victory over sin, bearing the fruit and characteristics of the power of the Holy Spirit.

The Apostle Paul prophesied in II Thessalonians and II Timothy about Christians being overcome or conquered in these last days. **"But mark this: There will be terrible times in the last days. People will be lovers of themselves, lovers of money, boastful, proud, abusive, disobedient to parents, ungrateful, unholy** (immoral), **without love, unforgiving, slanderous, without self-control, brutal, not lovers of the good, treacherous, rash, conceited, lovers of pleasure rather than lovers of God—having a form of godliness but denying its power. Have nothing to do with them"** (II Timothy 3:1-5).

Paul saw into our day and called it terrible times. Why? Because of the characteristics he saw that would be so prevalent in Christians. This message is to Christians and Paul says he is talking about the last days. He is not saying that each one of these characteristics of our old sinful nature will be found in every Christian, but we each will continue to demonstrate some of them far more than we should. What does this mean? It means we are denying the power of the Holy Spirit that is given to all who believe to overcome our sinful nature. It means we are living defeated spiritual lives. It means the influence of the beast-system has spiritually overcome or conquered us.

The fruit of our society reveals that it has lured us into a spiritual stupor—that we lack spiritual power. This is a good description of the spiritual condition of our country. Satan is winning the war for the hearts and minds of Americans, and many Christians are not concerned. We do not recognize the enemy's tactics; therefore we don't know what to expect from him. Too often we speak and act contrary to basic godly principles and do not know that we have been victimized by spiritual deception. We have been captured and have surrendered many of the biblical ideas and standards to worldly standards.

The majority of Christians today in our society are not living out God's principles in their family and business relationships, entertainment desires and material needs. Defeated Christians have trouble recognizing Christian morality and values. Our apathy toward sin is a true barometer of this condition. Pastors, in addition to the many professional counseling organizations that have appeared in recent years, expend great resources to help needy Christians. Contemporary Christians seem helpless to keep their families together. As we have mentioned before, the divorce rate is reported to be over 50 percent.

The fulfillment of this prophecy refers to a general state or condition that prevails. Conquering the saints does not mean that Satan will immobilize every individual. Speaking of the last days, Jesus says that the deception will be great, but not great enough to deceive everyone. **"For false Christs and false prophets will appear and perform great signs and miracles to deceive even the elect—if that were possible"** (Matthew 24:24).

How has the beast-system been so effective in spiritually overcoming many of the saints in their commitment to the teachings and standards of Scripture? The Bible gives us the answer. This next prophecy is the key to the beast's ability to conquer the saints in our day. Paul says, **"Concerning the coming of our Lord Jesus Christ and our being gathered to him, we ask you, brothers, not to become easily unsettled or alarmed by some prophecy, report or letter supposed to have come from us, saying that the day of the Lord has already come. Don't let anyone deceive you in any way, for that day will not come until the rebellion occurs and the man of lawlessness is revealed, the man doomed to destruction. He opposes and exalts himself over everything that is called God or is worshiped, and even sets himself up in God's temple, proclaiming himself to be God"** (II Thessalonians 2:1-4).

Paul's opening statement, **"Concerning the coming of our Lord Jesus Christ and our being gathered to him,"** indicates that he is talking about the last days. Evidently, the Thessalonians (a body of believers living in Thessalonica) misunderstood the coming of Christ, and Paul warns them not to be fooled. Paul says that Jesus will not come until two things happen: (1) **"the rebellion occurs"** and (2) **"the man of lawlessness is revealed."**

The Greek word Paul used in this verse for rebellion is *apostasia*. It means to defect or fall into apostasy. To fall into apostasy is to abandon or renounce a belief in following the standards of biblical Christianity. We may wrap ourselves up in acts of religious service, but by our lifestyle and fruit we reveal that we no longer are committed to the standards of Christ. That is rebellion!

In using the word apostasy, Paul is not implying that dedicated Christians won't make their share of mistakes. That is not his point! He knows that will happen. By using the word apostasy he is warning that in the last days, many who go by the name of "Christian" will fall away from being committed to following true biblical standards. They display no conscience against many of the sins in the world, no fear of God, and no attachment to Scripture.

Paul continues his prophetic warning in the third verse by calling those who fall away or rebel against following the biblical standards of God—**"the man of lawlessness."** In modern English a more suitable phrase might be to call such a person a "lawless man." The reason Paul uses the phrase **"man of lawlessness"** is because from a biblical viewpoint, anyone who does not respect the laws of God is a person with a lawless spirit.

It has often been taught that the **"man of lawlessness"** refers to one person. But that interpretation does not really fit because Paul is addressing a general condition that affects many people, not just one person and the cause of their falling away. The Greek word translated as man in this verse is *anthropes*. This word often appears in the New Testament referring to mankind in general. Some examples are, **"So that the man** (anthropes) **of God may be thoroughly equipped"** (II Timothy 3:17). **"What is man** (anthropes) **that you are mindful of him?"** (Hebrews 2:6). **"So that by the grace of God he might taste death for everyone"** (anthropes) (Hebrews 2:9). **"Everyone** (anthropes) **should be quick to listen, slow to speak and slow to become angry"** (James 1:19).

We are the only society in the world today that meets the full description of Paul's prophetic warning of a people in the end-times who followed God's standards, then rebelled against His standards. Therefore, we can conclude that his warning must apply to the United States as much or more so than to any other country. In verse 4, Paul tells us how Satan will develop this spirit of rebellion or lawlessness against God's standards in the minds of the people of our country. It states, **"He** (which refers to the man with a lawless spirit) **opposes and exalts himself** (his own being) **over everything that is called God or is worshiped, and even sets himself up in God's temple, proclaiming himself to be God"** (II Thessalonians 2:4). This is a significant verse about our society. It describes the basic characteristic of our society that has led to the rebellion and identifies how the rebellion will occur.

Notice that the pronoun "himself" occurs three times in this verse. That is the key! It describes the method of seduction that has brought about the rebellion or apostasy from Christian standards in our society. It reveals the spiritual reason why our society has developed a spirit of lawlessness against God's standards in this last generation. It has swept across our nation like a flood. It has been the age old trap of deception that has caused us to set man "himself" up— good ole' me, myself, and I—to decide right from wrong, serving himself as though he was a god.

The Bible says Satan had this same attitude and this is why God cast him out of heaven. Speaking of Satan, God's Word states, **"You said in your heart, I will ascend to heaven; I will raise my throne above the stars of God; I will sit enthroned on the mount of assembly, on the utmost heights of the sacred mountain. I will ascend above the tops of the clouds; I will make myself like the Most High'"** (Isaiah 14:13-14). "I," "I," "I," I will do this, I will do that. I will set my own standards, which means to be my own god. That is rebellion! That is lawlessness! That is how Paul describes the

"man of lawlessness," he speaks of in verse 3. And there is more than just one person who rebels and falls. Paul is addressing the general state of apostasy from Christian standards that take place in the central area of Christianity in the last days.

This prophetic warning from Paul is powerful! It gives insight to the question many people have been seeking an answer to in the Christian community! Why have the moral values in our country crumbled? Where have we gone wrong? Why has all the time, effort, and expense that has been put into trying to reverse and correct the rapid deterioration of our moral values had no success? This verse gives us the truth we need. The Scripture says man sets himself up in the temple of God. Where is the temple of God in Christianity? It is man himself.

There are some who say that Paul's use of the word temple in verse 4 is referring to the temple in Jerusalem. In order to be sure he could be talking about man himself, I did a word study on the word temple. There are two Greek words in Scripture for temple. One is *hieron*, which refers to the entire temple building in Jerusalem. The other is *naos*, which is used for the inner sanctuary where only the priests could enter, but when used in Christianity *naos* is always the Greek word that refers to mankind being the temple of God.

For example, **"Don't you know that you yourselves are God's temple** (Greek word *naos*) **and that God's Spirit lives in you?"** (I Corinthians 3:16). **"Do you not know that your body is a temple** (Greek word *naos*) **of the Holy Spirit, who is in you, whom you have received from God?"** (I Corinthians 6:19). **"What agreement is there between the temple** (Greek word *naos*) **of God and idols? For we are the temple of the living God"** (II Corinthians 6:16).

The same is true when Jesus says, **"'Destroy this temple** (Greek word *naos*), **and I will raise it again in three days.' The Jews replied, "It has taken forty-six years to build this temple, and you are going to raise it in three days?" But the temple he had**

spoken of was his body" (John 2:19-21). When the human body is referred to as the temple of God throughout the New Testament, the Greek word *naos* is always used.

In II Thessalonians 2: 1-4, Paul is warning people living in the last days of a rebellion that will take place. The cause of the rebellion is that man sets himself up in the temple of God and serves himself as though he is a god—deciding right and wrong. In verse 4, Paul used the Greek word *naos,* not *hieron,* for temple, which means he could be talking about the human body, not the temple in Jerusalem. Paul is writing to Christians, and in Christianity mankind is the temple.

Out society has developed tremendous resources to influence us to accept worldly standards, to decide right and wrong, creating a powerful temptation for everyone to <u>serve themselves as a god</u>. Though the majority of people in our country once respected and lived by many of the laws of God, in this last generation many have discarded biblical moral standards that were once considered normal, and have placed their own self interests above their regard for God's laws. That is setting ourselves up in the temple of God, the human body, by our actions and the way we serve ourselves, to be a god. It is idolatry!

II Thessalonians 2:4 is a perfect description of the religion of humanism and the new age movement. It has swept through our country in recent years and has become the main philosophy that is taught in our schools, and is used to establish the standards by which the majority of people live. Using the powerful influence of our society to serve ourselves like a god, above the true God, Satan has seduced and deceived the American Christian. To serve ourselves as though we were a god above the true God fits Paul's description of **"the man of lawlessness."**

This warning from Paul tells us that the most important things we need to be concerned about in spiritual warfare are not the open and blatant sins we see taking place. Christians are being seduced and deceived in our society to serve ourselves above what is normal. That is the trick Satan is using. He is tempting us by appealing to our basic physical needs or by attracting us to something that appears good and legitimate. However, it leads us to be disobedient to the Word of God, just as Adam and Eve were in the Garden. We can be assured that he is going to set his traps in his endeavor to get us to fall through disobedience. Today our mind has become so seared through the influence of the world our conscience no longer feels any, or very little, guilt when we disobey God's Word. <u>Deception is the way that seducing spirits work</u>.

One of the greatest ways we can dishonor the Lord is to put Him in a secondary place in our life. It is a slap in God's face to allow the things of the world to become more important to us than being obedient in carrying out His will and seeking to follow His standards. Paul warns that we need to change our way of thinking because it can lead us into apostasy. That is the substance of what he is saying in this prophetic warning about the last days.

God has equipped every born again Christian with the power of the Holy Spirit to fulfill our responsibility of being faithful to His standards. **"You, dear children, are from God and have overcome them, because the one who is in you is greater than the one who is in the world"** (I John 4:4). **"...in all these things we are more than conquerors through him who loved us"** (Romans 8:37). **"No temptation has seized you except what is common to man. And God is faithful; he will not let you be tempted beyond what you can bear. But when you are tempted, he will also provide a way out so that you can stand up under it"** (I Corinthians 10:13).

WAR AGAINST THE SAINTS

Paul is addressing the power that the beast-system has to overcome the saints. We learned the method and tactics that Satan is using by examining another prophecy about the same subject in II Thessalonians 2:1-4. This prophecy was about how last-day

Christians will fall away, be overcome or conquered, as they are influenced by the beast-system to the extent they exalt and serve themselves by deciding right and wrong above God and His Word.

Satan knows that our greatest weakness is to serve "self." It is a part of our sinful nature. As Satan observes the strength of God's people in any area, he strikes out against God by maneuvering his worldly systems to attack. This attack may be direct and obvious through persecution as we saw throughout the history of the church and still taking place today, or he may use deception. Through Satan's use of deception, he creates an overpowering temptation to serve the flesh or self by getting mankind to use his own reasoning to determine right and wrong. Since America gained the throne of the world after World War II, Satan has been able to use this method of attack, working through the influence of our society, which has been very deceptive and successful. It has resulted in the moral values of our country not only deteriorating more in this last generation than all the years combined since we became a nation, but we also have experienced the greatest deterioration in the shortest period of time of any society in the history of mankind.

Satan's objective in a society that has a strong Christian influence, like America's where persecution is not immediately possible, is to develop a strong worldly influence to trap and deceive those who serve the Lord. Using all the things in the world which our society has developed in this past generation that are so attractive, professional advertising to promote them, the electric media to present them, beautiful malls in which to shop, and easy credit to pay for them, makes it difficult to resist and not become committed to these things of the world over and above our commitment to serve God. If in our heart the things of the world become more important to us than our commitment to serve the Lord, then the "spirit of merchandising" has conquered us spiritually. We will find ourselves beginning to yield to the enemy's temptations and we will start establishing our own standards, taking the place of God in our being, so that we can serve the desires of the flesh above God's Word.

Another major trap the enemy is using in America is that of sexual immorality. History proves that this has always been one of Satan's major traps of deception to bring spiritual defeat, including spiritual leaders. It certainly has captured the minds of the American people, including Christians. King David would be an example that most of us are familiar with in the Bible and it has reached an epidemic level in our society today. The standards of sexual permissiveness that is being taught to the American people through TV, movies, books, the Internet, magazines and so on has destroyed the biblical standards in the minds of most. Just the laxity in dress standards, including Christians, grieves the Holy Spirit.

We need to realize that the degree to which we are being influenced by the spirit of Satan does not have to be expressed by some kind of satanic worship. It can be, and usually is, expressed by the degree to which we serve ourselves by establishing standards of our own making rather than Scripture.

The late Dr. Bill Bright, founder of Campus Crusade for Christ stated in his book, *The Coming Revival, "America is under siege. Tens of millions of Americans seem ensnared by an evil mind-set. The evidence is everywhere we look.*

Crime, abortion, divorce, violence, suicide, drug addiction, alcoholism, teen pregnancy, lust, pornography, fornication, adultery, and sodomy run rampant.

Airwaves carry sordid sex into the living room. Condoms are distributed to our children in the public schools. Militant homosexuals parade half-naked down the streets of our nation's capital demanding approval and special rights as a minority.

America is slaughtering tens of millions of its unborn babies in the womb and arresting those who try to peacefully stop the bloodshed.

Officials have fought vigorously to expel God from our schools.

The Ten Commandments cannot even be placed on the walls of most classrooms.

Powerful forces within our country want to make it illegal to mention the name of Jesus, carry Bibles, display religious pictures, or wear Christian emblems in schools and in the workplace. They argue that to do so creates an "offensive environment of harassment."

As a nation, we have spent our way into a $3 trillion national debt. It is still climbing at an alarming rate, threatening to bankrupt our nation in the next few years.

In many instances, our state and local governments are accused of linking arms with organized crime by legalizing lotteries and gaming houses. They are joining the ranks of the largest gambling operators in the world.

Selfishness has become a hallmark of the people. Americans are growing more cynical and less compassionate. Their attitudes toward minorities, immigrants, and the poor have hardened.

This sharp decline into decadence can be traced back to the day when secular humanism began to take control of our country. The level of America's sins would have astounded even ancient Rome whose own moral decay resulted in her self-destruction.

The Church is Asleep

And where is the Church? For the most part, it is asleep. Polluted with the desires and materialism of the world, she knows little about spiritual discipline and living the Spirit -filled life. She is complacent and at ease, thinking she has everything and is in need of nothing.

This picture is a mirror image of the churches at Ephesus and Laodicea portrayed in Revelation 2:1-7; 3:14-21, to whom the Lord spoke these sobering words:

"You have forsaken your first love. Remember the height from which you have fallen! Repent and do the things you did at first. If you

do not repent, I will come to you and remove your lampstand from its place" (Revelation 2:4,5).

"I know your deeds, that you are neither cold nor hot. I wish you were either one or the other! So, because you are luke-warm—neither hot nor cold—I am about to spit you out of my mouth. You say, 'I am rich; I have acquired wealth and do not need a thing. But you do not realize that you are wretched, pitiful, poor, blind and naked" (Revelation 3:15-17).

These pictures of America and the Church are but a few of the alarming snapshots of our nation. As I thumb through the pages of our national album, I cannot help but feel a sting of shame. Our great and God-blessed nation has forsaken its once solid foundation of biblical principles. And much of the Church is spiritually impo-tent—void of a vital, personal, and intimate walk with God. Having fallen into the cult of the comfortable, the Church, for the most part, is no longer a power to be reckoned with. It has largely lost the respect of the masses; it is often the object of ridicule. Tragically, it has become the last place our nation would turn for help.

Our Great Resource

America is a great resource providing more money, technology, and manpower to help fulfill the Great Commission than all other countries combined. If the enemies of the gospel had their way, America would no longer be a great sending nation; Satan would take away all of our religious freedoms.

God does not tolerate sin. The Bible and history make this pain-fully clear. I believe God has given ancient Israel as an example of what will happen to the United States if we do not experience revival. He will continue to discipline us with all kinds of problems until we repent or until we are destroyed, as was ancient Israel because of her sin of disobedience.

The Lord sent all sorts of calamities upon Israel, trying to get her attention and cause her to repent:

And still you won't return to me," says the Lord. "Therefore I will bring upon you all these further evils I have spoken of. Prepare to meet your God in judgment, Israel. For you are dealing with the one who formed the mountains and made the winds, and knows your every thought ...Jehovah, the Lord, the Lord Almighty, is his name" (Amos 4:11-13, TLB).

This idea is reinforced with terrible warning in Deuteronomy 28:58-62:

"If you refuse to obey ... refusing reverence to the glorious and fearful name of Jehovah your God, then Jehovah will send perpetual plagues upon you and upon your children ... The Lord will bring upon you every sickness and plague there is, even those not mentioned in this book, until you are destroyed. There will be few of you left, though before you were as numerous as stars. All this if you do not listen to the Lord your God" (TLB).

God is calling the Church to rise up and lead the nation to repent and follow Him. Our only hope is a supernatural visit from God."

Satan's enemy is God. Therefore, his most enticing and least detectable attacks will be against God's children in the geographical area where Christianity is strongest. Satan is no dummy; he attacks where it will hurt God the most. We learn this from Adam and Eve, Israel, Jesus, and the early church. And in our earlier review of Matthew 4:1-10, we discovered that Satan did not tempt Jesus with the obvious vices of the world. He didn't tempt Him to deny God or to quit being religious. He tempted Jesus instead with self-serving attractions to step out on His own, to become independent and make his own decisions.

In Revelation 13:7 John states: **"He** (the beast-superpower) **was given power to make war against the saints and to conquer them."** The beast-system has been given power to make spiritual war against the saints and has overcome many, causing them to fall away from following true biblical Christian standards. This is another prophecy, given by John about the end-time beast superpower, which we are seeing fulfilled in America before our eyes.

"**M**en worshiped the dragon because he had given author-ity to the beast, and they also worshiped the beast and asked, "Who is like the beast? Who can make war against him?"** (Revela-tion 13:4).

Worship means to serve, venerate, or hold in awe. In this verse, John describes the attitude of the people on the Earth toward the last-days empire. The phrase, **"Who is like the beast? Who can make war against him?"** indicates military might without equal. John fore-tells of the time after this superpower recovers that it demonstrates awesome military power, and commands the respect and fear of peo-ples throughout the world.

The United States achieved this distinction on July 16, 1945, when scientists working near an old ranch house outside Alamo-gordo, New Mexico, detonated the first atomic bomb. Yankee tech-nological know-how and industrial might advanced scientific knowl-edge beyond anything that had gone on before. At 5:30 in the morn-ing, American and exiled European scientists triggered humanity's first nuclear weapon of war. With a blinding flash of light, a wave of heat ripped past the observers as they watched a giant mushroom cloud rise above the desert that day.

On August 6, 1945, a B-29 bomber named the *Enola Gay* dropped an atomic bomb on the city of Hiroshima. People and buildings be-came a black, boiling mass. Survivors of the blast wan-dered the streets in tattered clothes crying out for water. Seventy thousand people died in five minutes. Countless more died from burns and cancer in the next few months. Three days later, the United

States dropped a second bomb on Nagasaki. Another 80,000 died instantly. Japan surrendered unconditionally, pleading only for the emperor to remain on his throne.

Why President Truman decided to make the United States the only country in world history to use a nuclear weapon during a war remains something of a mystery. Marshall, Eisenhower, and MacArthur believed nuclear weapons to be unnecessary. Japan's war machine teetered on the brink of collapse; its factories idled for want of raw materials, its people starving on less than subsistence rations. But one truth is clear. Americans exacted revenge on the Japanese for the humiliation at Pearl Harbor. One nation alone possessed the power to convert cities into ashes and shadows, and the other nations of the world took notice. "America stands at this moment," said Winston Churchill in 1945, "at the summit of the world."

The attitude that prevailed after World War II, which John prophetically calls an attitude of worship or to "hold in awe," certainly describes the world's thinking after America defeated both Japan and Germany. Few would question the prophecy given in this verse. And still today, regardless of what people around the world think of the United States, they stand in awe of our lifestyle and our world leadership position.

"The beast was given a mouth to utter proud words and blasphemies and to exercise his authority for forty-two months. He opened his mouth to blaspheme God and to slander his name and his dwelling place and those who live in heaven" (Revelation 13:5-6).

In these two verses, the beast engages in three activities: (1) **"to utter proud** (haughty) **words,"** (2) **"to exercise authority for forty-two months,"** and (3) **"to blaspheme God."** We will look at each of these in turn.

To **"utter proud words"** is to promote ourselves as being better than others. It is to display a haughty attitude or arrogance in personal accomplishments. We Americans are a proud people, taking great pride in our worldly position, accomplishments, and conquests. **"There are six things the Lord hates, seven that are detestable to him: haughty** (proud) **eyes, a lying tongue, hands that shed innocent blood"** (Proverbs 6:16-17).

"To exercise authority for forty-two months." In the second verse of this chapter, John says that the superpower receives three worldly positions: power, worldly throne, and great authority. This superpower exercises this authority for a period of time and while doing so it uses the name of God irreverently in a way that misrepresents and injures His Holy name, which is blasphemy.

The phrase **"forty-two months"** adds up to three and a half years. In other prophecies the Bible has used this same period of time in a figurative sense, as was Hebrew custom, to mean a period of time the Lord does not make known. In the Hebrew tradition the period of 1260 days, the phrase **"time, times and half a time,"** and 42 months each equal the same period of time using the Jewish calendar. John used 1260 days and the phrase **"time, times and half a time"** this way in Revelation chapter 12.

"And he (the beast-superpower) **was given authority over every tribe, people, language and nation. All inhabitants of the earth will worship the beast—all whose names have not been written in the book of life belonging to the Lamb that was slain from the creation of the world"** (Revelation 13:7b - 8). John foretells of our effect on people all over the world. Throughout Scripture prophets often foretold of a condition or general state of affairs, even though the literal fulfillment of a happening may not fully occur. Daniel, for example, wrote of empires that controlled the world, yet Babylon, Persia, Greece, and Rome controlled only a limited part of the Earth's topography. They influenced the mainstream of civilization as will be the case with any superpower. Daniel is illustrating the power of these empires and their worldly influence over all peoples.

For John to write that this superpower in the last days of the

Church Age will exercise **"authority over every tribe, people, language, and nation"** does not disqualify America. Clearly, we do not directly control every person on the globe. Yet we do influence, in a general sense, nations and peoples throughout the world through the authority of our leadership in world politics, economics, military, and industrial power. The inhabitants of remote places receive American foreign aid, products, and American visitors. Those who do not speak English learn about American culture through music and the electronic media. Countries without formal political ties to the United States cannot escape our foreign policy. We are somewhat like a giant surrounded by tiny people; whether the giant walks, stands, sits, or lies down, others are affected. The phrase, **"all the inhabitants of the earth will worship the beast,"** is an expression similar to **"every tribe, people, language and nation."**

This completes our study of the descriptive characteristics in Revelation 13 that the Lord has used to prophetically describe the end-time beast superpower prophesied about in this chapter. I will discuss the rest of the verses in Revelation 13 after I discuss the descriptive verses about this superpower in the last days that are in the book of Daniel.

DANIEL AND THE END-TIME BEAST SUPERPOWER

Daniel writes of a "beast" with "ten horns," with a mouth that spoke boastfully just as John did. Could two men who lived centuries apart be describing the same vision? The short answer is yes and no. Both Daniel and John write of the last days superpower, but they each have a different reference point.

Daniel had a dream (Daniel 7:1) and visions passed through his mind. In his vision God revealed the worldly empires from Daniel's day until the end of time that would have a strong effect on the people of Israel. Following the destruction of Jerusalem by Roman legions in

70 AD, a great dispersion of the Jewish people throughout the world took place.

It was not until May 14, 1948 that the modern state of Israel began. Therefore, Daniel would not have prophesied about empires between 70 AD and 1948, because Israel did not exist as a nation during that time. Therefore, his prophecy was of those beasts or superpowers before 70 AD and the end-time superpower that has a great amount of influence on Israel after it became a nation in 1948. It is essential to understand that Daniel's prophecies were centered around his people, their nation, and those superpowers that helped shape Israel's history.

"After that, in my vision at night I looked, and there before me was a fourth beast terrifying and frightening and very powerful. It had large iron teeth; it crushed and devoured its victims and trampled under foot whatever was left. It was different from all the former beasts, and it had ten horns. While I was thinking about the horns, there before me was another horn, a little one, which came up among them; and three of the first horns were uprooted before it. This horn had eyes like the eyes of a man and a mouth that spoke boastfully" (Daniel 7:7-8).

In these two verses Daniel describes a ten-horned beast that is similar to the beast John describes. Daniel, however, is not describing the same beast as John. Daniel wanted to know the identity of this fourth beast, the unnamed beast with iron teeth. He wanted to know about the ten horns, and the horn that came up, before which three horns fell (Daniel 7:19-20). In the verses that follow, Daniel receives his answers. **"The fourth beast is a fourth kingdom that will appear on earth. It will be different from all the other kingdoms and will devour the whole earth, trampling it down and crushing it. The ten horns are ten kings who will come from this kingdom. After them another king will arise, different from the earlier ones; he will subdue**

three kings. He will speak against the Most High and oppress his saints and try to change the set times and the laws. The saints will be handed over to him for a time, times and half a time" (Daniel 7:23-25).

History and Bible scholars agree that the "fourth beast" is the Roman Empire. "Horn" and "king" refer to nations with substantial power and influence, but not a superpower. We discussed the prophetic meaning of "horn" earlier when studying verse one of Revelation 13. "Little horn" has the meaning of a young or new nation. The little horn grew out of the ten horns but remained *distinct* or separate from them. This is the meaning of the Hebrew word translated as "among" in verse 8.

Daniel prophesied of those world empires in existence from his time until the end of time that greatly influenced Israel as a nation. The little horn or nation he introduces in chapter 7, which arises out of the countries from the Roman Empire, will be that super power influencing Israel after she regains her position as a nation near the end of time. **We are that young new nation** and have been the ruling influential power over Israel since the historical event of their regaining their homeland in 1948.

DANIEL'S PROPHECY

Putting these interpretations together reveals a prophecy that unfolds like this:

1. Out of the Roman Empire emerges a bloc of prominent countries.

2. Out of this bloc comes a new country comprised of people from the Roman Empire.

3. This new country defeats three of the other countries in order to achieve its separate status.

4. This new country gains power and influence to an extent greater than any of the countries from which its people came.

5. After reaching the status of a power with worldwide influence, this new country begins to turn on the saints. The nation wears down the saints to the point of overwhelming them.

6. Christians are worn down or defeated for an unknown period of **"time, times and a half time."**

During this period as a part of this new nation oppressing the saints, the government begins changing its laws. This we have done in this last generation; i.e. abortion, public prayer, censoring use of the name of God in government facilities and the classroom, lack of censorship in the electronic media, etc.

These six events describe America quite well. Europe emerged from its position as the northern region of Rome's empire, and the United States came together from the peoples of Europe. We defeated three of the nations from the Roman Empire in the development of our nation—England, France, and Spain. We went on to become a superpower, after which our government began to turn against the saints by changing the laws of its society. Daniel even prophesied that Christians would be overwhelmed by the spiritual attacks the enemy works through the influence of this superpower.

No other country even comes close to fulfilling these prophecies. America, barely 200 years old, became a superpower—the mightiest empire in world history. As a worldwide empire, we have had a unique influence over both the Jewish people as prophesied by Daniel and Christians as prophesied by John in Revelation 13. John and Daniel both prophesied of this last government superpower, and their approach is similar, but from different points of reference.

REVIVED ROMAN EMPIRE

The beast that John and Daniel prophesied about is without a doubt the ancient Roman Empire reappearing upon the world scene. Many historians and scholars have described a resemblance between the old Roman Empire and contemporary American society. The two societies share common characteristics, such as government, commerce, militarism; and an emphasis on hedonistic things, such as food, pleasure, athletics, building, and deterioration of moral standards. So similar are the two that a recent President commissioned a study to learn why Rome collapsed so that America might avoid the same collapse.

It is interesting to note that many of the first to settle North America trace their ancestors to the ancient Roman Empire. Rome controlled central Europe along with Britain, and many of the first immigrants were of German, Dutch, French, and English stock. John indicates that Rome's reappearance will display a particular characteristic. In Revelation 12:17 he saw Satan standing **"on the sand of the sea."** Indicating that this new superpower, which Daniel says comes up out of the Roman Empire, takes place across the sea.

The spirit of the revived Roman Empire bears a similarity to the fulfillment of a prophecy during the time of Jesus. When Jesus walked the Earth, Jewish scholars anticipated the reappearance of the prophet Elijah because according to Old Testament the prophet would precede the coming of the Messiah. Scripture says that this prophecy was fulfilled by John the Baptist (Matthew 11:14, Luke 1:17). John the Baptist fulfilled the prophecy because his personality and character, or spirit, were like that of Elijah's. In this same way the United States fulfills the prophesied reappearance of the Roman Empire. The same spirit that prevailed in pagan Rome characterizes contemporary American society. And just as religious leaders in Jesus' day failed to recognize the fulfillment of the prophecy concerning Elijah, many Christians do not realize that we fulfill the description of the prophecy concerning the reviving of the ancient Roman Empire.

A DRAGON JOINS THE BEAST

As we return to Revelation 13 the last verse we discussed was verse 8. The next two verses in this chapter, verses 9 and 10 state, **"He who has an ear, let him hear. If anyone is to go into captivity, into captivity he will go. If anyone is to be killed with the sword, with the sword he will be killed. This calls for patient endurance and faithfulness on the part of the saints."** We'll come back to these two verses later.

"Then I saw another beast, coming out of the earth; it had two horns like a lamb, but it spoke like a dragon" (Revelation 13:11). The first beast arose out of the sea (Revelation 13:1). This represents the United States becoming a superpower. This second beast that John now prophesies about arose out of the earth. It is subject to, and serves the interests of, the first beast. This second beast symbolizes the power of American society; specifically the teaching influence and values that develop through modern technology after the first beast gains the throne of the world. Its influence is so powerful, so dynamic, that John also makes reference to it as a beast. This second beast appears harmless, like a lamb, but represents the perverted values that accompany the first beast's ascendancy to power, and it speaks like a dragon—promoting values alien to what should be in a normal society (Daniel 7:25). Reading John's prophetic words, this second beast has the appearance of a false prophet, proclaiming godly interest while teaching false values about spiritual matters and standards.

We are, it cannot be denied, engaged in another revolutionary war. This revolution is a cultural war fought over the hearts and minds of the American people and their lifestyle. Our government occupies a central place in this unholy war against the saints. Each year, tens of thousands of new regulations appear, designed to control more aspects of American lives. They want Americans to believe that these measures are for our betterment. The truth is there is really very little truth presented by the government and the media.

The call for the emancipation of children, the abolition of the family, the promotion of promiscuity, the obliteration of private life and the installation of Orwellian controls over every aspect of life are things that have been on our government's agenda in what can only be called the greatest onslaught against American Christianity since the birth of our nation.

THERE IS A MIND BEHIND THE SYSTEM

This cultural war, this uprooting within a single generation of America's traditional way of life has not happened on its own. Our values have not slipped by accident or morality spontaneously decayed. No, not at all! John identifies the spiritual force behind the corruption of America. This second beast has orchestrated the transformation of this nation for a purpose, by means of a strategy intended to destroy the will of those who would resist. The strategy is to permanently alter the way in which people think about social problems and individual actions.

Satan has utilized the material world, the people of the world, and the value systems of the world. He has raised up in our society, a society that exalts itself far above all the other societies of the world. American society has perfected all of the characteristics of this world system, and consequently has developed great power to tempt Christians to step outside of God's Word. The result is many Christians are now preoccupied with serving self: my well being, my pleasures, my desires, my ambitions, things being done my way. It has been the influence of our society-system that is causing people to set themselves up in the temple of God serving themselves as if they were a god (recall our study of II Thessalonians 2:1-4).

The church has often presented the concept that the beast in the book of Revelation is some kind of monstrosity. One of the oldest literary devices is to make good things beautiful and evil things ugly. In the stories and legends we learned as children, bad things are represented by monsters, hags, and subhuman figures, while good things are presented by handsome young men and fair maidens. Artists use a scaly, horned figure with a tail to depict the Devil himself, yet the Scripture reveals that he appears **"as an angel of light"** (II Corinthians 11:14). As John prophetically describes in Revelation 13:11, the teaching power (two horns) of our society (beast out of the earth), may appear harmless (like a lamb) but the spirit of the philosophy being taught (spoke like a dragon) in our culture since the first beast came to power has been an overwhelming influence to develop the anti-Christ characteristics centered in serving self. This is the very character and teaching of Satan! (See II Timothy 3:1-5 and Isaiah 14:12-14.)

"It (the second beast) **exercises all the authority of the first beast in its presence, and makes the earth and its inhabitants worship the first beast, whose mortal wound had been healed. It works great signs, even making fire come down from heaven to earth in the sight of men; and by the signs which it is allowed to work in the presence of the beast, it deceives those who dwell on earth, bidding them make an image for the beast which was wounded by the sword and yet lived; and it was allowed to give breath to the image of the beast so that the image of the beast should even speak, and to cause those who would not worship the image of the beast to be slain. Also it causes all, both small and great, both rich and poor, both free and slave, to be marked on the right hand or the forehead, so that no one can buy or sell unless he has the mark, that is, the name of the beast or the number of its name"** (Revelation 13:12-17 RSV).

In the past, great empires or superpowers have relied on military might and political clout to dominate and control other countries. They would plunder the goods of the people and often place heavy taxes on them. Even in modern times, communism, for example, ruled through the barrel of a gun. But the beast superpower of Revelation 13 uses a uniquely different method of power to influence and dominate other peoples. It rules through the technological power of its society (the second beast which came up out of the earth) to produce and supply other nations with their goods and services.

Since World War II, our society's tremendous advancement in world leadership has primarily been the outgrowth of our electronic technology. Most of these developments we take for granted and consider commonplace, but John accurately describes what he saw which have been great and miraculous signs, even causing fire to come down from Heaven to Earth in full view of men—space shots, etc., for example done on behalf of the first beast—our government.

I am not saying that there is anything inherently wrong with electricity or electronic technology. It is a part of God's creation; electric power can be used for many wonderful things. But Satan controls the world; therefore, many of the things electricity makes possible are going to be part of his system. Television provides a direct means of mind control, a powerful means of influence that may appear harmless, but deceives because it overdevelops the sense of serving self. Anything that has the ability to plant thoughts in our minds is a teacher, a potential deceiver.

The creation of electronic media in the last generation has allowed Satan to capture human imagination as never before in human history. It has provided Satan with a medium of teaching influence for every minute of every hour of every day. The idea that there should be a time and space reserved for family life hardly exists. And being by far the largest exporter of TV programming we impact people around the world with our immoral lifestyle presenting our perverse values through the power of the second beast.

An Image

John states that our society will fashion an "image" for the first beast. Since our main source of power has been developed through the technology of electronics, it would be logical that the kind of image would be an electronic image. The Greek word used for image is *eikon*, a word that means "representation" and "manifestation." It is a representation or manifestation of the first beast which is crafted by the second, and is used, as John says in verse Revelation 13:17, **"so that no one could buy or sell unless he has the mark."** John's prophetic language is not as incomprehensible as it may appear. John is saying that out of our society (the second beast) there will be a product developed that will give the ability for our Government (the first beast) through some means (the image) by which the government (the first beast) can control (by use of the mark) the commercial activities (the buying and selling) of its citizens.

Consistent with the description given by John's prophecy, it appears this image has been developed; more specifically, the electronic computer. No other machine in human history matches the influence of the computer. Since World War II, when America began to reign over Satan's kingdom—the world—this amazing machine has become part of every facet of public and private life. Computers perform such an astonishing array of activities that modern life, as we live it today, would be impossible without them. They possess a powerful technological brain, the microchip.

The entire world of commerce and industry now functions by use of computers. Transportation, from interstate trucking to airlines, relies on computers for everything from navigation to the scheduling of maintenance. Medicine, from diagnosing illness to filling prescriptions to cure them; department stores, banks, hospitals, utilities, post offices, universities, every modern institution, and so on function by means of computer technology. The electronic computer is truly an image, or representation and manifestation, of a human creation using modern-day technology that fulfills John's prophecy.

I know very little about computers. It is not difficult to see, however, that the harnessing of the Earth's electromagnetic force of electricity, which appeared solely as lightning in the sky just a few hundred years ago, has resulted in devices capable of performing complex human activities, including reproduction of the human voice. This fits John's references of the second beast's ability to make fire come down from Heaven to Earth and give breath to the image of the first beast, so that it could speak. Several years ago Time Magazine, January 3, 1983, announced its man of the year for 1982 was not a man, but the computer.

Earlier I said that I would delay making a comment about Revelation 13 verses 9-10, this is because John's statement in Revelation 13:15b is similar. In verses 9-10 he said, **"He who has an ear, let him hear. If anyone is to go into captivity, into captivity he will go. If anyone is to be killed with the sword, with the sword he will be killed. This calls for patient endurance and faithfulness on the part of the saints."** In Revelation 13:15b he says, **"to cause those who would not worship the image of the beast to be slain."** It appears from John's statement in these verses, that some day in the future those who remain loyal to Christ and refuse to be controlled by a computer system could face prison and persecution.

"Also it causes all, both small and great, both rich and poor, both free and slave, to be marked on the right hand or the forehead, so that no one can buy or sell unless he has the mark" (Revelation 13:16-17a RSV). Some day in the future it will be necessary for the superpower to control economic transactions. I don't know what all these commercial regulations will entail, but some kind of marking system will be imposed. Did you know that computers read marks not numbers? A marking system of the kind John describes has already been developed. It can be found on practically every item on grocery and retail store shelves. It is called the Universal Product Code (UPC), which to the consumer looks like a series of vertical lines covering an area about the size of a large postage stamp. The UPC symbol technology has been in use in our country since 1973.

What is of interest from the perspective of Bible prophecy is that every UPC code contains at least three unidentified marks that correspond to the number 666. Students of Bible prophecy know that sixes are among the secrets of the economy destined to close out this, the Gentile Age. These three unidentified marks that you will see in any UPC code are the key working numbers for every version of the UPC code. Computer experts I have consulted told me that the triple-six pattern has become a universal design standard; it cannot be changed.

Why is the number six the key in reading the marks on a UPC code? Computer technicians say that 6 is the perfect computer number. It is the perfect number because computers work on a series of six cores that allow current to change direction in order to perform switching operations. The formula for this system is 6 60 6. The six cores work in conjunction with 60 displacements X 6 (one character—one bit of information). To number a card, person, or item, the transaction must be prefixed six hundred, threescore, and six, just as John said in Revelation 13:18. Apple Computer Inc. celebrated the number 6 when it introduced the Apple 1 which retailed for $666.66.

Although the bar codes on grocery items are the most noticeable, credit and bank cards also make use of bar codes. These are micro-encoded along the magnetic strip on the back of the card. When these marks are scanned by laser light, the optical pattern is converted to an electrical signal (analog), which is converted in turn to a digital signal, then decoded by a microprocessor. Literally tens of thousands of characters can be micro-encoded on the three by one half inch magnetic strip on a single card. It is possible to record a personal record of every person's purchases, transactions, and so on.

The question is always asked, when do I think our system of economic control will unfold? That I don't know! The technology for a cashless society already exists. Credit cards make the introduction of a national identification card possible right now. In addition, existing technology could be used to implant information beneath the skin on the head, arm, or some other place on the body. And new technology is constantly being introduced. The manipulation for using such technology for social control might follow a major social or political event, appear in the aftermath of a natural disaster, or result from the fallout of a major economic shake-up.

HEAVY DEBT

I am not an economic whiz, but it is not difficult to understand why many economists are warning that the heavy debt we have incurred over the last 15 to 20 years will some day have to be paid back. For some, this heavy debt is a matter of greed. They already have more than most people in the world, but still are not satisfied. However, for most Americans, heavy indebtedness is a matter of ignoring economic reality. We have grown accustomed to the material possessions that make up what we call "the good life" and few seem to realize that they have become victims of a worldly deception that ensnares people through irresistible advertising and product availability.

We have been led to expect a lifestyle that is getting harder and harder to achieve. Therefore, the widening gap between expectations and capabilities has created a nearly irresistible dependence on credit. Buying on credit is the only way for many Americans to get what we now think of as our birthright. Few understand the reality of our nation's economic position in comparison to the rest of the world. We have fallen into heavy debt. Personal debt has reached a record high; savings an all-time low. Government is in the same boat. Cities, states, and the Federal Government must borrow in order to maintain public services. Credit has put a stranglehold on our economy.

As a result we have dug ourselves into an economic black hole. During the 1980s, our country shifted from being the largest creditor nation in the world to being the largest debtor nation. People face huge personal debt. Corporations juggle massive business debt. Government operates with huge deficits.

Because we supplied the rest of the world with many of its goods and services after World War II when other countries lost their industrial infrastructure, huge amounts of dollars poured into our country. America developed a standard of living that was unheard of. That was not the case before World War II. But in recent years we have artificially maintained this living standard through credit. The insurmountable debt that has resulted does not look good.

Few politicians and corporate chieftains seem willing to admit this, but our years of unconscious overspending cannot be eradicated. No matter what the politicians promise, record indebtedness could ultimately result in financial judgment.

In a larger sense, what the government does or doesn't do at this point won't make much difference. Current "solutions" to the debt crisis amount to economic fiction rather than sound economic thinking. Take the idea of consumer spending. The notion is that the economy will be healthy as long as consumer spending remains strong. In other words, everybody will be poorer unless people spend more than they can afford. That just doesn't make sense!

Many economists predict there is no way to spend our way out of this economic crisis—that is the bottom line. Whether consumers spend more, or spend less; whether the government taxes more, or taxes less, the debt will continue to grow. Traditional methods taken to prop up the economy simply are not feasible. No conventional solutions are available because this is an unheard of economic problem.

The "spirit of merchandising" has grabbed people's hearts and many American families now depend on two incomes to meet their debt obligations. The loss of one income even for a brief period would tilt them dangerously close to financial ruin. At the root of this economic vulnerability is our failure to live within our means. Consumer debt, mortgage debt, government debt, plus corporate debt and other private debt has risen in a vain effort to maintain our present standard of living. <u>We have mortgaged the future to pay for the present.</u>

At some stage we will reach that critical point where the rising debt collides with falling earnings. When the right portion of debt goes unpaid, the credit system that drives our economy will falter. What will break the camel's back—the shock that will trigger a major economic change is unknown.

I do know that there could be significant social and political fallout to a major economic catastrophe. A major financial panic might bring civil disorder, violence, and unimaginable chaos, not necessarily because Americans will lack basic necessities, but because we will be denied the things we want. This is not the same in our country as it was during the Great Depression. During the 1930s, the majority of people were accustomed to working hard for simple necessities. The generation that survived the Depression was glad to have enough to eat, something to wear, and a roof over their heads. But our self-centered, materialistic, technology dependent generation will not be content with that.

If this should happen few Americans will resist government intervention; in fact many will probably demand it. It will open the door that will give our government great incentive to eliminate perceived threats to the economy by extending control over buying and selling. It could be easy for government leaders of the beast-system to promise social order in return for absolute compliance.

It is difficult to say what these commercial regulations will entail, but Bible prophecy clearly points to that day when our superpower government will control economic transactions. A marking system of some kind will be imposed as John prophesied, **"...so that no one could buy or sell unless he has the mark, that is, the name of the beast or the number of its name"** (Revelation 13:17 RSV). He tied the marking system with the numbering system of the beast society as the method used for control. As stated earlier, a computer reads "marks" not numbers. Only by the wisdom of God could John have known this.

"This calls for wisdom: let him who has understanding reckon the number of the beast, for it is a human number, its number is six hundred and sixty-six (666)" (Revelation 13:18 RSV). I have mentioned the Universal Product Code, which is not only used in retail trade, but is now used throughout most industries. The number 6 is the key to the computer's ability to read the UPC. Is this what John saw when he wrote this prophecy and stated the number is 666? It could be. It fits.

However, beyond the physical application of this prophecy I think there could also be a spiritual application. The number 6 throughout Scripture is the number for man; his doings, coming and going. The fact the Lord used three 6's in closing out this spiritual warfare prophecy is something that needs to be considered when seeking to find a spiritual application. I will give you something to ponder.

The make-up of a human being consist of three parts; body, soul, and spirit. The number of man in Scripture is 6. Three 6's would indicate the whole of man; all three parts. According to this prophecy, a time is coming when the beast-system will implement the control of buying and selling by requiring people to receive a physical mark. The reason why we would be open to receive this mark is because of our desire to serve ourselves, a condition that has captured the hearts of many people in our country. It is a spiritual condition that the enemy has been able to work through the beast-system to constantly tempt us to develop, which is to serve ourselves over and above what is normal; a spiritual condition that we discussed earlier. It causes us to oppose the laws of God by setting ourselves up in the temple of God so that we can serve ourselves as if we were a god. That is how the beast-system has overcome the saints. We studied through this in our review of Revelation 13:7a and II Thessalonians 2:1-4.

If we tied this prophecy of receiving the mark of the beast to the prophecy in II Thessalonians 2:1-4 this would indicate that if we reach a spiritual condition to serve ourselves like a god, then our spiritual condition is such that we would be more open to receive the physical mark when that time comes. Could this understanding be the wisdom called for in Revelation 13:18?

LIVING WITHIN THE BEAST SYSTEM

We don't want to make unwise decisions because we are living within the beast system of Revelation 13. We need to realize that the word "beast" as used in Bible prophecy is not referring to some kind of ugly, foul monstrosity. It is simply a word that the prophets used to refer to a superpower. Daniel also used animals as a way to describe a superpower's authority and so did John. At times we in the church have depicted the word beast to mean some kind of monster. That is false!

We are to live in the physical world, even though we are no longer a member of the spiritual kingdom of the world. Believers should not attempt to escape from the beast-system, but we must learn to live the successful Christian life within its dominion. We were bought at a price, reborn spiritually, and are now members of God's Kingdom to be the **salt of the earth** and the **light of the world**. You may wonder then, what specifically, is the responsible attitude that a Christians should have living under the beast-system?

The answer is found in the book of Romans where Paul instructs those Christians living under another superpower, called a beast in prophetic Scripture, the Roman Empire. In the first seven verses of Chapter 13, Paul explains the nature of a Christian's citizenship in this world. Paul did not teach believers to be anarchists, or to revolt. He taught those who feared God to respect the institution of government. God had instituted human governments to promote peaceable society and restrain selfishness and greed. This principle of respect applies to all governments. ***"Everyone must submit himself***

to the governing authorities," Paul writes, **"for there is no authority except that which God has established"** (Romans 13:1).

I understand why it may be difficult to respect a government
that performs its God ordained mission so poorly. Since our government gained the throne of the world after World War II as John prophesied (Revelation 13:2), it has allowed the spirit of lawlessness to grow
worse and worse. American society has become violent and lawless,
and our government seems powerless to control this violence. Too
many of those living in the United States fear nothing. No longer does
the fear of government exist because our government has proven inca-
pable of retribution. The United States government is failing its God-
ordained responsibility to maintain order.

Nevertheless, Paul says that Christians must not contribute to
this disorder. **"He who rebels against the authority is rebelling
against what God has instituted, and those who do so will bring
judgment on themselves"** (Romans 13:2). Government, no matter
how terrible, is not necessarily a warning of bad news for those who
fear God. Government is **"God's servant, an agent of wrath to
bring punishment on the wrongdoer"** (Romans 13:4), and
Christians must **"...submit to the authorities, not only because of
possible punishment but also because of conscience"** (Romans
13:5). Only if we are told to deny the Lord and go against His teachings would we take a stand and then it should not be with a rebellious
attitude but with the love and nature of God.

Christians are to live in a law abiding, respectful, and cooperative
manner. The ideal Christian concept of citizenship is to be a model subject of earthly authority. **"Give everyone what you owe him: If you
owe taxes, pay taxes; if revenue, then revenue; if respect, then
respect; if honor, then honor"** (Romans 13:7). It is much easier to criticize this nation's leaders than to pray for them, but pray for them is what
believers must do. **"I urge, then, first of all, that requests, prayers,
intercession and thanksgiving be made for everyone —for kings**

and all those in authority, that we may live peaceful and quiet lives in all godliness and holiness" (I Timothy 2:1-2).

WHAT DOES IT ALL MEAN

This concludes our examination of this end-time spiritual warfare chapter Revelation 13. Understanding the prophecy in this chapter is the root cause of Satan's success in his warfare against America and is the central core of my corrective action plan for Campaign Save Christian America. This is a spiritual truth that if you believe and apply it, will set you spiritually free in your heart from the bondage of our world system that has spiritually imprisoned many Christians.

CHAPTER EIGHTEEN

Y ou have now read my corrective action plan for my campaign. Knowing the truth, how then shall we live? Is there a certain formula that should be followed for these last days? Actually I caution you against any kind of physical action as your primary goal. Most of us will think of some good practical suggestions in the physical realm and they may be important, but it involves a lot more than that. The situation before us is of a spiritual, not physical nature, although spiritual guidance is carried out in the physical like the <u>spiritual characteristics</u> that I discussed earlier from The Sermon on the Mount. Jesus illustrated how they would physically be expressed in our life by what He said in the balance of this sermon after first stating these spiritual characteristic of the Kingdom of Heaven.

In Luke 17:26 Jesus said as it was in the days of Noah so shall it be in the last days. **"By faith Noah, when warned about things not yet seen, in holy fear built an ark to save his family"** (Hebrews 11:7). Noah was <u>moved by holy fear</u> to build an ark. Having a proper and healthy holy fear of the Lord is the key for building your ark for these last days.

I have shared that it was in the fall of 1969 that the Lord directed my wife and me to take six children into our home whose parents had been tragically killed in an automobile accident. Being fairly young at the time, we became very dependent on the Lord to lead us in the task of raising our expanded family.

God began to open our eyes to the deceptive attacks of Satan's spiritual warfare in the early1970s. The Lord showed my wife and me through various prophetic Scriptures why Satan would be as successful as he has been in accomplishing his objective of overcoming Christians. By faith we believed what the Lord was showing us. The fruit of our society over this past generation clearly shows that what the Lord began to teach us in early 1970 has now come to pass.

More than anything else, the insights from the Lord about these prophetic Scriptures along with my own research and study became the building materials we needed, to build our spiritual ark to raise godly children in an increasingly godless society. These building materials are what I have shared in this book. At the writing of this book, we have 54 in our family including children and their spouses, grandchildren and great grandchildren. Every one of them, except the few that are still too young, has made a commitment to serve the Lord.

I have now written 6 books, along with several small booklets and newsletters that pertain directly or indirectly to the spiritual warfare in our country. Nearly two million copies have been distributed. In addition to my writing, I have served several years as an elder and teacher at church. In 1974 my wife and I founded Paradise Valley Christian School in Phoenix, Arizona, which today is one of the major Christian schools in the Phoenix area serving Christians from all Christian denominations (visit web site www.paradisevalleychristian.org). In 1991, we founded Christian Life Outreach, which publishes Christian materials (web site www.christianlifeoutreach.org) and has an outreach project called Help the World Direct, a missionary outreach to help the poor and needy in Kenya, East Africa through medicine and health care (web site www.christianlifeoutreach.org). In 1988, we founded Golden Eagle Christian Center, a fully equipped Christian retreat center in Palestine, Ohio that churches and Christian groups use for training and fellowship retreats (web site www.christianlifeoutreach.org, then click on Golden Eagle Christian Center). My work employment since 1959 has been in the aluminum industry where most of the time I have served at the executive level of management. In 1997 I founded my own company, ALEXCO, a manufacturing company that produces high tech aluminum extruded alloys for the aerospace industry that are used in the manufacturing of airplanes (visit web site www.alexcoaz.com).

Recently I was called by the Lord to start a campaign on a much larger scale than in the past, to share with people the spiritual warfare principles that the Lord has been teaching me and my wife since the early 1970s. I am calling this effort Campaign Save Christian America (web site www.campaignsaveamerica.com).

I mention these things because I don't know of any better way to communicate how the Lord can work through our lives after we have been set free from our attachment and bondage to the ways of the world. Not one of these efforts has been a burden to us and our family. We have experienced many miraculous blessings along the way in the development of each one and they continue to happen!

As you can see by our activity, we are not to take ourselves out of the world, but learn to live the Christian life as best as we can within its dominion. I caution you about this because it is normal to react in a physical way of taking ourselves away, out of the beast's system of influence. However, that is not the answer. We are to follow the principles taught in the Bible that teach us how to spiritually prepare ourselves to live in the world, but not be a part of the world's ways.

Spiritual preparation is the key. We need to know the mind of the Lord in these trying times of heavy spiritual warfare. And there is no set formula for everyone, everybody's situation is different. Therefore, we need guidelines or spiritual principles to follow that can apply and work for every person.

I will share with you a word the Lord gave me about living in these last days: FEAR NOT THE DAYS TO COME, BUT FEAR THIS ONLY: THAT YOU SHALL WALK IN A MANNER PLEASING TO THE LORD. According to Scripture a holy fear is spiritually proper and healthy, one that is pleasing to the Lord.

There was a major spiritual deterioration of God's standards in Noah's day and according to the prophecy of Jesus in comparing our day to the days of Noah, it is a great concern for the Lord in our day. It is obvious by the fruit of our society and in the body of Christ that few of us are prepared to meet the spiritual challenges of the vicious spiritual warfare that has come upon America during this last generation.

If our day is similar to the days of Noah, then a good source for gaining wisdom about preparing for our troubled times in these last days is to review the attitude and activities of Noah. The Bible says, **"By faith Noah, when warned about things not yet seen, in holy fear built an ark to save his family"** (Hebrews 11:7).

The **first** thing that motivated Noah to prepare himself and his family was his faith. He believed God's warning! Before anything else, to spiritually prepare ourselves to live in these last days Barbara and I had to believe what God taught us through the prophecy recorded in Revelation 13. Before being able to understand and accept direction from God and His Word about how we should live in these last days we first had to have faith in His warning. All things in our relationship with the Lord begin with our faith. The same truth applied in this situation. If we don't believe, would we be willing to step out in faith to follow the Lord's direction in how we should live to be pleasing to Him?

The **second** important thing we learned about Noah's preparation was his attitude. After receiving a warning from God, which he believed, he stepped out in faith with an attitude of *holy fear* within his character and took action. This is critical! Holy fear is what motivates us to adhere to God's standards and not give in to worldly standards. Believing the warning we received about America becoming the superpower of Revelation 13 in these last days put within us a healthy holy fear in our walk with the Lord.

As it is in our day, Godly standards had been lost in Noah's day. But possessing a holy fear of God in his character, Noah cultivated a deep reliance on God and a love for God's standards. This verse says of Noah, **"... in holy fear built an ark to save his family."** Walking in holy fear led him to take action to save his family. Obedience was the key to his success and it is our key to live a victorious Christian life. He trusted in God and His Word completely. His obedience was foremost in his mind because he had a proper fear or respect for the Lord. This same attitude is what will keep us and help save Christianity in America.

" ... Learn to fear the Lord your God..." (Deuteronomy 31:12). **"The Lord confides in those who fear him..."** (Psalm 25:14). **"Let all the earth fear the Lord"** (Psalm 33:8). **"But the eyes of the Lord are on those who fear him..."** (Psalm 33:18). **"The angel of the Lord encamps around those who fear him, and He delivers them"** (Psalm 34:7). **"...for those who fear him lack nothing"** (Psalm 34:9). **"... through the fear of the Lord a man avoids evil"** (Proverbs 16:6). **"To fear the Lord is to hate evil..."** (Proverbs 8:13). **"He who fears the Lord has a secure fortress, and for his children it will be a refuge"** (Proverbs 14:26). **"Then the church ... was strengthened; and encouraged by the Holy Spirit...living in the fear of the Lord"** (Acts 9:31). **"...live your lives as strangers here in reverent fear"** (I Peter 1:17).

There are several other verses that touch on the subject of having a proper fear of the Lord. To have a holy fear is to stand in awe of and have a deep respect for God's holiness and His standards. Possession of this characteristic is what gives us that inner desire to avoid sin. It gives us a conscious desire to avoid anything we are aware of that would displease the Lord. Obedience to the Lord becomes our utmost priority.

To have a proper holy fear of the Lord means to seek His will in all things—to examine every aspect of what is going on in our life with God's Word. To be in God's will is a deep concern and a driving force behind every thought and action.

Holy fear develops the desire to subject everything in our lives to the same exacting standard: <u>Is this pleasing to God?</u> Holy fear develops a heart that is pure, open to conviction and repentance. It allows the Lord to open our spiritual eyes. <u>Holy fear gives us discernment.</u>

To stay in line spiritually, we need to have a proper fear of the Lord. If we don't, we will take certain things for granted. We will lose our sensitivity and alertness to the influence of the world around us. We can easily develop spiritual pride and take liberties, which will not only affect our spiritual walk but will hurt others. Without holy fear, our heart can quickly become hypocritical in certain areas. We won't have a fear of sinning as we should. We become negligent in seeking righteousness.

Holy fear is needed for a healthy spiritual walk. Jesus always kept His eyes on the mark. He avoided sin at every turn. He never wavered. A proper holy fear will help keep us from straying from God's standards and towards worldly standards. It will help keep us from being easily led astray by those who have gotten off the track.

It is a sure indication that we don't have the kind of holy fear towards God that Noah had and that Scripture talks about, if our standards as a Christian allow us to walk along the edge of the darkness in the world. We must strive to stay as far away as possible from worldly values and give no advantage to Satan. We must have a strong desire to avoid sin at every turn, to walk uprightly in a manner pleasing to Him, and to live in awe of the Lord. This is what it takes to build the spiritual ark we need to keep us from the pressures, temptations, and trials of our day.

Those who have a fear of the Lord have nothing to be afraid of from the world in the days to come no matter what happens. In God's family, great courage against the enemy begins with a proper <u>holy fear of the Lord</u>. According to Scripture, the Lord will protect us regardless of the circumstances if we have a <u>healthy fear of the Lord</u>.

Another Scripture that is worth our consideration when discussing how then shall we live in these last days is II Chronicles 7:14. You hear this verse quoted quite often these days. I like it because at the time God gave this Word to Solomon for the Israelites it was during a time of great prosperity. The conditions then were similar to those in America; we are living in a time of great prosperity. It states, **"if my people, who are called by my name, will humble themselves and pray and seek my face and turn from their wicked ways, then will I hear from heaven and will forgive their sin and will heal their land"** (II Chronicles 7:14).

This verse is obviously directed to God's people, which today would be Christians. It is important for us to see the Lord's direction in this verse is prefaced with the word **"if."** There are several conditions we must follow before the promise at the end of the verse will be fulfilled.

The **first "if"** condition is: **"will humble themselves."** You may recall that humility, or meekness, was one of the key heart characteristics that Jesus emphasized in His "Sermon on the Mount."

The characteristic of pride in the American people has definitely become a problem and has made a heavy contribution to the moral conditions we now find in our country. Pride stands in the way of true spiritual love, the ability to give of oneself without recognition, which is the very nature of God. Pride is the opposite of being broken. God revives a humble and broken heart: **"The sacrifices of God are a broken spirit; a broken and contrite heart, O God, you will not despise"** (Psalm 51:17). **God says, "...I hate pride and arrogance..."** (Proverbs 8: 13). **"Pride only breeds quarrels ..."** (Proverbs 13:10). **"The Lord detests all the proud of heart..."** (Proverbs 16:5). **"Before his downfall a man's heart is proud..."** (Proverbs 18:12). **"Live in harmony with one another. Do not be proud, but be willing to associate with people of low position. Do not be conceited"** (Romans 12:16). **"...God opposes the proud but gives grace to the**

humble" (James 4:6). Pride has become one of the greatest spiritual problems in the American church.

The **second "if"** condition in this verse is to **pray**; the **third "if"** is to **seek God's face**. There is a lot of good material available about both prayer and seeking God's face. It is important that we become well-informed about these two subjects.

The **fourth "if"** condition, **"turn from their wicked ways."** To turn from means to repent. Their wicked ways means that God's people must turn from following the ways of the world and seek His righteousness. I have fully discussed this subject in this book.

For the next Great Awakening to take place in America all of the **"if"** conditions must become a daily part of our Christian life. This principle applies to an individual, a church, or even a nation.

For Christians to prepare themselves to fulfill God's mission for America in these last days to be salt and light: We must have faith in God's warning, develop a holy fear in our hearts, follow His instructions of humbling ourselves, praying, seeking His face, repenting, and seeking His righteousness. It is then He will heal our land. Is this going to happen? Only the Lord knows! Regardless if it does or does not, our call, as with the plan of salvation, is to commit to seek the Lord to see what we can do to help make it happen. God's relationship with mankind since the day Adam and Eve fell has always been to save. Every Christian is called to be a soldier in God's army. There is no option. We can only be one of three things: A warrior, a deserter, or a POW. Would you choose to become a warrior and help us save Christianity in America? The least we can do is to commit to save Christian standards and values in the American church.

A personal word to you from the Lord: **"In righteousness you will be established: Tyranny will be far from you; you will have nothing to fear. Terror will be far removed; it will not come near you. If anyone does attack you, it will not be my doing; whoever attacks you will surrender to you. 'See, it is I who created the** blacksmith who fans the coals into flame and forges a weapon fit for its work. And it is I who have created the destroyer to work havoc; no weapon forged against you will prevail, and you will refute every tongue that accuses you. This is the heritage of the servants of the Lord, and this is their vindication from me,' declares the Lord." (Isaiah 54:14-17).

Books & Booklets by Bob Fraley—Order Form

Books

Qty.	Title	Each	Total
_____	Salt & Light-Fulfilling God's Mission ....$14.95.........		_____
_____	The Last Days in America ....$ 8.95.........		_____
_____	Holy Fear ....$ 7.95.........		_____
_____	Prepare Yourself (10 copies @ $1.00 each) ....$ 2.00.........		_____
_____	Caught in the Web of Deception (Hardback) .....$14.95.........		_____

Booklets

_____	Campaign Save Christian America ....$ .30¢.......		_____
_____	It Will Be Worth it All ....$ .15¢.......		_____
_____	Could You be Caught in the Web of Deception .....N/C..........		_____

Postage & Handling

Prices, Postage & Handling Are Subject to Change Without Notice		
Orders up to $15.00	=	$ 2.00
$ 15.01 - $30.00	=	$ 4.00
$ 30.01 - $50.00	=	$ 6.00
$ 50.01 - $80.00	=	$ 8.00
Over - $80.00	=	10%

Subtotal _____

Postage/Handling _____

My Donation _____

TOTAL _____

NAME _____

ADDRESS _____

CITY _____ STATE _____ ZIP CODE _____

YOUR EMAIL ADDRESS _____

Phone Orders call: 1-480-998-4136 or e-mail:

xnlifeout@yahoo.com

Website: www.campaignsaveamerica.com

Or tear out this page and mail to:

Christian Life Outreach,

6438 E Jenan Dr., Scottsdale, AZ 85254

These books can also be purchased at your bookstore

Please Note: Christian Life Outreach is a 501(3c) non-profit ministry. All proceeds from the Sale of these books are used for this ministry. You will receive a tax-deductible receipt for that amount allowed by the Internal Revenue Code.